Warriors

To my children, Carrie, Dan, and Amy, and my first grand-child, Dakota Ruth Christensen. I pray your lives be filled with peace.

To Howard, a warrior who had been in Vietnam only a few weeks before the rockets came.

To those men and women warriors with whom I shared a tour on the Portland (Oregon) Police Bureau during my 25 years, who fell in their prime.

To the men and women warriors who today fight in foreign lands and patrol the streets of urban and rural America.

On Living with Courage, Discipline, and Honor

edited by Loren W. Christensen

PALADIN PRESS • BOULDER, COLORADO

Warriors: On Living with Courage, Discipline, and Honor
Edited by Loren W. Christensen

Copyright © 2004 by Loren W. Christensen

ISBN 10: 1-58160-454-8
ISBN 13: 978-1-58160-454-2
Printed in the United States of America

Published by Paladin Press, a division of
Paladin Enterprises, Inc.,
Gunbarrel Tech Center
7077 Winchester Circle
Boulder, Colorado 80301 USA
+1.303.443.7250

Direct inquiries and/or orders to the above address.

Visit our Web site at www.paladin-press.com

Contents

We sleep safely in our beds this night,
because rough men stand ready in the night
to visit violence on those who would do us harm.

—George Orwell

Preface

I'm an idea guy. Mostly I get them in the middle of the night as I fight my cursed insomnia. The majority are like bubbles that work their way to the water's surface and pop, never to be anything but a rising bubble. But every so often, one rises to the surface and bobs about demanding attention. Those are the ones that become books, magazine articles, newspaper columns, and training ideas. *Warriors: On Living with Courage, Discipline, and Honor* is the result of one of those bubbles that didn't burst.

It was my friendship with Lt. Col. Dave Grossman, who lectures about warriorhood all over the world, and our association working together on the book *On Combat* that got me thinking even more deeply on the subject and led to that bubble's rising to the surface at 2 A.M. one night and not going away. When I started bouncing it around, I saw the structure of this book: warrior and warriorhood defined by those who live and function in it.

I ran the idea by my friends Dr. Alexis Artwohl, Lieutenant Colonel Grossman, and Paladin Executive Editor Jon Ford. "Do it," they said, and began supplying me with names of top people in the warrior community—the ones that appear under the essay titles throughout this book. I must admit that at first I was somewhat shy, even apprehensive, about contacting them, but nearly every one of them agreed without hesitation to contribute. Actually, all were overjoyed to have the opportunity to tell the world what warriorhood means to them.

The task of compiling and editing their work was a humbling one for me. For years I have read their writings; heard their names spoken with respect, even awe; seen their appearances on CNN, the *Today* show, *Larry King Live,* and *Oprah;* and watched movies they have scripted or appeared in. The writers who graciously contributed to this work are some of the finest warrior scribes, warrior trainers, and warrior scholars today. They've been there and done that. Many have fought on the edge of death's yawning orifice, survived, and now teach others to do the same. They do it because it's their duty, their destiny.

During the last two weeks of working on this book, I got to hold my first granddaughter, Dakota Ruth Christensen, for the first time. Although she was already a month old, I had been sick for several weeks, and we didn't want to risk her getting my bug. But I was finally well enough to hold the delicate flower in my arms, and my tired old warrior face became smiles and wet eyes. Ralph Waldo Emerson said, "We find delight in the beauty and happiness of children that makes the heart too big for the body." For sure, mine was hammering frighteningly hard at that moment.

Many of the warrior writers in this volume talk about children and family—because it is for them that we fight. Yes, we fight for our buddies, the ones on our right and on our left who go with us into harm's way, because they too are family. But it's our children who tug hardest on our warrior hearts. It's looking at them after we have just peered into death's door that makes our hearts too big for our bodies and our faces smile with tears. George Eliot said, "Little children are still the symbol of the eternal marriage between love and duty."

Duty. It's what a warrior does. Because . . . well . . . it's what he does. "It's my destiny," many have said. They train continuously. They learn their craft continuously. They prepare themselves physically and mentally continuously. They prepare. George Washington said before Congress in 1790, "To be prepared for war is one of the most effectual means of preserving peace."

It's what a warrior does. He does it for his children, for my new granddaughter, and for a million others he will never meet and never know.

The word "warrior" is not new; those who function in the warrior community have always used it. But outside this community, the word was always just a word with no great significance attached to it. That is, before September 11, 2001. After those planes smashed into the Twin Towers, the Pentagon, and that field 80 miles outside of Pittsburgh, warrior became a buzzword, a household word. Most often it's used properly, though in some cases its use has been a stretch of the definition.

Many people define warrior as "man engaged or experienced in warfare." I do too, but in a broader interpretation of those words. Some define a warrior as one who goes toward the sound of gunfire while everyone else flees. I do too, but again, in a broader interpretation of those words. Still others have said that a warrior is one who does what needs to be done. Again I agree, broadly.

In the broad interpretation of these definitions, I believe that a warrior is also

- A single mother of three who works two jobs but still lives on the poverty line and, though exhausted, fights daily to keep her kids out of street gangs, off drugs, and on the honor roll.
- That courageous spouse and older children who wait for the warrior cop or soldier to return home, always with that nagging doubt that this time, *this time,* he might not come home.
- The terminally ill patient who fights to the very end, not just to ward off death, but to ensure that loved ones are comforted, taken care of, and can look forward to a bright future.
- Those who stand up for what is right, even when the odds are against them: the 80-year-old woman who stands up in a bus and threatens to clobber an obnoxious, loudmouth gangbanger with her umbrella; the mother who pickets a neighborhood drug house in spite of numerous death threats; the secretary who blows the whistle on corporate corruption.

- Those who face injury and death because they love the risk: boxers, full-contact martial artists, skydivers, and extreme-sports enthusiasts of all kinds. We might not all agree with what they do or with their motivation, but they can teach us something about facing fear.

The purpose of this book, written by those who have experienced warfare in its many forms, is to help us all understand who our warriors are and what they do, so that in the end we might understand ourselves a little better.

> *Cowards die many times before their deaths;*
> *the valiant never taste of death but once.*
> —Shakespeare, *Julius Caesar*

Acknowledgments

Lt. Col. Dave Grossman—thank you for your inspiration, teaching, encouragement, and friendship.

To the warrior writers, scholars, thinkers, and teachers who graciously and enthusiastically shared their thoughts in this book. Thank you for your powerful words, inspiration, and teaching.

A WORD ON THE WRITING

While the authors fully recognize and respect the outstanding work done by women in the military and law enforcement today, for ease of reading, we generally elected to use masculine pronoun forms, rather than the awkward *he/she* and *him/her*. In addition, *soldier* is used most often to mean all warriors in the military, and *police officer* and *cop* are used to refer to the many types of law enforcement officers. We hope no one is offended.

Warrior Defined

And although we may do our best to avoid trouble, sometimes trouble insists on finding us. When that happens, when the time for talk is over, warriors act. They flip the switch and act decisively—ruthlessly if necessary—to preserve and defend the things they hold dear. And when the fight is over, they turn off the switch and continue to cherish the things they valued enough to defend. That's what makes them warriors. And that's what makes them the good guys.

—Michael D. Janich,
from "You Can't Always Get What You Want: Why Being a Warrior Starts with Accepting the Limitations of Peace"

ON SHEEP, WOLVES, AND SHEEPDOGS

by Lt. Col. Dave Grossman and Loren W. Christensen

Lt. Col. Dave Grossman *is a West Point psychology professor, professor of military science, Army Ranger, and author of* On Killing: The Psychological Cost of Learning to Kill in War and Society; Stop Teaching Our Kids to Kill: A Call to Action Against TV, Movie, and Video Game Violence, *coauthored with Gloria DeGaetano; and* On Combat: The Psychology and Physiology of Deadly Conflict in War and in Peace, *with Loren W. Christensen.*

Lieutenant Colonel Grossman's research was cited by President Clinton in a national address after the Littleton, Colorado, school shootings. He has testified before the U.S. Senate, the U.S. Congress, and numerous state legislatures, and he has served as an expert witness and consultant in state and federal court cases, including United States vs. Timothy McVeigh. *He helped train mental health professionals after the Jonesboro, Arkansas, school shootings, and he was also involved in counseling or court cases in the aftermath of the school shootings in Paducah, Kentucky; Springfield, Oregon; and Littleton. Lieutenant Colonel Grossman wrote the entry "Aggression and Violence" in* The Oxford Companion to American Military History *and three entries in the Academic Press Encyclopedia of Violence, Peace and Conflict. He has presented papers before the national conventions of the American Medical Association, the American Psychiatric Association, the American Psychological Association, and the American Academy of Pediatrics. Lieutenant Colonel Grossman is the director of the Killology Research Group (www.killology.com). In the wake of the 9/11 terrorist attacks, he is on the road nearly 300 days a year training elite military and law enforcement organizations worldwide about the reality of combat.*

Loren W. Christensen's *biography can be found at the back of this book.*

"On Sheep, Wolves, and Sheepdogs" was taken from the book On Combat *and has been edited slightly for this book.*

❖

One Vietnam veteran, an old retired colonel, once said this to Lieutenant Colonel Grossman: "Most of the people in our society are sheep. They are kind, gentle, productive creatures who can only hurt one another by accident." This is true. Consider that the annual murder rate is six per 100,000, and the annual aggravated assault rate is four per 1,000. What this means is that the vast majority of Americans are not inclined to hurt one another.

Some estimates say that 2 million Americans are victims of violent crimes every year. While this is a tragic, staggering number, perhaps an all-time record rate of violent crime, we must keep in mind that there are almost 300 million Americans, which means that the odds of being a victim of violent crime are considerably less than 1 in 100 in any given year. Furthermore, since many violent crimes are committed by repeat offenders, the actual number of violent citizens is considerably less than 2 million.

Thus there is a paradox, and we must grasp both ends of the situation: we may well be in the most violent times in history, but violence is still remarkably rare. This is because most citizens are kind, decent people who are not capable of hurting each other except by accident or under extreme provocation.

Let us call them sheep.

Now, we mean nothing negative by calling them this. Think of a pretty blue robin's egg. It is soft and gooey inside, but someday it will grow into something wonderful. But the egg cannot survive without its hard, blue shell. Police officers, soldiers, and other warriors are like that shell, and someday the civilization they protect will grow into something wonderful. For now, though, civilization needs warriors to protect the sheep from the predators.

"Then there are the wolves," the old war veteran said, "and the wolves feed on the sheep without mercy." Do you believe there are wolves out there who feed on the flock without mercy? You'd better believe it. There are evil men in this world who are capable of evil deeds. The moment you forget that or pretend it is not so, you become a sheep. There is no safety in denial.

"Then there are sheepdogs," he went on, "and I'm a sheepdog. I live to protect the flock and confront the wolf."

If you have no capacity for violence, you are a healthy, productive citizen, a sheep. If you have a capacity for violence and no empathy for your fellow citizens, you are an aggressive sociopath, a wolf. But what if you have a capacity for violence and a deep love for your fellow citizens? Then you are a sheepdog, a warrior, someone who walks the hero's path. You are able to walk into the heart of darkness, into the universal human phobia, and walk out unscathed.

One career police officer wrote the following to Lieutenant Colonel Grossman after attending one of his "Bulletproof Mind" training sessions:

> I want to say thank you for finally shedding some light on why it is that I can do what I do. I always knew why I did it. I love my citizens, even the bad ones, and I had a talent that I could return to my community. I just couldn't put my finger on why I could wade through the chaos, the gore, the sadness, if given a chance try to make it all better, and walk right out the other side.

Let us expand on the old soldier's excellent model of the sheep, wolves, and sheepdogs. We know that the sheep live in denial; that is what makes them sheep. They do not want to believe that there is evil in the world. They can accept the fact that fires can happen, which is why they want fire extinguishers, fire sprinklers, fire alarms, and fire exits throughout their kids' schools. But many of them are outraged at the idea of putting an armed police officer in their kids' school. Our children are thousands of times more likely to be killed or seriously injured by school violence than fire, but the sheep's only response to the possibility of violence is to deny that it could happen. The idea of someone coming to kill or harm their children is just too hard for them to fathom.

The sheep generally do not like the sheepdog. He looks a lot like the wolf. He has fangs and the capacity for violence. The difference, though, is that the sheepdog must not, cannot, and will not ever harm the sheep. Any sheepdog that intentionally harms the lowliest little lamb must be punished and removed. The world cannot work any other way, at least not in a representative democracy or a republic such as ours.

Still, the sheepdog disturbs the sheep. He is a constant reminder that there are wolves in the land. They would prefer that he didn't tell them where to go, or give them traffic tickets, or stand at the ready in our airports in camouflage fatigues holding an M16. The sheep would much rather have the sheepdog cash in his fangs, spray-paint himself white, and go, "*Baa*."

That is, until the wolf shows up. Then the entire flock tries desperately to hide behind one lonely sheepdog.

The students, the victims, at Columbine High School were big, tough high school students, and under ordinary circumstances they would not have had the time of day for a police officer. They were not bad kids; they just had nothing to say to a cop. When the school was under attack, however, and SWAT teams were clearing the rooms and hallways, the officers had to physically peel those clinging, sobbing kids off of them. This is how the lambs feel about their sheepdog when the wolf is at the door. Look at what happened after September 11, 2001, when the wolf pounded hard on the door. Remember how America, more than ever before, felt differently about its law enforcement officers and military personnel? Remember how many times you heard the word *hero*?

Understand that there is nothing morally superior about being a sheepdog; it is just what you choose to be. Also understand that a sheepdog is a funny critter: he is always sniffing around out on the perimeter, checking the breeze, barking at things that go bump in the night, and yearning for a righteous battle. That is, the young sheepdogs yearn for a righteous battle. The old sheepdogs are a little older and wiser, but they move to the sound of the guns when needed right along with the young ones.

Here is how the sheep and the sheepdog think differently: the sheep pretend the wolf will never come, but the sheepdog lives for that day. After the attacks on September 11, 2001, most of the sheep, that is, most citizens in America, said, "Thank God I wasn't on one of those planes." But the sheepdogs, the warriors, said, "Dear God, I wish I could have been on one of those planes. Maybe I could have made a difference." When you are truly transformed into a warrior and have truly invested yourself into warriorhood, you *want* to be there. You *want* to be able to make a difference.

While there is nothing morally superior about the sheepdog, he does have one real advantage. Only one. He is able to survive and thrive in an environment that destroys 98 percent of the population.

Research conducted on convicts serving time for serious, predatory acts of violence—assaults, murders, and killing law enforcement officers—found that the vast majority said that they specifically targeted victims by body language: slumped walk, passive behavior, and lack of awareness. They chose their victims like big cats do in Africa when they select one out of the herd that is least able to protect itself.

However, when potential victims gave cues that indicated they would not go easily, the cons said that they would walk away. If the cons sensed that the target was a counterpredator, that is, a sheepdog, they would leave him alone unless there was no other choice but to engage.

One police officer told me that he rode a commuter train to work each day. One day, as was his usual, he was standing in the crowded car, dressed in blue jeans, T-shirt, and jacket, holding onto a pole and reading a paperback. At one of the stops, two street toughs boarded, shouting and cursing and doing every obnoxious thing possible to intimidate the other riders.

The officer continued to read his book, though he kept a watchful eye on the two punks as they strolled along the aisle making comments to female passengers and banging shoulders with men as they passed.

As they approached the officer, he lowered his novel and made eye contact with them. "You got a problem, man?" one of the IQ-challenged punks asked. "You think you're tough, or somethin'?" the other asked, obviously offended that this one was not shirking away from them.

The officer held them in his steady gaze for a moment, and then said calmly, "As a matter of fact, I am tough."

The two looked at him questioningly, blinked a couple of times, and then, without saying a word, turned and moved back down the aisle to continue their taunting of the other passengers, the sheep.

Some people might be destined to be sheep, and others might be genetically primed to be wolves or sheepdogs. But most people can choose which they want to be, and more and more Americans are choosing to become sheepdogs.

Seven months after the attack on September 11, 2001, Todd Beamer was honored in his hometown of Cranbury, New Jersey. Todd, as you recall, was the man on Flight 93 over Pennsylvania who called on his cell phone to alert an operator from United Airlines about the hijacking. When he learned of the other three passenger planes that had been used as weapons, Todd dropped his phone and uttered the words, "Let's roll," which authorities believe was a signal to the other passengers to confront the terrorist hijackers. In one hour, a transformation occurred among the passengers—athletes, business people, and parents—from sheep to sheepdogs, and together they fought the wolves, ultimately saving an unknown number of lives on the ground.

Here is the point Lieutenant Colonel Grossman likes to emphasize, especially to the thousands of police officers and soldiers he speaks to each year. In nature the sheep—real sheep—are born as sheep. Sheepdogs are born that way, as are wolves. They did not have a choice. But you are not a critter. As a human being, you can be whatever you want to be. It is a conscious, moral decision.

If you want to be a sheep, then you can be a sheep and that is okay, but you must understand the price you pay. When the wolf comes, you and your loved ones are going to die if there is not a sheepdog there to protect you. If you want to be a wolf, you can be one, but the sheepdogs are going to hunt you down and you will never have rest, safety, trust, or love. But if you want to be a sheepdog and walk the warrior's path, then you must make a conscious and moral decision every day to dedicate, equip, and prepare yourself to thrive in that toxic, corrosive moment when the wolf comes knocking at the door.

For example, many officers carry their weapons in church. They are well concealed in ankle holsters, shoulder holsters, or inside-the-belt holsters tucked into the small of their backs. Anytime you go to some form of religious service, there is a very good chance that a police officer in your congregation is carrying. You will never know if there is such an individual in your place of worship until the wolf appears to massacre you and your loved ones.

Lieutenant Colonel Grossman was training a group of police officers in Texas when, during a break, an officer asked his friend if he carried his weapon in church. The other officer replied, "I will *never* be caught without my gun in church."

Lieutenant Colonel Grossman asked him why he felt so strongly about this, and the officer told him about another police officer he knew who was at a church massacre in Ft. Worth, Texas, in 1999. In that incident, a mentally deranged individual charged in and opened fire, gunning down 14 people. He said that that officer believed he could have saved every life that day if only he had been carrying his gun. His own son was shot, and all he could do was throw himself on the boy's body and wait to die.

The officer telling the story looked Lieutenant Colonel Grossman in the eyes and asked, "Do you have any idea how hard it would be to live with yourself after that?"

Some individuals would be horrified if they knew this police officer was carrying a weapon in church. They might call him paranoid and scorn him. Yet these same individuals would be enraged and would call for "heads to roll" if they found out that the air bags in their cars were defective, or that the fire extinguisher and fire sprinklers in their kids' school did not work. They can accept the fact that fires and traffic accidents can happen and that there must be safeguards against them. However, their only response to the wolf is denial, and all too often their response to the sheepdog is scorn and disdain. But the sheepdog quietly asks himself, "Do you have any idea how hard it would be to live with yourself if your loved ones were attacked and killed and you had to stand there helplessly because you were unprepared for that day?"

It is denial that turns people into sheep. Sheep are psychologically destroyed by combat because their only defense is denial, which is counterproductive and destructive, resulting in fear, helplessness, and horror when the wolf shows up.

Denial kills you twice. It kills you once, at your moment of truth when you are not physically prepared: You didn't bring your gun; you didn't train. Your only defense is wishful thinking. Hope is *not* a strategy. Denial kills you a second time because even if you do physically survive, you are psychologically shattered by fear, helplessness, horror, and shame at your moment of truth.

In Gavin de Becker's superb post-9/11 book *Fear Less*, which should be required reading for anyone trying to come to terms with our current world situation, he says,

> Denial can be seductive, but it has an insidious side effect. For all the peace of mind deniers think they get by saying it isn't so, the fall they take when faced with new violence is all the more unsettling. Denial is a save-now-pay-later scheme, a contract written entirely in small print, for in the long run, the denying person knows the truth on some level.

And so the warrior must strive to confront denial in all aspects of his life and prepare himself for the day when evil comes.

If you are a warrior legally authorized to carry a weapon and you step outside without that weapon, then you become a sheep, pretending that the bad man will not come today. No one can be on 24/7 for a lifetime. Everyone needs downtime. But if you are authorized to carry a weapon and you walk outside without it, just take a deep breath and say this to yourself: *"Baa."*

This business of being a sheep or a sheepdog is not a yes-no dichotomy. It is not an all-or-nothing, either-or choice. It is a matter of degrees, a continuum. On one end is an abject, head-in-the-sand sheep, and on the other end is the ultimate warrior. Few people exist completely on one end or the other. Most of us live somewhere in between. Since 9-11 almost everyone in America took a step up that continuum, away from denial. The sheep took a few steps toward accepting and appreciating their warriors, and the warriors started taking their job more seriously. The degree to which you move up that continuum, away from sheephood and denial, is the degree to which you and your loved ones will survive physically and psychologically at your moment of truth.

STAND AND NEVER YIELD
HOW RICK RESCORLA
SAVED 2,700 LIVES ON 9-11

by Dan Hill
(as told to Fred McBee)

Dan J. Hill, captain of infantry (retired), Airborne Ranger – Special Forces, is legendary in the special warfare community. He enlisted in the army when he was 15 years old, and by the time he was 21 he'd seen action in Beirut, Hungary, and the Belgian Congo. After graduating from officer candidate school (OCS), he served two tours in Vietnam and later fought with the mujahidin in Afghanistan. Along the way, he did many deeds that he officially didn't do. He is still active as an independent security consultant.

Fred McBee is a writer and retired university instructor. He was also a close friend of Rescorla's and a charter member of Rescorla's brain trust.

❖

Rick Rescorla predicted 9-11. He also predicted the 1993 World Trade Center bombing. It is a matter of record. Rescorla was the vice president for security for Dean Witter Corporation when he foresaw the bombing of the World Trade Center in 1993. Two years before this first attack, he predicted it would be a truck bomb exploding in the unsecured basement parking area. He went to the New York/New Jersey Port Authority with his warnings and was told to "be concerned with the security of the 40 floors that Dean Witter leases from us and leave the rest to us." Dean Witter/Morgan Stanley received about one-quarter billion dollars in settlement fees for the Port Authority's negligence in failing to heed the informed warnings of the coming 1993 attack.

Still ignorant, arrogant, and flat-out stupid, the Port Authority and Dean Witter/Morgan Stanley refused to heed

Rescorla's second warning—a very specific warning—that another attack was coming—this time from the air—in the form of commercial aircraft. Rescorla was a hair off. He thought it would be cargo aircraft out of Europe or the Middle East loaded with explosives.

Asked by his superiors what could be done to prevent such an attack, Rescorla replied, "Nothing. Get out of this building. It's nothing but a big, soft target. And they intend to hit us again. Move across the river to New Jersey. Build, buy, or rent a group of low-rise buildings. Spread out into smaller targets. In this computer age we could do our business from the middle of North Dakota. We don't need Wall Street anymore."

How does a man come to possess this ability to so accurately predict future events? He had no crystal ball. He was not clairvoyant. He was a professional in the arts of intelligence, security, and counterguerrilla warfare. He had spent his entire life centered on these things. Over a lifetime, Rescorla accumulated knowledge and experience that allowed him to know how, when, why, and where his enemy would strike.

Rescorla was born in May 1939 in Hayle, Cornwall, England. His childhood memories were of commando raids by British forces, OSS (Office of Strategic Services) operations, and the French Resistance. As a youth he read about these events, studied them, analyzed them, criticized them—like a Monday morning quarterback. He was virtually nurtured at the tit of war and special operations.

In his teens he joined the British army, became a paratrooper, and then went into intelligence and led a unit fighting guerrillas and insurgents in Cyprus. Then he went to Africa—Northern Rhodesia (now Zambia), where he fought more guerrillas and insurgents. After that, he joined the London police force as a member of the Scotland Yard Flying Squad, where he was much involved in anti-IRA operations. In 1963, he came to the United States and enlisted in the U.S. Army as a private. In April 1965 he was commissioned as a U.S. officer of infantry out of the OCS course at Fort Benning, Georgia. Five months later he was commanding a platoon of 44 men in Vietnam with the 2/7th Cavalry Battalion of the 1st Air Cavalry Division. Two months after that he was one of the most distinguished heroes of the battle of Ia Drang Valley (see the Joe Galloway/Lt. Gen. Hal Moore book *We Were Soldiers Once . . . And Young*).

After the war, Rescorla left active army service (although he stayed in the National Guard until he retired as a colonel). In 1967 he became an American citizen. He had paid his dues. He went to college at the University of Oklahoma, where he studied literature and writing. Then he went to law school and became a lawyer. He taught criminal justice at the University of South Carolina in Columbia for a while, but the academic life was too tame for him. He went into the banking/financial security business and quickly advanced to the top ranks of his profession.

Over the course of his life, Rescorla developed a corps of men he could rely upon: thinkers, soldiers, politicians, writers, law enforcement officials—second-class, politically incorrect, belligerent men who saw things as they actually were and not what they seem to be. From these he developed his own brain trust—his own intelligence unit, his own staff and group of counselors. He kept in contact with them by telephone. He posed questions—hypothetical situations concerning international developments and problems. He collected, consolidated, and analyzed the input from this net of agents and thus came to logical conclusions. Some he hired for short periods as consultants. One, a natural insurgent/guerrilla/warrior, he brought to New York to make an estimate of the situation and the likely plan of attack upon the World Trade Center. In 1990–91, all this produced the prediction of the 1993 bombing. In 1995–96, it predicted the 2001 air attack.

See? No horoscope, no crystal ball, no tarot cards, just plain and simple intelligence and professional expertise and logical projection, i.e., "If you want to know what a terrorist is likely to do, just ask a terrorist—or one whose mind works like that of a terrorist."

Now, why was Rick Rescorla a hero on 9-11?

Because after being told by Dean Witter/Morgan Stanley

that they could not relocate—that their lease ran to 2005 and maybe after that the move would be possible—Rescorla planned and drilled the Dean Witter/Morgan Stanley staff and employees in the evacuation of the World Trade Center offices that they occupied.

Despite criticism and intimidation, despite ridicule and denigration, Rescorla forced his people to drill. Without warning, he'd sound an alarm and then lead the entire company through a mandatory, rapid, efficient, and safe evacuation practice. They grumbled and they griped, but they did it.

Rescorla installed generators and stair lighting in case of power failure (which came to be). He assigned office and floor wardens to ensure control and accountability of personnel in evacuating. Rescorla insisted on buddy teams—people were to go two-by-two down the stairs in an orderly and rapid manner. Rescorla made sure that elderly and handicapped persons had three or four others to assist them. And he drilled them—over and over, again and again—until it became a conditioned response, like that of "a soldier going into an antiambush drill," as Rescorla put it.

On the day of the crisis, when the first tower was hit, the Port Authority ordered everyone in the second tower to stay at their desks. Rescorla made a command decision to countermand that order. "Bugger that!" he said. And then he initiated his conditioned response plan. Evacuation began immediately.

Trained, conditioned, the Dean Witter/Morgan Stanley employees responded. They implemented Rescorla's plan; 2,700 people followed his drill. Rescorla was everywhere—the halls, the stairwells—from the 10th to the 70th floor. His voice could be heard above the near mayhem, keeping everyone calm, responsive, moving in a controlled and orderly manner. At times he sang to them over his megaphone. He sang "God Bless America" in that booming deep baritone of his. And he sang the defiant "Men of Harlech," just as he'd done when the 7th Cavalry was surrounded in the Ia Drang Valley, just as the British army had done when surrounded by the Zulus at Rourke's Drift.

Men of Cornwall stop your dreaming;
Can't you see their spearpoints gleaming?
See their warriors' pennants streaming
To this battlefield.
Men of Cornwall stand ye steady;
It cannot be ever said ye
for the battle were not ready;
Stand and never yield!

All but six of Dean Witter/Morgan Stanley's employees survived. They got out—alive. They live today. They live because Rescorla was watching out for them.

Dean Witter/Morgan Stanley was not comprised of its equipment, computers, files, fixtures, furnishings, or potted plants. It was comprised of its people—those 2,700 individuals, their minds and talents and experience. When Rescorla saved their lives through his foresight and actions, he also saved the largest financial institution in the nation, in the world, on this earth.

But Rescorla did not survive. After shepherding the 2,700 out of the building, Rescorla knew there were still a few left above—the confused, the disoriented, the injured. And as everyone who knew Rescorla knows, he would leave no man behind.

And so he went up into that tower of death in an attempt to save them. He knew it was a forlorn hope. He knew that he would probably die in his attempt. But Rescorla was a man who could never live with himself in the future if he did not try to save those few who were left. So he went up. And the tower came down. And Rescorla is no more.

I know this is true. I was Rescorla's best friend, confidant, and comrade-in-arms throughout our entire adult lives. I fought with him in Africa, went through OCS at the same time he did, fought in Vietnam with him. I am the guerrilla/insurgent/terrorist-at-heart he hired as a consultant. My children called him "Uncle Rick." My wife thought of him as the brother and sibling she'd never really had. I was best man at both of his weddings. From 1970 until his death, we spoke on the telephone three or four times a week. His children called me "Uncle Dan."

Not by blood or birth but by choice, we were brothers. (For a full account of Rescorla and Hill's legendary exploits and amazing friendship, read *Heart of a Soldier* by James B. Stewart.)

On 9-11, as he went through that trial, we spoke over the cell phone as things progressed from the initial aircraft hit until he went up looking for the few survivors who may have been left behind. After he started up, he called his wife, Susan. His last words to her were, "You made my life." Susan and I were both watching our TV when Rick's tower went down, taking him and his life with it.

I have wept only one time over the loss of my one true friend, brother, and companion—and that, unfortunately, was on national television while being interviewed by Jane Pauley. She asked me then if that was the first time I had cried over Rick. I replied, "Yeah. I've been too busy being proud of him. I've been too busy cheering."

I have vowed to never again cry over Rick Rescorla and his death. It was not an event to weep over. It was a noble ending for a noble man. I choose to rejoice in that. I will continue to cheer.

Such magnificent men are rare. They appear every few eons or so, and they are a gift to mankind.

Rescorla died the death for which he was destined—standing for the principles of honor, integrity, and valor. He was a man who considered everyman to be as important as himself. From bush natives in Africa to the barons of Wall Street, he considered every life as valuable as his own. In the end, he died as he lived—in service to his fellow man. Like the Good Book says, "Greater love hath no man than this, that a man lay down his life for his friends" (John 15:13).

There was no better man in history. There probably never will be better. I give you 2,700 survivors of the 9-11 World Trade Center disaster as witnesses.

THE WARRIOR

by Harry Humphries

Harry Humphries's *vast experience in the warrior community includes:*

- *Former Navy SEAL with more than 200 combat operations as a SEAL operator and a provincial reconnaissance unit (PRU) advisor with Phoenix Program's counterterrorist units.*
- *An engineer with operational and security consulting experience in the United States and many foreign lands, including Germany, Austria, Russia, Commonwealth of Independent States (CIS), Albania, Kosovo, Africa, the Middle East, Colombia, and Mexico.*
- *Recognized counterterrorism authority specializing in tactics of post-modern terrorism and weapons of mass destruction (WMD) preparedness.*
- *Lecturer in modern law enforcement training techniques and improvised explosive device (IOD) awareness.*
- *Accomplished trainer in combat tactics, small arms, and edged weapons.*
- *Owner/operator of Global Studies Group, Inc. (GSGI), former tactical instructor at the Advanced HRT (hostage rescue training) Instructors program at Eastern Michigan University, former tactical instructor at Gunsite Training Center, and participant in Illinois University's Police Training Institute's Master Instructor program.*

Humphries has a working relationship with the criminal justice and military special operations communities in an effort to amalgamate their technologies in a modern training philosophy.

❖

Historically, the warrior class has been recognized as a unique entity within civilized societies, either loathed or loved, depending the observer's mind-set or exposure to threat. John F. Kennedy's "Ask not what your country can do for you—ask what you can do for your country" hit on the core of warriorhood: those selflessly willing, if not obsessively driven, to go in harm's way for the sake of others within their tribal or social sphere.

Unfortunately, a vast element of naive liberals associates today's warriors with guns, gangs, bombs, killing, and comic books. Idealistic, some well meaning, these liberals have little tolerance for any sort of violence, justified or not, as an ultimate means of neutralizing evil. Carl von Clausewitz's concept of war being a continuation of politics by other means is lost on them. They view the warrior as a dinosaur in a civilized urban environment. They would negotiate ad infinitum seeing only the good in humankind, seeking peace, while evil continues to kill, pillage, and torture as a means of gaining or maintaining power. They fail to recognize the limits of diplomacy—logical negotiations between logical parties require that logic prevail in the final decision process. Their argument for diplomacy does not apply to humans who illogically seek power at any cost. These creatures understand only fear delivered through violence of action. The warrior, the ultimate pacifist, avoids conflict, yet continually prepares for it. In *Hamlet*, Shakespeare epitomized the warrior attitude: "Beware of entrance to a quarrel; but being in, bear't that the opposed may beware of thee."

Who are the warriors and how do they find themselves? In many ancient cultures, the transition into manhood required some form of rites of passage preparing the young adult for warriorhood or dangers in the wild. This phenomenon has evolved into modern-day trials by fire, such as participation in a lesser form of the combat experience. Relatively risky activities, such as contact sports and sky diving, and on the other side, the dark side, drugs, gang membership, and so on have all substituted for the traditional character testing and painfully demanding rites of passage in primitive cultures.

For other would-be warriors, the pursuit of law enforcement and military careers has served as their rites of passage. By definition, these professions require one to prepare for and possibly make the ultimate sacrifice on fields of honor. It is here where one will most probably be tried at the highest level of warriorhood—at one's trial under hostile fire, wherein the limits of man's inhumanity toward his fellow man are exposed. Here is where the ubiquitous haunting question of the quality of one's performance under fire is answered. It is at this point that the would-be warrior discovers his composition. After this event, one either finds comfort with one's warrior image or becomes cursed with the memory of failure under fire.

It is my great honor to have been accepted by and served with the men of the SEAL community during wartime. I have seen some of the best of the best-trained individuals fail while some of the lesser trained performed valiantly under fire. The warrior finds himself only after answering the ultimate question. This is an inevitable truth, independent of the training experience.

My good friend Lt. Col. Dave Grossman talks of the sheepdogs and wolves in our society. I won't endeavor to touch his treatment of the subject, as I doubt anyone can do so as well. There is no question, however, that the warrior is of the sheepdog species, instinctively protecting the flock.

The professional warrior internalizes combat experience and prowess. For instance, I can usually smell the real deal through his body language and silence. The true sign of the pretender, or failed combatant, is loud verbosity and stories of exploits. No doubt a defensive syndrome or shield hiding past failures.

Those of the Silent Proud truly know who they are and need not have others judge. That is not to say that they are without inner conflict and flaws. They are never sure if they owe their lives to combat skills, luck, or divine intervention. There are even those who are willing to expose themselves to high risk for the sake of others while seeking recognition or reward. I have seen men in combat display extreme bravery, only to push for military award, which seems to me a curious character trait.

Some view the warrior as a warmongering killer. They would say he kills out of some primal urge, but nothing could be further from the truth. He is driven by the concept of "Good Sword versus Evil Sword"; in his mind, he fights the "Just War" espoused by the Romans, a fight for just reasons. This begs the questions, What are the reasons? Where is the bar? He will not independently make that decision, as he is the consummate good soldier who does not reason why; he will do or die for his accepted authority. Ancient warrior societies may not have had honorable reasons for war; however, those warriors, in their minds, followed the accepted authority, selflessly willing to sacrifice their lives for what was perceived as just. Ernest Hemingway, a self-imposed warrior, had a toast I believe appropriate: "To all the dead soldiers of all the wars, and to the women they had loved and lost." He implies that all warriors on all sides have an honorable commonality; I heartily agree.

Business schools and executive boardrooms recognizing the value of warrior mentality design commercial strategies based on the works of Sun Tzu (*The Art of War*), Clausewitz (*On War*), Niccolo Machiavelli (*The Prince*), and others.

Business managers come away from these works appreciating the value of the warrior mentality devoid of conventional restraints. They can equate business conflicts with military strategy, which should not be a lengthy action plan, but rather an evolution of a centralized idea working within an ever-changing environment. The warrior will seize unforeseen opportunities as they arise, setting the broadest objectives, realizing the detailed plan will fall apart after the first enemy contact. He or she stresses leadership and morale and thrives on an instinctual savvy. Business managers might do well to emulate these traits; however, I cannot suggest the warrior's mind-set is completely applicable to sound business management. There is a compulsive drive to completely destroy hostile forces, which will not work in a win-win compromise when two competing enterprises logically come to a mutually advantageous agreement. This sort of thing will probably be considered as a defeat—something short of complete victory—to the warrior.

Warriors are, after all, human, demanded by society to maintain a civilized sense of decency on fields of horror—the world of kill or be killed. They are the Dragon Slayers, precariously teetering on the brink of becoming the dragon. Even the hardened will carry demons, silently reliving memories of extremes beyond belief.

WHAT IS A WARRIOR?

by W. Hock Hochheim

W. Hock Hochheim is a military and Texas police veteran and former private investigator who holds black belts in Japanese, Filipino, and Hawaiian martial arts. Bridging the gap between the police, the military, the martial artist, and the aware citizen, he teaches hand, stick, knife, and gun combatives courses in 40 cities around the world each year. Mr. Hochheim also publishes Close Quarter Combat Magazine. *Check out his Web site at www.HocksCQC.com*

❖

Hunting the cagey, courageous elephant is an arduous and dangerous expedition. The beasts will stand their ground, charge, and fight back. So much so that the term "seeing the elephant" in certain circles has come to mean surviving some type of real-world badge of courage. This experience is often the key criteria when someone defines a warrior, elevates a hero, or selects some kind of hand, stick, knife, or gun instructor.

There is an old parable about three blind men touching an elephant at different parts of its body. One feels the elephant's side and determines it's like a wall; the second one feels the trunk and says the elephant is like a snake; and the last one feels a leg and determines it's like a tree trunk. Due to blindness, all three are wrong. When we ask the question, What is a warrior? do we perceive the big creature itself, or just one part?

Specifics must be investigated. What exactly was this badge of courage, this combat experience? Where was it? How much was it? When was it? What exactly was done? Who was the enemy? Many aspects need surgical examination in order to better understand what the blind may miss.

Today, the word warrior is used in many abstract ways. There are road warriors and weekend warriors, and those dedicated to training for karate tournaments have been called warriors. There are even prayer warriors at churches.

Dictionaries define a warrior first as *a person engaged or experienced in warfare*. Next, they define the term broadly as a person engaged in some kind of struggle—and therein slip in these other, abstract categories. Authors Robert Moore and Douglas Gillette of *King, Warrior, Magician, Lover* use a common symbol for readers to relate to—Yul Brynner in *The Magnificent Seven:*

> The warrior's energy is concerned with skill, power and accuracy, and with control, both inner and outer, psychological and physical, with training thoughts, feeling, speech and actions. Yul Brynner's character in *The Magnificent Seven* is a study in trained self-control. He says little, moves with the physical control of a predator, attacks only the enemy and has absolute mastery over the technology of his trade. He has developed skill with the weapons he uses to implement his decisions.

People seeking these warrior accolades are often insecure about the lack thereof, making excuses for it. Some lie about it, desiring the psychological and often momentary value of this badge of courage. They pretend to be Navy SEALs, Gurkha soldiers, black bag operators, international martial arts contestant winners . . . the list is endless.

Joseph Campbell, the leading expert on the blend of mythology, religion, and history, has reminded us how badly we need our warrior heroes and mentors. With lines reaching back to the powerful monks of China, the jettis and Kshatriyas of India, the Zoroastrians of Persia, and the Japanese samurai, there is much reference and talk of the warrior spirit. Even the ancient gladiator "sports" meant life or death. We love, create, and covet heroes, and in our wantonness, therefore, have created a landscape of heroes and veteran teachers from karate tournament champs to Medal of Honor recipients.

Police? Corrections? Security? Military? Martial? These days there are only a few ways to gain this tribal christening of manhood. One joins the military or becomes employed by a law enforcement agency. One might work in a corrections facility. The easiest street access to the elite club is to become a bouncer or security guard of some type. Some seek adventure in crime—negative warriors. Some people's only claim to the Tough Guy Hall of Fame is that they grew up on the tough side of town. Left with few options to gain experience and respect, people resort to beating each other senseless in sport arenas to earn their warrior mettle.

What actual experience does a person holding a position in these fields garner? In police work there is introspection about the life of a 20-year veteran. Did he see 20 years of varied experience, or just one year, 20 times over? Did he sit in a records room for 11 of those years? Were those 20 years in a Mayberry R.F.D. agency with Sheriff Andy? Did he, in only one day in those 20 years, prove heroic in a *High Noon* gunfight against multiple opponents and win the day? Or was there one High Noon a year? Was that one High Noon gruesome enough to qualify for a lifetime? Did that bouncer work at Slugger's Bar and War Zone, or at Lady's Finger Café? How many kills in Vietnam make a warrior? 1? 10? 25? What about the sniper who killed 50 from a tremendous distance and never took return fire? Or was never in hand-to-hand combat? How many bullets must you duck to be so classified? 20? 30? Hundreds? Does one tour count or do three tours? Where do you draw the line?

The commanders and generals who receive the most respect are the ones who frequently appeared on the front lines or fought beside their men, such as King Leonidas of Sparta. Gens. Douglas MacArthur and George Patton appeared there from time to time. Many true warrior/leaders wanted to but were ordered not to risk their leadership skills in the bigger effort.

There are plenty of elite special forces military types who served 20 years and, due to the politics of the times, never once saw a day of combat. They struggled through that special forces obstacle course, they parachuted, they swam deep and long, and they shot well. They wanted to fight! But no fight! Are they still . . . warriors?

The line is gray. This curious mystique is projected even amongst the warrior groups. I've attended gatherings, seminars, and expos where police and military personnel were present. The police as a whole were enamored with the Rangers, Green Berets, and SEALs and projected upon them their own macho vision of the complete warrior package. Conversely, the military gazed upon the SWAT officers in the same way, visualizing them with guns drawn, kicking in doors twice a week, and seeing all kinds of action. Citizens were enamored with both groups. Most—not all mind you, but most—wanted to rub shoulders with everyone else, trying in some way to touch that elephant, capture and define that mythical magic.

Prof. James William Gibson of California State University said,

> The fact that even the men who had military service of some kind, or who were policemen, or in the security business were so quick and some often anxious to distinguish themselves from those they saw as lesser men, points to a deeper problem at the core of the warrior's ideal, namely: How much war does it take to make a warrior? No matter where one stood in terms of combat experience, there was always someone who had seen more action, taken more risks, and killed more enemies.

I think that someone like Col. David Hackworth (U.S. Army, Ret.) is a true warrior in body and spirit, a veteran of close-quarter battle in Korea and Vietnam. He trained, fought beside, and led many successful warriors. Then, in spite of his beliefs, he even fought his own army to try to fix it, against such odds that he was compelled to leave his own country. He was right, and he is obviously back, still the most decorated army soldier in our country's history. I think it is only fair that I offer up Hackworth as one example, because I now challenge you to consider all these issues, these questions that I have raised.

Ask yourself. What is a warrior?

MIND-SET OF
THE WARRIOR

An interview with Tony Blauer by Loren W. Christensen

Tony Blauer, one of the world's foremost authorities on personal safety and fear management, has traveled extensively sharing his research with top combatives, defensive tactics, and self-defense instructors around the globe. His four-volume audio CD package on the subject of mind-set, fear management, and killer instinct has been a best-seller among martial artists and trainers for more than a decade. You can learn more about his programs at www.tonyblauer.com, where you can subscribe to Mr. Blauer's free Combatives *newsletter by clicking on the "Contact Us" section.*

Loren W. Christensen's biography can be found at the back of this book.

❖

LWC: How do you define a warrior?

TB: That's such a hard one to answer because warriorlike action can manifest itself in so many ways in so many places: the courage to face battle, the courage to face fear, and the courage to face reality. I suppose, at the core, a warrior is defined by his willingness to face adversity and do what is right.

One of my favorite quotes from Emerson sums it up: "What goes on around you compares little with what goes on inside you." In other words, the true mark of a warrior is often defined by his personal virtues. That is the philosophical answer. Combatively, or, more specifically, "athletically" speaking, I see warrior essence demonstrated in contact sports, such as boxing and football. However, many of these athletes haven't balanced that skill and responsibility with some of the more Renaissance virtues that once made the warrior a coveted class.

LWC: Why are warriors needed?

TB: There are many ways to answer this. Perspective will influence an answer, and I don't know if I should focus on the philosophical or the tactical—that is, the actual combat realm. But I feel that sheer ability and toughness are only two components of a totality. At the meta level, I think the warrior class creates balance in society. There is also the DNA aspect to consider: some of us are hunters, while others are farmers, artists, doctors, and so on. There is room to have a little warrior in every calling. There have always been warriors, from caveman times to the present. So, for me, it's not so much *why* are they needed, but rather *when* weren't they needed.

LWC: Who influenced you as a warrior?

TB: So many people have influenced me over the years—and continue to. I've become friends with many people who are professional warriors and risk their lives every time they go to work. Though I've met them through my courses, I'm like Angelo Dundee, and they are like Muhammad Ali or Sugar Ray Leonard. They are fighting in the arena, and I'm outside the ropes. These men inspire me to stay razor-sharp and continually innovate new drills to address their concerns.

For me, my first warrior heroes were on television. When I was a youngster, it was Bruce Lee as Kato who transfixed me. Bob Conrad in *Wild Wild West* was super cool. Sylvester Stallone as Rocky and Sugar Ray Leonard during the Roberto Duran/Tommy Hearns years. All these men shaped or formed some idea of what toughness meant, or they exhibited something special in the way they handled violence and adversity. While I realize that three of these people were actors on television and in the movies, if you study their real, personal stories, you come to realize that what made them successful were some of the virtues and elements of conviction, tenacity, and will that are requisites for any warrior. Robert Conrad was a good boxer, as well as a martial artist. Bruce Lee was years ahead of his time as a martial artist, and Sylvester Stallone trained hard and was actually a decent fighter.

Leonard pulled off tactics and strategies in the ring with real competition that most fighters can only fantasize about. I remember throughout the 1980s getting up early in the morning, going out to run, and then coming home and watching a Sugar Ray fight. I would study his ring generalship, footwork, and combinations, and then I would create drills around them for my students. Incredibly, I was to meet and develop relationships with each of these men over the years, except for Bruce Lee, who had passed away when I was 13, though I ended up being good friends with his son, Brandon. I was able to share my experience and really connect with these people who had so inspired and driven me.

I have also studied the mind of the samurai, a great deal of Gen. George Patton, and other great leaders who've shaped our world.

LWC: Why do you, Tony Blauer, do it week after week, year after year?

TB: Loren, it's just what I do. I go 24/7 dreaming about drills. I'm constantly tearing apart courses and training principles and searching for a deeper reality. Sometimes I have no idea where ideas come from. When I was 13 my mother asked me what I was going to study when I was older, and I told her that I wouldn't really need school because I was going to develop my own martial art system and be like Bruce Lee. She smiled, patted me on the shoulder and said, "OK, Sweetie, we'll talk about this when you're older." That was 30 years ago. I know she's proud of me, but I don't think she quite knows what I do.

LWC: Why are warriors a different breed?

TB: A real warrior just *is*. It's about the DNA I mentioned earlier. A real warrior, at the tactical level, finds himself gravitating toward training, analysis, and the what-ifs. Emotionally, warriors are different because they are able to focus on the bigger picture, such as determining what is the right thing to do for another person or for society. This goes back to my answer to the question, why are warriors needed? I really think the warrior class is part of a huge human ecosystem that keeps us all in check, so to speak. I don't think there ever was a time when there weren't warriors, nor do I think there will be a time when the warrior will be extinct. After all, only another warrior can really stop a warrior. When the proverbial duel is over, metaphorically speaking, a warrior still stands.

LWC: Why is the "average" warrior willing to risk everything—from embarrassment when screwing up, to injury, to loss of life—for the mission, whether it's chasing down a purse-snatcher or going into an Afghan cave?

TB: Most likely because of the calling, because warriors are goal oriented, and because a true warrior is somewhat selfless. So the mission, the objective, the chance to verify the training is of tantamount importance to the lifestyle.

LWC: How should a warrior's mind-set be each time he trains?

TB: That really depends on what phase of training he is in. Training should always serve the ultimate objective. One of my favorite maxims is attributed to the Roman legions: "Training should be like a bloodless battle, so that battle is just like bloody training." Years ago we coined a concept called "cerebral calisthenics," and *Martial Arts Training* magazine ran a feature on it in the 1990s. The premise is quite simple: all training should be three-dimensional, i.e., it should blend the emotional, psychological, and physical arsenals; anything you work on should connect to some sort of scenario so that, irrespective of the drill, there's an emotional and psychological rationale for the exercise. This way the training triggers and creates connections between all three arsenals. Also, we remind warriors that to have theoretical confidence in training, it must be three-tiered. This means that there must be physical conditioning, skill development, and, lastly, strategic and tactical conditioning.

LWC: What should a warrior's mind-set be as he moves into danger?

TB: Loren, all our training is geared toward performance enhancement protocols. I was once asked what is the most important element of a fight, and I smiled and said, "The result."

To achieve this, we begin all of our training by attacking fear, since fear is the fist opponent. One of our maxims is this: "It's not the danger that makes us afraid, it's the fear of danger." In other words, to fully engage a threat with resolute focus, we need to understand what the risk is and train for that risk. This eliminates fear of the unknown. When we are in the tactical arena, meaning we are engaged in a real fight, we strive to be focused totally on the task and the opponent. A huge part of our training encompasses more than two decades of research into fear, especially how it afflicts performance, and we always integrate these behavioral realities into our training. Every single one of our drills blends emotional and psychological components so that danger is just another aspect of the training. In fact, we built our HIGH GEAR scenario equipment (see our Web site for details), so that the dispersion properties of the gear allow for the transfer of energy on impact. This causes pain, and pain causes fear. If you don't blend pain management and fear management into your training, you are not preparing yourself completely.

We have another drill called Emotional Climate Training, a six-stage drill that allows anyone to apply a researched formula to identify startle/flinch points and apply pain management and other conditioning aspects to almost any attack. This helps the warrior stay in the proverbial Zen moment and just focus on the threat. The bottom line is that real danger evokes and inspires emotional and psychological reactions. Fighting systems that focus mostly on the physical don't prepare for the totality of an assault.

LWC: What should a warrior's mind-set be regarding the risk of getting hurt?

TB: Here is a good maxim about training: "Training must hurt at times but should never injure." Hurt heals; injuries are permanent at some level. This mind-set carries over to real-world activities. Provided the drills replicate reality, realistic training attitude and effort create a form of stress inoculation for the real world.

LWC: What should a warrior's mind-set be regarding the risk of getting killed?

TB: This is just an extension of the mind-set of moving into danger and the risk of getting hurt. I come back to the psychology of fear and the need to manage it during intense stress and danger. Dan Millman, a former world champion athlete, college professor, and best selling author, once said, "If you face just one opponent and you doubt yourself, you're outnumbered." I love that because it sums up the simplicity of it all. In the heat of the moment, the warrior athlete must focus on the dynamic of the game, because any and every distraction can potentially derail the effort.

LWC: What should a warrior's mind-set be regarding having to kill?

TB: The scenario should always dictate the choices one makes in a confrontation. If the situation is credible, if the requisite level of force to achieve safety requires it, then killing should be approached simply as another tactic.

I'm not trying to sound cavalier about it. In more than 20 years of teaching, I have seen the graphic result of people choosing to fight back too late or not taking a threat seriously. Having had the honor of working with sport warriors like mixed martial arts fighters and boxers, as well as working extensively with real-world warriors like soldiers and cops, I've seen my intuition proven right about the importance of mental preparation in conjunction with realistic training. In the real world, force must parallel danger.

YOU SCARE ME!

by Dave Rose

Dave Rose retired from the Placer County (California) Sheriff's Department after 25 years of service, with 28 years total law enforcement experience. He is a certified instructor in defensive tactics, impact weapons, firearms, survival shooting, less-lethal munitions, submachine guns, distraction devices, Tasers, incident command, and WMDs. Mr. Rose has 23 years of SWAT experience, including entry team, entry team leader, assistant team leader, team leader, and team commander. He has received three Silver Stars for Bravery from the American Police Hall of Fame, two Bronze Medals of Honor and one Bronze Medal of Valor from the Placer County Law Enforcement Awards Program, and the J. Edgar Hoover Gold Medal for Distinguished Public Service from the American Police Hall of Fame. Mr. Rose served in the U.S. Army as a military policeman and received a Bronze Star during his Vietnam service.

Mr. Rose is a published coauthor of numerous articles printed in several law enforcement periodicals. He is the coauthor of Police Use-of Force Case Law: The Complete Trainer, Instructor's Guide *published by Varro Press. He is also the coauthor of* Paradigm of the Moral Warrior, *currently being considered for publication.*

Mr. Rose has testified as an expert witness in both California and federal courts in the areas of police practices, use of force, deadly weapons, training, firearms, and electronic control devices.

❖

"You scare me!" "He scares me!" If only I had a thousand dollars for every time I heard one of those comments, or similar ones regarding me or directed at me, I could pay off both my truck and car loans and have some money left over!

What is it about being a warrior that genuinely makes the average person queasy or uncomfortable? Why are warriors looked at as a lion or tiger is by herds of prey animals? I'm not just talking about those who don't actually know you personally, but coworkers and family members. What characteristics or qualities do warriors possess or exhibit that leave the average person uneasy and fearful? Should warriors learn to curb or suppress these qualities or character traits in order to set the rest of society at ease?

Often warriors are told, "I saw you take a stance and could tell by your posture that you were going to do something," though the more mature warrior isn't consciously aware of doing the action that is ascribed to him. This is a result of the action having become ingrained to the point that it is a natural response to any high-risk situation. To achieve that level of competence, the warrior needs to process and respond on automatic mode. Thus, his character and qualities of action must be natural and could only be consciously stuffed down, which is unhealthy in the long term.

Society and the families of warriors are ever so grateful for the warrior immediately following his protective actions. We saw this very behavior immediately after the September 11, 2001, terrorist attacks. Yet over time, those feelings become eroded. The warrior is not completely trusted by society. Warriors are tolerated by most of society, including their superiors, as a necessary evil. What is the cause of this intolerance to warriors and warrior ways?

Fear, real or imagined. Not just physical fear of the warrior's capabilities, but fear of the power he can wield by force of his integrity, and the following this integrity generates among society's members when the going gets bad. I believe there is also an inherent fear among members of society that they too could be capable of delivering violence or even death to a predator in the proper circumstances. That reality is frightening to the majority of them. Just the acknowledgment that warriors and warrior ways are needed for the protection of that society is often offensive to today's public. This causes many top administrators and politicians to fear telling the truth to citizens.

Some members of society actually consider a warrior to be no different than a violent predator criminal. This is most often demonstrated by those who protest why a warrior had to be "so violent" in suppressing the actions of a violent societal predator. These same societal members assail the warrior for not expressing heartfelt sorrow for using force on an aggressor. Most often the warrior's superiors or political leaders wield this particular slanted attack on the warrior society.

Part of the issue can be attributed to the warrior's ability to discuss, explain, train, and apply force when required. Warriors do this with calm intellect and matter-of-fact emphasis. Most members of today's society have been trained to think emotionally with their hearts instead of their brains. That is, for them it is more important to *feel* than to evaluate intelligently and respond appropriately. Because warriors tend not to demonstrate an emotional response to violence, but rather a practical and decisive action, others are oftentimes intimidated. What if the warrior decided to use his capabilities against society?

Over the course of my 28-year law enforcement career, I have been described as the "point of the spear" of the department. My superiors have actually used the "warrior" word when describing me or my fellow trainers or SWAT members. At the same time that these accolades, such as they were, occurred, there immediately followed a comment that we were to be kept out of the public view until needed to act or intimidate. Many times I have been told that when the "dogs of war" are needed we will be activated and are expected to win. Public acknowledgment, however, is relatively unheard of. This did not make me depressed or angry, but rather surprised and resigned to the fact that some people are just not emotionally or intellectually wired to be warriors.

My father, a World War II navy combat veteran, often quizzed me on why I continued to practice martial arts and remained part of the SWAT unit for most of my career. He properly pointed out that there was no financial benefit, or much public recognition, for all of the sweat, pain, and blood involved. I did it because it was the right thing to do for me, and the acknowledgments received from my fellow warriors were worth more than money or public acknowledgment. Warriors pride themselves on being able to respond in emergency situations and being counted on by their families and society.

A fellow warrior-trainer, Lt. Col. Dave Grossman, equates the warrior to a sheepdog and society to a flock of sheep. The sheep tolerate the sheepdog but don't particularly like or trust him. But when the wolves come looking for meat, the sheep all flock around the sheepdog for protection. I like to use the analogy of lions and their interactions with hyenas. When the lions are in a pack, or a strong solitary lion makes a kill, the hyenas stay away. When the strong lion leaves or the pack is weakened somehow, the hyenas come around in force. I liken the lion to the warrior and the hyenas to the predators of society. The superiors or political leaders who are quick to criticize the warrior's actions are three-legged dogs.

Most warriors are also considered fine leaders, particularly by the rank and file. This is why they are feared by many of their peers and superiors. Those who gained their positions by being "nonwarriors" fear the warrior and his capabilities. Animosity is also directed at warriors by the "wannabe warrior" who doesn't want to commit physically to attaining the title of warrior. This is especially acute when the warrior has trained many others and they now represent an opposing force to the whims and wants of those nonwarriors in the organization or society. Warriors represent a strong opposition force to those who would advocate political correctness over the harder, right thing to do.

All of this should fortify the warrior to continue the tradition and train those who follow to maintain the ethos of the way. There will always be fear of, animosity toward, or jealousy of the warrior and warrior ways. We have seen this in American law enforcement to the point that most agencies have organized opposition to warrior training and even use of the word "warrior." Part of the tradition of warriors is tenacity. Trainers need to continue to pursue every avenue to train upcoming warriors to be properly prepared to defend society against the predators, regardless of whether society expresses its appreciation or understanding of who they are and what they do. We need to ensure that society always has a group of warriors ready to defend them and our way of life.

To ensure the adequate supply of future warriors, it's important that the retiring warrior and warrior trainer educate members of society on the value and importance of the warrior class. One way is to write articles and books and to lecture on the subject. Educating judges and juries is another excellent method. Every opportunity should be taken to explain why a warrior action was taken and/or why a certain level of force or violence was needed in a particular incident. Most importantly, we must allow ourselves to be seen and perceived as part of the fabric of society.

The main difference between the warrior and the sheep is that the warrior will place his life in jeopardy for society, an ideal, or a principle, knowing it might be his ultimate, final act. He knows that, should he survive, his reward will more likely come from within than from those he serves.

THE HEROIC SET
OF SHOULDERS

by Sgt. Rocky Warren

Rocky Warren is a U.S. Army veteran, former SWAT operator, and law enforcement veteran of more than 28 years, having worked as a military policeman, sheriff's deputy, detective, jail supervisor, and patrol sergeant. He has received two Bronze Medals of Valor. Mr. Warren is now employed part time for two community colleges, where he teaches defensive tactics, impact weapons, and firearms; officer-safety field tactics; SWAT; and immediate entry/active shooter response. Mr. Warren retired recently from active law enforcement to pursue his training, teaching, writing, consulting, and use-of-force expert witness services.

Mr. Warren has written three books that are available through BarnesAndNoble.com, Amazon.com, and other Internet outlets, or upon request at any major bookstore: Behind the Badge: Real Stories from the Police Beat, *by Rocky Warren (Varro Press);* Police Use of Force Case Law, *by Dave Rose and Rocky Warren (Varro Press); and* Paradigm of the Moral Warrior, *by Dave Rose and Rocky Warren (www.ebookstand.com, a division of CyberRead).*

You can learn more about Mr. Warren through his Warren Consulting Web site at www.rockywarren.com.

❖

Throughout history, heroic people were apparent by the set of their shoulders.

The fighter slides in closer to his opponent with his left shoulder hunched in front of his vulnerable jaw. Yet there are also degrees of finesse in the positioning and set of the shoulders. It's all open to situation and interpretation. The fencing swordsman extends and ranges his shoulder to use as a pivot point for his wrist and the snake-fast flick of the blade. Yet the wielder of a broadsword uses the sweep of his shoulder to hack away, meat-axe style. Which is most efficient? Who is the best at his craft? As with anything in life, only time will tell.

In these modern times, there are many heroic sets of the shoulders. Sometimes it takes a very good eye to tell where and who the heroic are.

❖

Doctors leave the surgical suite and fling their bloody gloves into the blind cloth sack marked "biohazard." The top surgeon removes the shapeless, ugly, blood-spattered gown, never realizing that blood has soaked through the outer gown so that a smear spreads across her stomach. She's too bemused to notice the blood smear until later, and then it causes her to say a bad word. Her shoulders are stooped forward with fatigue from the hours-long operation. Our doctor's bemused state is because she's saved someone when she just knew that the patient would die. Incredibly, her surgery hasn't killed the young man, and if she knew just why, she'd be able to save more of them. But the doctor has been at her craft long enough to know that it was God's will, or fate, that kept the patient alive. In the future, she'll save more she thought lost and lose a few she was sure she could save. No rhyme or reason. It just is.

The doctor works her shoulders back and forth, trying to ease the stiffness, as she turns down the corridor. There's a family in the surgical waiting room that still has to receive the news.

❖

The flare of rotating lights gives the car crash site a surreal glow every half second. The gurney is ringed with firefighters and emergency medical technicians, as the screaming teenager writhes in agony with a broken back. Strong hands support the extremities, and one fireman kneels at the head of the gurney. In a grotesque turn of phrase, this fireman's position is crucial. He holds the wailing teenager's head straight and solid on the gurney; firefighters and emergency medical technicians (EMTs) call it "being married to the head."

No matter which way the body turns, the fireman holds the head steady to the shoulders so the rough edges of the spine don't saw through the spinal cord, killing the patient or making her a quadriplegic. The fireman has a daughter the same age as this girl, and the two look very much alike. When the cervical collar is strapped around the patient's neck and her head is firmly strapped to the board, the fireman can finally relax.

He stands, his shoulders slumped with fatigue. His eyes are dry now, but they weren't a couple of minutes ago. No one on the scene will ever know . . .

❖

In the full pitch-blackness of night, a man, a police suspect, lies on his back on the ground. One uniformed officer kneels over him, alternately pressing on his chest and breathing for him. Another officer comes over and takes over the chest compressions. Naturally, he takes the clean job. He leaves the breaths to the original officer, and the reason becomes obvious when the gunshot suspect vomits explosively, spraying the one giving him the breath of life. That officer earns his pay when he too vomits, wipes the face of the suspect, and then returns to giving breaths between bouts of gagging.

His shoulders hunch forward with his effort to breathe life into another human.

❖

The 14-year-old girl pants heavily as she runs through the field. She is nude and blood streams down the front and back of her body from 13 knife wounds. Behind her, a psychopathic rapist gives chase. After he had imposed his evil, twisted will upon her body, he tried to kill her, but she fought back and ran. The girl dives through a barbed-wire fence and veers across the county roadway toward oncoming headlights. A woman and her children see the young victim suddenly appear from nowhere, naked and bleeding in their headlights. The young woman's shoulders rise and fall with exertion as she drops into the welcome safety of the Good Samaritan's car seat. The driver speeds away to the hospital.

The girl survives. Later, when she takes the witness stand in court, she feels shaking and tension in her shoulders. She faces her attacker, identifies him, and tells everything . . . everything he did to her. In a calm, rational, and orderly fashion, she makes sure the sexual predator will never make a victim of any other living soul.

When she steps down from the witness stand, there is strength and dignity in her shoulders, a set of shoulders that once trembled with fear and shame.

❖

Inez stands on her front porch, smoking quietly. She figures she owes herself a short break after the days, months, and years of work. The sound of a guttural grunting inside the tiny house reaches her ears, and she snaps her cigarette into a coffee can with a set expression.

Inez squares her shoulders and plants a wry smile on her face. She's been with her husband for more than three decades. For more than two of them, his small progressive strokes have put him into a hospital bed under total-care conditions, with all that that entails. Her shoulders are straight and proud as she walks through the door and into the bedroom. A lopsided grin on his face tells her that he is awake. In the cruelest of ironies, his mind is sharp but the body is wrecked. He needs to be changed, fed, his bed cleaned, and medicines given. Not just today, but tomorrow, and the day after, and the day after that. For as long as they both last.

The small smile on her face is unchanging as she teases her husband a little. He enjoys the interaction as much as she does. It is what they have left, and they both treasure it. Inez goes about her tasks with a small smile and squared shoulders.

Until death do us part means something more than average to this woman.

Her squared shoulders reveal her firm determination and her commitment to love and duty.

❖

In historic times, there were many obvious heroes, and they were easy to single out. But if we were to take any of the people in these true stories away from their settings and scatter them among other people, would you be able to tell which one was the hero?

Everyone has the capacity to be a hero, and the vast majority of people have been one at some time in their lives. There is no race, religion, color, sexual orientation, or other factor that makes people heroes. Treat each person you meet with the dignity he or she deserves. You can never tell when you'll be face-to-face with a hero.

Even when you're looking in a mirror.

WALKING WITH WARRIORS

by Chris Lawrence

Chris Lawrence began his career as a police officer in 1979. His experience included walking a beat, general patrol, serving on a Marine unit boat crew, assignments to the dive team, serving in a tactical and rescue unit, working in a criminal investigation bureau, and instructing in the training bureau. Since 1996, he has served as an instructor at one of Canada's largest police training schools as a specialist in defensive tactics. Mr. Lawrence is a graduate student at Royal Roads University in Victoria, British Columbia. He has been training warriors since 1983.

❖

It was a pleasant surprise and an honor to be asked to provide a chapter for this book. I do not think of myself as a warrior; however, on reflection, I know what it is like to walk with them.

The root of the word warrior is war, conflict: a subject that readily conjures up images of strength, willingness to engage the enemy, prowess as a fighter, commitment to battle. These are common elements of the traditional portrait of the strong, courageous, battle-ready warrior—the kind of individuals Jack Nicholson's character speaks of in his famous courtroom scene in *A Few Good Men* when he says, "We live in a world that has walls, and these walls have to be guarded by men [and women] with guns."

Preparing to write this essay required me to examine this stereotype beyond a first impression, and in the process my original concept of what a warrior is and what he does went through a transformation. This reflective process led to my realization that the former view lacked appreciation for the depth possessed by those who meet the criteria to be defined as true warriors. A psychopath may have the ability to fight effectively. Likewise, an individual may possess Olympian strength yet lack personal courage. Neither could ever be considered a warrior.

To get to the essence of what makes a person a warrior, I weighed the qualities of individuals known to be warriors. What became apparent is that fighting ability is only a small part of what makes one a warrior. Although strength does indeed play a part, the measure of strength goes well beyond muscular development.

A true warrior knows that his most effective weapon is his mind. He possesses the ability to engage an enemy and is prepared to fight to the death when necessary, yet he also appreciates the value of avoiding battle because he is keenly aware of the human cost. Fighting is not as much fun as it looks. The reality is that one who looks for a fight has seldom, if ever, been in one, or he has been involved in too many. Lost on him is Sun Tzu's precept: "To conquer the enemy without having to resort to war is a greater achievement than fighting to win every battle."

My reexamination of the concept of warriorhood also brought to light that warriors exist in roles other than those traditionally associated with the word. Among the examples that spring immediately to mind are individuals found within the ranks of corrections officers, firefighters, nurses, and paramedics. Consider the collection of society's citizens within any prison, or the furious nature and unpredictability of a fire. Some warriors battle foes not human, yet just as deadly. These warriors contribute greatly to our safety and provide for the diverse lineaments of our lives.

Warriors are complex individuals with much greater depth than one can appreciate from a first impression. They are truly people of quality, and, above all else, they are human beings in every sense of the word. Warriors are still subject to human frailties and are thus capable of making mistakes.

Warriors sometimes take for granted the people they love and who love them dearly. They will always respond to a call for help, secure in the knowledge that their families are safe and will stay that way until they return. Warriors' families learn to accept this fact, although their acceptance does not mean they like the choice made. Those who understand the warrior's philosophy know that it is not for lack of love that he leaves his family, but rather for what *seems* to be a temporary shift of mission. At times something must be done, and that something requires the warrior's full attention. It is done out of a love of others—a love not limited by sanguinity. Those who love their warriors understand that there is no shift in mission at all. They understand that what warriors leave to do is in fact part of their greater purpose: service to and protection for their families and community.

Warriors often fail to share their burdens, fears, and concerns with others. Because of the sense of selflessness warriors possess, we can expect to encounter those who are blind to their own circumstances (or maybe it would be more accurate to say that they choose to ignore them for the sake of others). A warrior can be as blind as any other human being. I recall a situation where a warrior and friend lost his wife to cancer. A couple of days after the funeral he returned to his duties, confident in his ability to continue his mission. I watched as he struggled with his situation over time. He never once asked for consideration, nor did he admit to needing time for himself. He carried his burden alone, blind to his worsening condition. I watched in frustration as time passed and this warrior continued to attend to the needs and desires of everyone except himself. When I finally determined that I could no longer stand by, I spoke with my friend and told him what everyone else could see. He had been so focused on getting from one day to the next that he was unable to see the state of the bigger picture.

Warriors are subject to being tempted like any other person. In times of weakness they can fall to their humanness. Unlike others, a warrior can pick himself up and resume the path. He will also allow himself to be picked up by others who possess the capacity to lift him from where he is and place him where he needs to be. A warrior thanks the one who does this, and he will lift those who stumble nearby without asking for acknowledgment, tribute, or ceremony.

Warriors make errors in judgment, and because they are *doing,* rather than watching or waiting, they can do so with greater frequency than others. Watchers and waiters are seldom wrong, but only because they are watchers and waiters, not warriors. Warriors add to life; watchers and waiters do not. A warrior will step forward and admit a mistake for what it is—a part of being human. Fellow warriors understand and forgive because they know that "there but for the grace of God go I." Watchers and waiters often demand that a penalty be inflicted upon a warrior for the error, because that is how watchers and waiters understand the world.

Warriors inherently possess a clear understanding of right and wrong. The rest of us must learn and study virtue under the title of ethics. Critics may argue that warriors should not be given understanding, leeway, or lenience when they commit errors or do what is seen—from the safety and cleanliness of a courtroom or from behind an editorial desk—as the wrong thing. These same critics often claim that a warrior's strong sense of right and wrong precludes mercy. The critics would do well to consider the context of the warrior's decisions. But often they are incapable of appreciating what a warrior does, for they do not—and likely never will—possess the necessary frame of reference. Two warriors named Theodore Roosevelt and John F. Kennedy made this point much clearer than I can:

> It is not the critic who counts: not the man who points out how the strong man stumbles or where the doer of deeds could have done better. The credit belongs to the man who is actually in the arena, whose face is marred by dust and sweat and blood, who strives valiantly, who errs and comes up short again and again, because there is no effort without error or shortcoming, but who knows the great enthusi-

asms, the great devotions, who spends himself for a worthy cause; who, at best, knows, in the end, the triumph of high achievement, and who, at the worst, if he fails, at least he fails while daring greatly, so that his place shall never be with those cold and timid souls who knew neither victory nor defeat.

Roosevelt made this speech at the Sorbonne in Paris on April 23, 1910. Kennedy paraphrased it in his remarks at the National Football Hall of Fame Banquet in 1961. I think their comments speak directly to the difference between the warriors and the watchers and waiters.

Warriors possess the strength and ability to rise to the task. They are capable of bulling through adversity and can become temporarily microfocused by mission—what is sometimes known as the "fog of war." The difference between one who is a warrior and one who is not is the warrior's ability to bull on while still managing to grasp the fruit of life with hands rather than smashing it with hooves.

A warrior's compassion extends to those he does not know and those he does not like. Who but a warrior responds to sounds and situations that instill fear in citizens, aids people unknown to him, and endures dangerous conditions to help others? Who else volunteers to fight, knowing well that sometimes warriors die while helping people they have never broken bread with?

A warrior will always assist others with their burdens and do so unencumbered by prejudice. While he may have personal views that conflict with others, he possesses a sense of purpose greater than himself. George Bernard Shaw concisely summed up this perspective when he wrote, "This is the true joy of life, the being used for a purpose recognized . . . as a mighty one . . . the being a force of nature instead of a feverish, selfish little clod of ailments and grievances complaining that the world will not devote itself to making you happy." Warriors add to the timbre of life.

Warriors are committed to community. I came to understand the true meaning of community by having the privilege of attending what was once a World War II warrior's school, the former Royal Canadian Naval College at Royal Roads on Vancouver Island, British Columbia. The wholeness of my understanding occurred while standing above Neptune's Stairs, a rally point where warriors once met, on the campus of what is now Royal Roads University. Warriors are committed to community—the community of warriors, coworkers, and citizens. They understand and are able to interact with each level as needed. They also understand intrinsically the importance and value of each person within the community.

Warriors have a capacity for commitment beyond that of the average person. They obtain training as warriors because they choose to attend schools like West Point, Annapolis, and the Royal Military College of Canada. It is said that such schools do not train warriors; they merely identify them. Not everyone who graduates from a warrior school will be one. True warriors are a combination of intelligence, spirit, integrity, and compassion. They must be able to make a commitment to assist others before they worry about themselves (an uncommon feature within our greater society).

A warrior follows commands and understands that people who have authority to give them do so with good reason. While respectfully following orders, warriors consciously as well as unconsciously align each order with their own moral compass. "I was only following orders" never spews from the warrior's mouth.

The difference between a mere fighter and a warrior is subtle, yet tangible. There is an aura about a warrior, if one simply pays attention, which can be seen from a distance as well as up close.

The greatest compliment one can receive comes from a warrior. For when he says that he was glad to have fought alongside you because he knew you would not abandon him, regardless the odds, or he tells you that he would place you on the right side of the line, the side of ancient battle formations unprotected by a shield, the place of the bravest, you too are being recognized as a warrior.

For one cannot claim the title. It is an honor bestowed by other warriors.

YOU CAN'T ALWAYS GET WHAT YOU WANT
WHY BEING A WARRIOR STARTS WITH ACCEPTING THE LIMITATIONS OF PEACE

by Michael D. Janich

Michael D. Janich has been studying and teaching self-defense and the martial arts for more than 25 years. A certified instructor of several martial arts systems and a member of the elite International Close-Combat Instructors Association (ICCIA), he is also a recognized expert in handgun point shooting and one of the few contemporary instructors to have been personally trained by the late close-combat legend Col. Rex Applegate.

Mr. Janich served nine years in the U.S. Army, including a three-year tour at the National Security Agency (NSA). He is a two-time graduate with honors of the Defense Language Institute in Monterey, California (Vietnamese and Chinese-Mandarin), a recipient of the Commandant's Award for Outstanding Linguistic Achievement, and one of only two U.S. Army Vietnamese linguists to have achieved professional certification from NSA as a voice language analyst. As a civilian, Mr. Janich served as an intelligence officer for the Defense Intelligence Agency's (DIA's) Stony Beach Program in Hong Kong and the Philippines. He also served as an investigation team leader for the Joint Casualty Resolution Center (JCRC) and Joint Task Force–Full Accounting (JTF–FA) and has led numerous investigations into remote areas of Vietnam and Laos in search of information regarding American prisoners of war and missing in action (POW/MIA).

Mr. Janich is the author of six books and twelve instructional videotapes on personal protection and exotic weapons. He is also the founder of the Martial Blade Craft (MBC) and Counter-Blade Craft (CBC) edged-weapon tactics programs and regularly provides targeted defensive tactics instruction to law enforcement officers, government agencies, and concerned civilians. Mr. Janich may be contacted at modtempest@aol.com.

Additional information on his background and training programs can be found at www.martialbladecraft.com.

War can only be abolished through war.

—Mao Zedong

The way of the warrior begins with acceptance of the fact that reason requires two willing minds. Whether the conflict in question is a struggle between two individuals or a true war involving many nations, a peaceful solution is always dependent upon the willingness of the opposing party to listen to reason. In the real world, violent, aggressive people who are immune to reason either get their way or are stopped by greater, more skilled, and more determined violence and aggression. While this viewpoint may seem pessimistic, it actually takes more strength to acknowledge the shortcomings of human nature than it does to place blind hope in it. And the way of the warrior is characterized by strength—strength of mind, strength of body, strength of conviction, and strength of action.

To be a warrior is to accept the inevitable reality of human conflict and prepare for it diligently while at the same time never sacrificing one's appreciation of humanity. It is the ability to respect life while actively developing both the will and the skill to ruthlessly take it when necessary. It is an incredibly fine balance that empowers good men to do horrible things for all the right reasons.

The quintessential warrior embraces both the mind-set and the physical discipline of war completely. For him, there is no separation between the will to win and the skill to win. While this concept of the warrior is often associated with classical martial cultures like the samurai, this type of intense individual discipline and commitment exists just as readily in modern soldiers, law enforcement officers, and hard-core self-defense practitioners. The true warriors of this breed realize that regardless of the scope of a particular conflict or the nature of an assigned mission, their *individual* survival may depend upon their skill and determination to fight. As such, they train themselves to be intimately familiar with the darkest aspects of physical combat and to value their lives above those of their enemies.

Once again, the reasoning behind this approach is not a lack of humanity or a morbid obsession with violence. It is the simple act of realizing which tools are required for which jobs and employing them without hesitation to get the job done. In extreme combat situations, mind-sets and skill sets that do not support the quick, efficient, and ruthlessly detached elimination of a violent enemy are simply inadequate.

Although modern combatants have a tremendous arsenal of weapons at their disposal, training in close-quarters personal combat remains one of the most effective—and important—means of instilling and cultivating the warrior spirit. By developing the skills and strength to take combat to a personal level, the warrior learns true self-reliance. He realizes that knives, guns, and other ordnance are merely tools and that the true weapon he wields is his own will. A warrior empowered by this understanding soon realizes that even without purpose-designed weapons, he is still a force to be reckoned with. He also learns that it is his will that enables something to *become* a weapon and begins to approach combat with an entirely new creative mind-set.

While some people may question the need for hand-to-hand combat training for modern combatants, I still feel it is unequaled as a means of developing warrior spirit and therefore a critical element of defining the ultimate warrior. It is also an incredibly effective way of identifying one's *own* shortcomings and, again, learning to approach conflict with an open mind. For example, a soldier forced to train with a larger, stronger partner may realize that he is physically outmatched. Rather than admitting defeat, he learns to overcome his disadvantage through a superior mental attitude, or he learns to cheat and introduce weapons of opportunity to even the odds. Believing oneself invincible can be a powerful tool; however, realizing one's own limitations and learning both how and when to stack the odds in your favor is even more powerful.

With this concept of the quintessential warrior in mind, it is easy to see how the term "warrior" can apply more readily to law enforcement officers, bouncers, prison guards, and street people than it does to a uniformed soldier who looks the part but lacks the will to fight with everything he's got. Curiously, this definition of the term also disqualifies many high-ranking martial artists who, due to an excessive focus on mysticism, unrealistic tournament competition, or cross-cultural experiences, have never made a substantial connection between their skills and any kind of combative reality. In short, the ultimate warrior is any person who, in the face of unavoidable conflict, jumps mind, soul, heart, and body into the fray and takes the fight to his opponent using any means at his disposal.

Although close-combat physical skills do much to instill the warrior spirit, they are by no means a prerequisite for warrior status. The modern, technological approach to conflict has created another type of warrior who uses sophisticated tools to enable him to wage war from a distance. This approach to combat may seem much less personal than a face-to-face engagement with an enemy; however, it is not necessarily any less difficult.

This class of warrior includes snipers, pilots, artillerymen, and anyone else who uses long-range weapons to destroy an enemy. This sanitized approach to warfare depersonalizes the concept of killing and greatly separates the act from the result. However, while markedly different from engaging an enemy in close-quarter combat, it nevertheless requires extreme levels of skill and commitment.

Warriors who engage an enemy at close range may be fighting for a mission or some greater cause, but they are very definitely fighting for their own survival. Whether willingly or unwillingly, they have ended up in harm's way and must apply their skills and will to ensure their own survival. This type of conflict presents extreme challenges, but at the same time it allows the reasonably efficient control of collateral damage. When fighting up close and personal, it's easier to know who's getting hit.

Tactically, a sniper takes this type of combat to the next logical progression. Although he is still able to maintain focus on specific targets, he is usually removed from the immediate threat of his targets' action. Through the application of extreme skill, he is able to engage the enemy from a safer distance. Although this "safety" may suggest less commitment on the sniper's part, that is not the case. Part of what defines a warrior is compassion and a sense of fair play. As such, the act of killing an opponent who does not have a realistic chance of "fighting back" can be much more mentally challenging than the act of engaging an opponent face to face. It therefore requires an even more highly evolved warrior mind-set and challenges the warrior even more to maintain the delicate balance between respecting and taking life.

Taking this progression one step further, we arrive at a class of warriors even further removed from the realm of personal combat, yet capable of delivering tremendous—and potentially indiscriminate—death and devastation. Like the sniper, pilots, artillerymen, and other warriors who deliver firepower from great distances must develop extreme skill to perform their jobs effectively. However, unlike the stray bullet of a sniper that may claim one unintended life, the shells, bombs, and missiles of the techno-warrior may—unintentionally or, if the situation warrants, by design—claim the lives of hundreds or even thousands of noncombatants. Despite the distance and insulation that this type of warfare provides, its effect is still very real, as are the challenges placed on the mind-set and conviction of the warriors who engage in it. The men who dropped the bombs on Nagasaki and Hiroshima were warriors in the truest sense. They realized the nature of the threat we faced and found within themselves the conviction to do something horrible for the sake of the greater good.

The final class of warrior, in my opinion, is the true leader of men. During my years of military and government service, I had many unique opportunities to learn the tremendous difference between rank and leadership. While working in the military intelligence community during the latter years of the Cold War, I observed great men manifesting every ideal of a true warrior as they led our efforts to survive and thrive as a superpower. Although the nature of their war was different, their mind-set and conviction were just as real and just as powerful as those of any battlefield warrior.

As an investigation team leader charged with resolving the fates of servicemen missing in action from the Vietnam War, I became intimately familiar with the heroic actions of thousands of true warriors who lost their lives fighting for what they believed. I also worked with dozens of honorable men who exemplified the warrior mind-set in their approach to that mission, silently suffering extreme personal hardships to do what was right and to honor the memories of the men we served.

At the same time, I was sickened and disgusted by the petty rivalries of many of the senior officers and politicians involved in that effort. I saw firsthand how a major general's abusive management of literally hundreds of personnel could be easily outshined by a sergeant's real leadership of a small team. And ultimately, I found it within myself to stand up against the generals, the government agencies, and the politicians, and fight that war my way.

Being a warrior has nothing to do with uniforms, weapons, or outdated military traditions. It has *everything* to do with believing that there are important things in life worth fighting for. And although we may do our best to avoid trouble, sometimes trouble insists on finding us. When that happens, when the time for talk is over, warriors act. They flip the switch and act decisively—ruthlessly if necessary—to preserve and defend the things they hold dear. And when the fight is over, they turn off the switch and continue to cherish the things they valued enough to defend. That's what makes them warriors. And that's what makes them the good guys.

The Journey

Graham Greene said, "There is always one moment in childhood when the door opens and lets the future in."

—Loren W. Christensen,
from "Discovery"

DISCOVERY

by Loren W. Christensen

Loren W. Christensen's biography can be found at the back of this book. "Discovery" was taken in part from Mr. Christensen's book Crouching Tiger: Taming the Warrior Within.

❖

As a teenager, I got into three fights that not only opened my eyes to violence but also revealed something inside of me that I didn't know existed. I was unaware of this thing called warrior spirit then, but I was to learn that fighting brought something to the surface that at once intrigued, frightened, fascinated, and repelled me.

I was about 15 years old and on a school bus when I got into my first fistfight. I stood toe-to-toe in the aisle with a big, older kid and exchanged a couple dozen face punches with him. Eventually, he knocked me across a seat, straddled me, and punched my face at will. Though I was the first to give up, he too was glad to see it end because his eyes, nose, and lips were swelling as fast as mine.

Afterward, everything on my body hurt, but I felt a strange exhilaration and a sense of pride for having given my best in a good fight. I lost, but I proved to myself—that voice of self-doubt in the back of my mind—and to those on the bus that I was not a coward. I wasn't anxious to get into another fight anytime soon, but if one happened, I knew I could give a good account of myself, even if I lost again. Author Graham Greene said, "There is always one moment in childhood when the door opens and lets the future in." But I didn't see that then.

Two years later, my best friend, Mike, and I slugged it out behind a grocery store where we both worked, a hugely one-sided fight in which I punched and kicked him at will. It lasted 20 minutes—18 minutes longer than the average fight. I didn't want it to go that long. Actually, I didn't want it to happen at all, but every time I tried to walk away, he pushed, shoved and encouraged me to continue. It ended with him lying in a fetal position, moaning and spitting up blood.

Later that night, I thought about why I let the fight happen in the first place. Although Mike started it (he was angry with me over something that happened in the store), he was my best friend, so I should have backed away and flatly refused to fight him. But I didn't. I fought him and . . . I liked it. It was exciting, and I enjoyed the strategy during the fight and the sense of power I felt afterward, feelings that were far more intense than the guilt I had.

When I was 19, about five months after I began studying karate, a drunk jumped me in the parking lot of a hamburger joint. The attack was unprovoked and caught me by surprise, but after I got my bearings, I kicked the man in the throat, sending him sprawling over the hood of a car. I leaped on him like a madman, grabbing his hair and repeatedly banging his head against the windshield, bringing screams of terror from the young couple in the car who were clutching each other desperately. A police officer cruising through the lot leapt out of his car, pulled us apart, and then unwisely stuffed us into his backseat without handcuffing us. When he went to interview witnesses, I resumed punching my attacker in the face, and the officer had to jump into the back to separate us again. Another police car was summoned so my attacker and I could be taken to jail in separate rides. An hour later he was taken to a hospital with a throat injury, and then a month later a judge found him guilty of unprovoked assault.

I learned from this fight that I was capable of great rage, especially when bullied. Once I hurt the man with my kick, I attacked him with ferocity, ignoring his throat injury and his inability to fight back. I was enraged by his attack and I wanted to punish him. If it hadn't been for the police officer, I don't know how far I would have gone.

I had never before felt this extraordinary rage and aggression, and it concerned and frightened me. Where did it come from? Would my martial arts training help? Would it make it worse by supplying a weapon for my rage and aggression?

My training quickly became a place to vent my energy and aggression. Along with my ability to hurt people came a respect for the fighting arts, for others, for myself, and a philosophy not to abuse the weapons and the power I'd worked so hard to develop. This didn't happen overnight; I made mistakes early on and hurt people.

I joined the army in 1967 and discovered quickly that I loved the training—the mud, sweat, fatigue, and camaraderie. I loved it and I was good at it. I did well in military police school, and after a few months of stateside duty, I volunteered for Vietnam. After studying Vietnamese at the Defense Language Institute in Arlington, Virginia, I ended up patrolling the very mean streets of Saigon as a military policeman.

Dealing with rocket attacks, terrorist bombings, anti-American riots, bar brawls, combative AWOLs, street fights, thefts, drug overdoses, assaults, and murder investigations kept us humping 12 to 14 hours every shift, every day. It was a marvelous, intense, enlightening, and horrific time to test, analyze, and adjust my warrior craft, to use my army training and my martial arts. There were times when I was proud of how I defined warriorhood through my actions—helping other American servicemen and Vietnamese, sometimes routinely, sometimes heroically, though I never thought then about being a hero, or really cared about the label.

There were also times when I was ashamed at how I performed.

I had been there only a couple of months when my old rage returned, sparked by an obnoxious Marine refusing with all his might to be arrested. When the struggle came to a place where I'd had enough, I punched him, a driving karate punch deep into his chest. He collapsed, falling straight to the ground, twitching at first, and then shaking violently as his heart went into fibrillation. It was a long night at the hospital waiting to see if he was going to survive. He did.

I was ashamed and embarrassed. I had abused my power, my physical power and the power of my position.

That wasn't the only time I acted wrongly. I learned from most of my mistakes—my stupidity, my power trips, and my ineptness—and tried to grow and progress from each of them. Sometimes it took repeat occurrences before I caught on.

I learned something else while I was in Vietnam. When all about me was chaos—a riot of horrific sounds, sights, confusion, and insanity—I discovered I loved it. I could function in it and do what I was supposed to do: my duty. I literally went to the sound of gunfire, as well as the sound of explosions, while everyone else took cover or fled. Through it all, I took care of my fellow MPs and they took care of me.

The day before I was to leave country and return home, there was some kind of demonstration at AFVN (Armed Forces Vietnam), the American radio station made popular in the Robin Williams movie *Good Morning Vietnam*. It was unknown whether it was Vietcong (VC) or South Vietnamese protestors, but it was known that an MP unit was trapped. My company went on alert, everyone into the trucks with flak vests, M60s, M16s, and grenade launchers. But I was ordered off. "You're short, Christensen. Get the hell off the truck. You're goin' home tomorrow." I wanted to go. I insisted. But I was literally pushed off the back. "You nuts, or what?" someone called out as the truck roared off.

"Might just be," I thought.

I flew home the next day, and 48 hours later I was a civilian, looking around my parents' house and thinking, "Talk about your culture shock."

Before I went into the army I had been in the theater, so I returned to the stage with hopes of . . . I hadn't a clue now of what I was in hopes of. I tried radio broadcasting, but I was too restless to sit there spinning records and babbling for hours. One of my karate training partners, a Portland (Oregon) police officer, talked me into taking the tests to get hired. I did, I passed, and a few months later I was patrolling the mean streets of Portland's Skid Row.

The Row—"a place forgotten by God," as one old cop described it—was the closest thing to Saigon this side of the Pacific pond, and I was right back into chaos again. There were no rocket attacks, of course, though there were bombings around town, mostly of military recruiting offices. It was the early 1970s. Like Saigon, Skid Row was a riot of violence: crowded streets of rage and intoxication, the almost constant wail of police and ambulance sirens, blaring music from dozens of Wild West saloons, and fights. Always there were fights, mostly with fists, broken bottles, and knives; sometimes with guns. I was in the middle of it all, fighting in the streets, on the sidewalks, and in the saloons virtually every night.

And loving every minute of it.

I worked on Skid Row for a while at the beginning of my career and for several years in the middle. In between and near the end of my 25-year stint, I worked street gangs, intelligence, patrol, and as a training officer. I worked as a bodyguard for presidents, vice presidents, political candidates, notorious criminals, and other "VIPs." During my career, I was confronted with shootings, riots, rapes, and robberies. In other words, I was just like every hardworking cop in a major city.

There were a few times when I abused the power of the badge, and there were times when I got accolades for doing good work. I was often scared, but still I went to the violence alongside my comrades, and always as others fled. I learned a lot about myself as a cop. Most of it I liked.

Except for those times when serious injuries prohibited it, I have maintained a rigorous martial arts workout schedule since 1965, training hard two or three days a week and enjoying easy sessions on the other days. It has kept me physically fit, confident, and in tune with my physical, emotional, and spiritual sides. The skill saved my skin more than once and has served as an outlet for anger, stress, depression, and bad memories.

I have had the wonderful opportunity to meet several martial arts masters during my years of study, men with 45 or more years of training. Every one of them has been gracious, humble, and knowledgeable, and all have possessed incredible skill. There is an almost tangible quality that envelops true martial arts masters, a quality that makes them stand apart from others. Call it a special aura, a presence, a dignified demeanor. By whatever name, I believe it's a characteristic of those who have faced that warrior within and tamed it.

It's been my honor to have learned from and been influenced by many great people I have met in all of the warrior community. I have often met them when I was complacent in my training or becoming smug that I had all the answers. These true warriors appeared just in time to knock me down a peg or two and remind me that I still had lots to learn, as learning never stops in all aspects of warriorhood.

I have faced the dragon in a war zone, in the mean streets of a major city, and in a tournament ring. I have known the copper taste of fear, the exhilaration of victory, the humility of defeat, and the agony of physical pain. Through it all I like to think I've grown and learned from the experiences. I know for sure that I have grown from the absolute privilege of knowing, working with, and learning from true *warriors* who have faced the dragon and tamed the warrior within.

THE LONG JOURNEY OF A SHORT WARRIOR

by Joseph "Little Joe" Ferrera

Joseph Ferrera (affectionately known as "Little Joe") began his law enforcement career in 1977 as a protection officer with the Federal Reserve Bank in Detroit, Michigan. He spent six years as a deputy sheriff (Corrections Division) with the Oakland County Sheriff's Department. He has been a police officer since 1985 in a 160-officer agency that borders Detroit. Mr. Ferrera has experience as a patrol officer, field training officer (FTO), directed patrol unit member, department training officer, Sheriff's Emergency Response Team (SERT) team leader/operator, detective (narcotics/vice/surveillance), and background investigator, and he has worked in the training unit doing research and development of training and equipment. He is currently assigned to afternoon shift patrol.

Mr. Ferrera is on staff at the Oakland County Community College Police Academy and Reserve Academy in Auburn Hills, Michigan. He has instructed across the United States and Canada training local, state, and federal law enforcement personnel in various aspects of use of force and subject control.

Mr. Ferrera is a technical consultant and on-air talent for the Law Enforcement Training Network and Caliber Press, the Professional Security Training Network. He is a subject matter expert and instructor trainer for the Michigan Commission on Law Enforcement Standards (MCOLES). In April 2003, Kentucky Governor Paul E. Patton commissioned Mr. Ferrera a Kentucky Colonel in recognition of his contributions to police training in that state.

Since 1974, Mr. Ferrera has made another career of teaching martial arts to civilians.

❖

For much of my 26 years wearing either a sheriff's department or police department uniform, I didn't consider myself a warrior. After all, Oxford's dictionary defines a warrior as "a person who fights in battle, a member of any of the armed services."

Then I began attending training seminars conducted by such people as Bruce Siddle, Dave Smith, Dr. Paul Whitesell, and even Lt. Col. Dave Grossman. There are many others I don't have space to list here, but all spoke of warriors and their training, missions, beliefs, and commitment to the people they serve. Still, I wasn't sure that I was some kind of warrior.

Then one day while on patrol I met a member of the U.S. military. He asked me how I could do what I did. I was puzzled and asked what he meant. He explained that his job was easy compared to mine. He was pretty much safe and sound on his base. When problems arose, he and his team members were told how to dress, what gear to bring, what their mission was, and what the enemy looked like. They would ship off to a hot spot, complete their mission, and return to their base.

He then told me that he and his teammates wouldn't do my job for anything. He asked how I could put on a uniform week in and week out for 25 years plus and work in a hot spot that whole time. He understood that our mission was to keep the peace and catch bad guys, but he couldn't understand how we could carry everything we need or identify our enemy. It amazed him that one moment we would be assisting a citizen, and a moment later we would be stopping a car full of gangsters and getting into a shootout.

If I met that soldier today, I would ask him how it feels, for in this day and age, with all the "peacekeeping missions" our military performs, he probably understands my job better.

After that chance encounter with what I considered a real warrior, I walked away with a better understanding of who I was and what I stood for. I started listening to trainers who were trying to get us to understand who we were and what we meant to the communities we serve. At one point after the death of a Detroit police officer, I wrote a poem called "The Thin Blue Line," in which there is this stanza: "Their battles lasted but a moment, but they were warriors just the same, and for those of us they fought for, their death was not in vain."

By this point I had looked at what we do as law enforcement officers, and I realized that the trainers were right. We go charging toward the sound of gunfire as everyone else is fleeing in fear. We race to a scene to assist anyone who needs us, no matter who they are or where they come from. We couldn't care less about their race, color, creed, or national origin. We don't care about their socioeconomic status or religious beliefs. All we know is that they need help, and we are compelled, because of who we are and what we stand for, to be there for them.

Many times "being there for them" means great danger. We might be called to violent situations where the victim's attacker turns on us, and occasionally, so does the victim. Soon, you either learn to accept these conditions or you leave the job. You come to accept that one moment you are a hero and the next a zero. There are days that you just can't win, and you wonder why you chose such a terrible career. Nevertheless, most of the time you realize you have the best job in the world.

For me, the desire to serve as a police officer started when I was a child. I am short (five feet, two inches), and because of this I was picked on and teased growing up. I learned to despise bullies and ruffians and at the same time respect the big kids who would occasionally come to my aid. As I grew older, I began to understand that standing up for those who needed help was not only the right thing to do, but it also made me feel good about myself. I came to realize that cops get paid to do just that—to stand up for people who can't defend themselves. It was the perfect career for me, once I could get a department to look past my size.

If you don't have size and strength, you'd better have skills. Actually, skills will help everyone, regardless of size and strength, but especially those who lack mass. Police warriors had better be able to back up their verbal commands with action, or they become useless rather quickly. Subject control is one of the most difficult parts of being a cop—much more difficult than television makes it look. Even worse is not being able to fight off an attacker. We still get assaulted to the tune of 60,000 to 80,000 times a year in this profession, and we had better be ready for it. Many times police officers forget that they are warriors and must be prepared for the possibility of a violent encounter. Unfortunately, we lose around 200 of our sisters and brothers every year *in the line of duty*.

As I look at these numbers, it confirms in my own mind that we are warriors in the battle for freedom: freedom from crime, especially violent crime, and the freedom of people to come and go when and where they please. My brothers and sisters have fought that battle for many years, on many different fronts in this great nation.

Generations of law enforcement families and rookies alike have made many sacrifices to fight the war on crime. They face violent people, often alone and without warning. Sometimes these aggressors are violently mentally ill and have a strength and endurance that seems superhuman. Sometimes this strength is chemically induced. Whatever the reason, these individuals wreak havoc on their own families and strangers alike. When they do, we get called.

If you have never fought people in this condition, you can't imagine the intensity. They are stronger than their stature indicates; it often takes several of us to control them, and even then they continue to struggle. In one case, more than 11 officers fought with one subject, and several got injured and had to be hospitalized whereas the subject barely received a scratch. You might ask why didn't we just bust him in the head with a baton or a flashlight. When we do, we are called brutal and are indicted as if we were common criminals. Our accusers have never had such a struggle and have no idea what it is like to fight to the point of exhaustion—fighting not to destroy or injure, but to subdue and control. This type of battle is much more difficult and exhausting. It usually requires multiple officers to control the subject safely, and then we are criticized for needing so many to control one person.

A typical scenario goes like this: A mentally ill individual stops taking his medications and, as the week(s) progress, becomes more and more unstable. Finally, he becomes violent toward family members, neighbors, or friends. Then someone calls 911 and says that he is out of control and to please send help. By the time we arrive, the subject is totally out of control and extremely violent. We team up, maybe using chemical sprays, batons, stun guns, or other intermediate weapons on him. If things go well, we finally control the subject and take him to a medical facility. Sometimes he falls victim to some aspect of sudden death syndrome, or he finds a weapon or grabs an officer's, and we end up dying or having to use deadly force on him.

Of course, the family can't understand how this could happen. It must be bad cops. They would never think to blame themselves for letting this go on so long without having their loved one medicated properly. They never consider that the longer such a person goes without medication the worse he gets. "Surely," they think, "he can be convinced to take his meds in the morning. Yes, that's it, we will tell him in the morning." Days turn to weeks, and weeks turn to tragedy, with law enforcement taking the blame for those who won't face reality. Believe me, battles with these types of people are intense. When it's over, you are completely exhausted and you hope it's the last time you have to fight this battle. Deep inside, though, you know it isn't, and you pray you will be ready for the next one.

The other type of violence the law enforcement warrior faces is much more evil. It might be a lone gunman on a crime spree or one who is just mad at the world. It might be a suspect we encounter on a traffic stop, in responding to a man-with-a-gun call, or during a robbery. It is what we saw in that April 11, 1986, shooting in Miami where hundreds of rounds were exchanged between two bank robbers and the FBI. When it was over, the two suspects and two agents were dead, and five other agents were wounded. And there was that February 28, 1997, North Hollywood, California, shootout between 350 LAPD officers and two heavily armed bank robbers wearing body armor. Such battles are completely different from the so-called routine situations cited in the first example. These are against armed—and sometimes heavily armed—individuals who would rather die than be arrested. Many times the suspects have plied their trade for some time and refined their technique. These are battles that would seem more familiar to our military brothers and sisters, not what the average law enforcement warrior expects on his watch.

Because of those who have gone before us, we are better prepared for these battles. We now have patrol rifle programs, carry new and improved handguns and ammunition, and receive technical and tactical training in anticipation of prolonged gun battles. Just as important as firepower and tactics is the improvement in our mental preparation. We not only better understand our adversary, we also better understand ourselves.

So it is that I have come back to the beginning. I started by talking about trainers like Bruce Siddle, Dave Smith, Dr. Paul Whitesell, and Lieutenant Colonel Grossman. Much of what they do is prepare the warrior's mind for the types of combat I have mentioned. I listened closely as they spoke of mind-set being as important as physical ability. As a smaller than average person as well as a police officer, I understood what they were saying. When I first started in this profession, I was literally and figuratively looked down on. In the early 1970s, a 5-feet 2-inch, 130-pound police officer was not in demand. I tested with approximately 18 departments before being hired by one.

I realized it was going to be tough to get hired, so I took a job as a store detective, figuring I could tell the interview boards that I had experience arresting people. It also helped that I began training in tang soo do in 1970, and later Yoshinki aikido. It helped more than I realized. As a store detective, I was hit by a car, stabbed in the hand, and—my personal favorite—shoved through a plate glass window. I learned to bounce back fighting and not quit until my partner and I were safe. Sometimes that meant the bad guy was in custody. Other times it meant that he escaped but we were okay (I just couldn't seem to stop that car I leaped in front of). I also learned that real warriors come in all shapes and sizes and are not to be judged by what they look like but by how they stay in the battle.

Take my first partner, for example. "Mama" is the only name I remember for her, the name everyone called her by. She was a senior store detective for the department store chain I worked for, a black woman in her late 50s, not much taller or bigger than I was. She would come to work and put her purse in a locker and pull out another purse to carry on duty. She took it to catch "thieves," as she called them.

One day we went out after a thief who had taken a bottle of Afro Sheen and a copper bracelet. I approached first and identified myself with my really cool gold badge. The over-six-foot-tall suspect just kept going. I grabbed his arm from behind, and the fight was on. I remember going over a shopping cart and the hood of a car, but I kept going back to the fight. I wasn't going to leave my partner alone, and I wasn't going to have a reputation of spending more time in the air than in the fight. I also thought that this guy was trying to kick our butts for about three dollars worth of nothing.

Mama wasn't thinking about anything but winning that battle. She had been through that kind of crap before and had learned hand-to-hand combat to be prepared for bigger, stronger, and faster enemies. That purse she always switched to for working didn't have handcuffs or Mace in it. It held half a brick—and she knew how to use it. While I kept him busy, she got in a good shot with the purse and ended our ordeal. I learned that day that the battle goes to the better-prepared warrior; the thief wasn't it because he had brought his hands to a brick fight.

Long before the "Big Dog" T-shirts came out, Mama taught me it's not the size of the dog in the fight, it's the size of the fight in the dog. Over the years I have had some great partners and trainees, and some who weren't meant to *be* the police but to *call* the police. They were all bigger than I, but none have been bigger than Mama.

Once I got on the job, another real warrior taught me that you couldn't pretend to be one. It's more than a job; it's who you are. Sgt. Lary Leadford spent several years with Detroit PD and was involved in his first shooting while walking a beat. Lary has several nicknames, and they are all good. My favorite is "Felony Lary," as the man is a major criminal-finding machine.

I had the chance to work with him in the department's Directed Patrol unit. We worked many different types of details together—patrol, plainclothes, and surveillance. Lary dedicated each day to a victim. Sometimes it was a fellow officer killed in the line of duty. Other times it was a local woman whose car was found on the side of the road—though she wasn't. Every day for more than 25 years he went out and did the job, no excuses and no complaints.

Lary lives to hunt evil people, and he enjoys it; it's why he is here and he knows it. Even after retiring from our department, he continues to control evil people. He now works for a federal agency transporting prisoners to and from court and lockups.

Lary recently rode a 10-hour shift with me. After briefing him on the latest procedures, we went out on the street, and his first statement (not a question or comment) was, "Let's find a hold-up man." We spent a rainy night trying to find a specific suspect. Lary is a living reminder to me that I will always be a police warrior, even after my ID card reads "Retired." I will always be looking for the predators who steal from fellow members of our society the freedom to live a peaceful, safe life.

My agency has been fortunate. We have not lost an officer to violent attack. Nevertheless, two were lost in traffic-related incidents many years ago, and we have lost several of our retired brothers to illness. These fine warriors taught me much about standing up for others who can't defend themselves. They kept me alive when I made mistakes and were there when I yelled for backup. I can never thank them enough but only pass the torch when my time comes.

Therefore, to my brother and sister law enforcement warriors past, present, and future, who make the ultimate sacrifice in the fight for freedom at home, I dedicate the following poem.

The Thin Blue Line

There are those who've gone before us, who we long to see again,
fathers, mothers, loved ones and some we just called friend.
They chose to make a difference, to walk the thin blue line,
they took a call to duty, but they just ran out of time.

Their battles lasted but a moment, but they were warriors just the same,
and for those of us they fought for, their death was not in vain.
I chose to take the gauntlet and to walk the thin blue line,
and for those of you who are strong enough, please join us anytime.

For the line it isn't easy, it's not safe for body or soul,
it will change forever who you are, if you're lucky you'll grow old.
And when our time has run out, and we're facing our own end,
we will walk a beat in heaven, with our loved ones and our friends.

—Joe Ferrera, 1995

DESTINY:
WALKING THE PATH LAID FORTH

by Kelly S. Worden

*A hometown street kid from the inner city streets of Tacoma, Washington, **Kelly S. Worden** found his path in life through fighting. Once introduced to the martial arts, he made training a way of life. Martial arts styles were only a vehicle he used to seek freedom in self-expression and personal fighting development.*

Several men in the martial arts were inspirational in guiding Mr. Worden's visions into reality—in particular, Edward Lewis, Jesse Glover, and Professor Remy A. Presas. It was Professor Presas who set him on the path of being an educator of the martial arts, an effort that earned Mr. Worden the coveted title Datu of Modern Arnis in 1988; he has the distinction of being the first American to receive the title from Professor Presas.

Mr. Worden is currently contracted to develop and instruct the U.S. Army 1st Special Forces combative hand-to-hand training program at Ft. Lewis, Washington.

Additionally, Mr. Worden is an internationally recognized seminar instructor, instructional video author, knife maker and designer, developer of the Impact Kerambit Travel Wrench self-protection tool and instructional book/DVD, radio talk show host, and the owner of Natural Spirit International.

Contact Mr. Worden at www.kellyworden.com or by E-mail at kellysworden@comcast.net

❖

As a martial artist and teacher, I'm approached by a multitude of people who are intrigued by the path I have chosen. In retrospect, I'm not sure if I had much to do with my current state of being. After years of pondering, I feel that the fighting arts somehow chose me. Surely, the raw essence of the martial arts can be defined as a developmental path to self-defense. I have always believed that this meant protecting myself and others from the devastating harm that can result from raw violence.

Strangely, though, in all of its challenges, confusion, and brief moments of glory, my study of the martial arts has evolved into a way of life. My walk down this path of unlimited potential has been driven by an inner consciousness that pushes me to seek self-acceptance and a sense of perfection through physical challenges. Without question, challenges in the physical realm are integral to the path to becoming a warrior. I'm sure that I am not alone in the universal experiences of adolescence through adulthood that produce in some a fierce determination not be intimidated or abused physically or mentally.

NATURAL BORN WARRIOR

When we cease to acknowledge our infancy and begin our unconscious efforts to rebel and resist domination, our warrior blood begins flowing, and the transformation of self-preservation begins. This transformation is imperative for one's personal growth as a warrior and transcends the limitations set forth by the social guidelines of formal education. Survival instincts are cultivated by fear and emotional disparity. Formal education has little to do with facing the reality of pain or the mental anguish associated with violently implemented pain. The powerful urge to question or confront uncontrollable circumstances that are unacceptable or detrimental is what distinguishes the natural born warrior from those who succumb to domination with compliance.

Labels are often attached to children with "unacceptable attitudes"—that is, those who question authority or adults. Terms such as bad boy, misfit, delinquent, troublemaker, and punk are used to describe young people who confront mainstream ideals. I believe that many of my colleagues who walk the path of the warrior were once labeled and categorized in this derogatory manner. Perhaps the apparent paradox between their current discipline and their former rebellion can be resolved by viewing their behavior and choices as nothing more than an ongoing effort to demonstrate individuality and uniqueness through blind spontaneity. Although the evolution of such attitudes requires walking a fine line between right and wrong, knowing some aspects of both offers insight into making critical choices that affect the balance of life. Rebellion is one of the many stepping stones on the path into warriorhood.

DEFINING WARRIORHOOD

I do not think there is a distinct answer to the question, what is a warrior? To many, the answer lies in the warrior's presence and energy. Many can relate to expressions such as "he walks the walk" when used in describing the warrior when the excrement hits the fan.

One thought that does pass by my bruise-riddled brain cells is that few can be self-appointed into the warrior society. If an individual pounds his chest and proclaims he is a warrior, he is probably a wannabe with an exaggerated sense of self-worth. The brotherhood of warriors is an elite class of individuals, and acknowledgment as part of this class can only come through the acceptance awarded by those who really do walk the walk and not just talk the talk. Such are those who have sacrificed a life of socially perceived stability and sought instead a life of inner consciousness, addressing life's complex and difficult issues with an intuitive sense of values, moral justice, and equality for the weak. This higher value of life and honor does not come without great sacrifice.

THE SPIRITUAL WARRIOR

Acknowledging those who have sacrificed so we could live is an aspect of the path that burns, yet breathes like a living entity within every warrior's soul. I believe that those who have passed on become spiritual guides and integral shadows in the reflections of our souls, sharing in our existence. The warrior might appear to be standing alone, but within the essence of spirit and brotherhood, he is never alone.

Although spiritual awareness cannot be measured in a physical form, it can be detected in one's physical presence. In many ways, spiritual strength is what allows the warrior to accept life as it is. Through perseverance, his internal spirit is refined—a process similar to the tempering of Damascus steel: it is layered, hammered, and forged from the core elements that form the earth and have sustained man from the beginning of time.

The Five Elements of Chinese Martial Theory—earth, wind, fire, water, and wood—offer a lens through which the warrior can view and apply the physics of existence to his life. From a purely martial arts perspective, the practitioner seeks to embrace physical, mental, and spiritual growth as developmental phases in the search for his own soul. He adheres to the premise "no limits or boundaries," leaving no stone unturned. A warrior is raw in the most primal state of being, yet outside the realm of physical challenges, he seeks to become a cultured life force emerging to face and resolve the quagmire of man's many-layered existence: hunger, pain, disparity, happiness, compassion, resentment, achievement, failure, obsession, defiance, love, hate, and war. And he has honed his primal instincts in seeking to conquer the many challenges to survival.

With conviction, a warrior confronts the anguish of physical battle; if need be he seeks an eye for an eye, a tooth for a tooth. Facing death head-on, he draws spiritual strength from the deepest part of his soul while seeking consolation in moral values and ethics that have been adhered to in war for centuries. Humbly, the warrior becomes self-realized through a committed responsibility to cherish all living things. He judges another man only when he has walked in his shoes. *Do unto others before they do unto you, your family, or your country* is his axiom of life. He does not grapple with it through his emotions. Rather, his firm grasp of it is born of his primal, instinctive sense of right and wrong. He stares fiercely into the eye of the tiger during that epigrammatic moment of truth. Few men control or manifest their own destiny without walking this path of moral conviction. Through the rigors of challenge and conquest, the warrior gains an understanding of what separates man from the nature of his inner beast. This progressive step toward maturity is imperative to gaining the recognition of and acceptance into the warrior society.

ONE WARRIOR'S BEGINNING

My introduction to the warrior path might have been the multiple ass-whoopings I received after school in an alley. The alley, a frequent hangout for all the local thugs, was a spit spray from Stewart Junior High School, my alma mater. Strolling down the alley was the equivalent of a challenge for those seeking recognition as being a cut above the rest.

I thought I was a tough SOB. I started boxing when I was eight years old, and, for the most part, I survived scuffles and confrontations with little effort. But things changed after I hit junior high school. Life was seldom if ever really good. It was the often-heard "poor white boy story"—I was poor, relatively small for my age, and, because I did not have many clothes, I was the target of humiliation. When countering verbal attacks, I would fight back physically. I became withdrawn from the very social scene that many others aspired to. I didn't understand my situation; it was just my way of life. Thus, fighting and rebellion became simpler solutions—and much easier to control—than interaction or social compliance.

I'm often asked who inspired me to the path of survival and later into the realm of warriorhood. There were many men who stood out in the crowd and paved the way. First and foremost was my dad, and, later, my older brother, who through great pain and undaunted spirit tempered the ground on which I walked.

My old man was a disabled veteran from World War II with six kids and no way to improve a life that was swept away in the turmoil and sacrifices of war. He was leathered and scarred by a life that was no doubt filled with more anguish and disparity than anything I or my generation of street urchins might have experienced. I've often wondered why he never shared his love, compassion, and shadowed life with me. What he did share was an ass-whooping every time I stepped out of line—a very thin line that I couldn't even see. Without question, it was his way and his gift: preparing me for a destiny of self-realization that began with the understanding that a man can only depend on himself, and that he must face his own path head-on.

These were hard lessons from a hard man, indeed. He taught me to fight for every grain of rice, every grain of respect, and every moment of tranquility in a life filled with violence and confusion. Bittersweet was the taste of intimidation, pain, humiliation, defeat, and my own blood. Yet even more so was the essence of vanquishing in a back-alley street fight. What he instilled was a warrior spirit—things he himself learned through blood, sweat, and tears. No matter the logic or reason; every day was a new lesson in survival.

My older brother trudged his own path of self-discovery. Early on, he ran with an outlaw motorcycle gang called the Satan Psychos, where he polished his expertise in sex, drugs, and rock and roll. His youth too was marked by personal turmoil and violence; indeed, his reputation as a back-alley fighter is still legendary on the streets of Tacoma. And the tangles he had with the police cultured him to become elusive in order to maintain a lifestyle that he controlled.

Using my brother as a personal template for the fine art of raising hell, I sought the same action-adventure thrill ride he lived daily. I did all that I could to mimic his attitude, embrace his indomitable spirit, and refine my own abilities as a street-fighting renegade willing to "rape, rob, and pillage" not only the neighborhood but all of society. It didn't feel as if we were doing anything wrong then because when everyone you know, fear, and respect walks the same path, it's just life in the fast lane.

It is certainly not a direction I would take today. Yet I would not change any of the things I experienced in the past, because they are what enable me to look my students in the eyes now and share the truth with them. In reality, survival of the street culture was something I lived to endure and exploit.

Today, lessons of my past still guide me as I walk a fine line between social consciousness and the darkness of street survival. I like the saying, "You can take the kid off the street, but you can't take the street out of the kid." I can attest to the truth of this. In reality, one slip in judgment, even today as an adult, could sever my spirit like a double-edged sword. Life is about fine lines, and those lines are borders that separate success and failure in all endeavors. One trip in either direction creates change, good, bad, or indifferent; it is all a form of evolution.

EDGED STEEL:
THE BIRTH OF A FIGHTING SYSTEM

From age 8 to 51, my years of training in a multitude of comprehensive martial arts systems shaped my determination and rebellion into a finely functional approach to hand-to-hand tactical technology. Years ago, I named this system the "Natural Spirit Way."

Today, I train mature civilian, police, and military operatives in a collaboration of personal protection options. "Sophisticated simplicity" describes the control tactics, lethal empty-hand striking, threat-response impact weapons, and down-and-dirty street fighting that comprise this system, which is based on raw and primal survival concepts. The nucleus of my fighting art is in the combative applications of the knife, man's oldest weapon. Knife techniques, when combined with knowledge of firearms, impact weapons, and empty-hand striking arts, allow the warrior to develop a complete personal protection system.

Centering a system on the art of the knife constitutes a moral challenge that transcends the physical realm of what is generally accepted as mainstream martial arts in today's society. In refining the inordinate power of the blade, one cultivates the warrior mind-set while stimulating growth through the act of confronting one's own fears. Learning to use a knife for protection forces the warrior to confront and understand the lethal power of the blade, not only its ability to inflict damage but its power to instill fear and intimidation. Intent is in the eyes, heart, and soul of the knife combatant.

Developing technical skill is a lifelong endeavor that few individuals commit to. In facing this challenge, the martial artist grows in his understanding of the personal accountability instilled through training in edged steel. Through the art of the knife, discipline, self-control, and confidence, as well as unsurpassed technical skill, can be cultivated. These are serious attributes that produce emotional stability and control during conflicts, balance physical attributes in everyday life, and impart symmetry to the warrior spirit.

Without question, a prepared society is a polite society! Those who want to harm others seek as victims only those who are reluctant to stand up against violence. If all citizens were armed with the knowledge and balls to defend their personal rights of self-protection, criminals would not be so eager. Citizens have the right to empower themselves against anyone wishing to do them harm. A knife in the hands of a distressed person of any physical stature instills in him the power to discourage most antagonists from stepping over the line. It does not take a killing wound to neutralize a threat; it merely requires confidence.

One must accept the emotional and moral challenge of self-protection when aspiring to develop survival skills with edged weaponry. Indigenous to many cultures, the knife is a symbol of manhood; sadly, few people in Western societies truly comprehend the value, art, science, and principles of edged weapons as a way of life. The development of knife skill for combat is a lifelong study requiring perseverance. The practitioner dissects the very core of his physical, mental, spiritual, and emotional existence, and in the process creates a tempered complexity as he finds the balance of life as a warrior.

Integral to knife tactics is the study of physical movement. This study challenges and dissects all preconceptions of tactical theory through physical analysis so that they become valid strategies to be integrated and executed without fear or hesitation. Generally speaking, geometric patterns such as figure eights, circles, diagonal intersecting lines, plus signs, boxes, and other diagrams form endless universal lines of movement, which are honed to become reactionary offensive and defensive fighting patterns.

Physically, it is imperative that a tactical system include direct explosive offensive techniques and evasive defensive maneuvers. Psychologically, it's critical that it develop an ability to utilize deception, creating the illusion of willing compliance or fear of confrontation in order to draw an aggressor into a mode of overconfidence.

Of immeasurable value in developing tactical proficiency in both impact and edged weapons is training that includes disarming and controlling techniques and specific vital killing point tactics. The insight into the real world of improvised weapons that such training imparts is critical to surviving a multitude of dangerous environments. Additionally, training with improvised weapons enables the warrior to recognize a potential threat from literally any object. This level of force escalation is as essential for the citizen protecting his home and family as it is for the professional protection agent, sentry, or threat abolitionist carrying out high-level security missions.

As an instructor, I strive to increase students' intestinal fortitude while honing their warrior attributes through the use of instinctual or neuromuscular response training methods. This combination is critical to establishing efficiency of movement.

One goal of a trained fighter is to conquer at all costs; if not he dies, and so do those who depend on his protection. Few martial training methods tap primal, killer instincts as does training to absorb and comprehend the power of the blade. The knife cultivates the warrior mind-set as it trains the individual to excel in developing offensive and defensive lethal-force skills. There is little room for error mentally, physical, or spiritually in knife training. How we train is how we shall respond.

Due to the success of today's "no holds barred" events, many practitioners place a majority of the emphasis on grappling in their training. Even military men have been drawn into this fallacy. In reality, whether in the streets of our inner cities or on the battlefield in a war zone, it takes nothing more than a simple boot knife or folding pocketknife to kill or maim a grappling strategist during a physical engagement. Warriors are survivalists and thus rarely depend on a single strategy or martial arts system. To survive a physical conflict, the warrior needs to cultivate common sense as well as technical skill.

Warriors know that survival is not about fair fighting or glorified cultural styles that claim to be "reality-based" yet create deception through half-truths. I tell the men I train, "We are American, and we are not bound by cultural glorification of martial arts styles." Simply put, *use what works*. Additionally, only foolish men would believe a fight for ideals, religion, life, freedom, or country is going to be fought without deadly weapons. Prepare for the worst and pray for quick resolution with minimal loss.

WARRIOR AXIOMS

There is an old axiom about steel: live by the sword; die by the sword. Most blade warriors eventually accept this as a verity of life on the path they have chosen. Although it is not necessary to die in a lethal encounter, it is crucial to face that potential reality. Here is another axiom: expect one man to depart this life and the other to bleed; both will be cut. This is a truth that many not cut from the cloth of the warrior ignore.

Though it is said that ignorance is bliss, one cannot hide behind the shimmer of steel. Only a mediocre practitioner or fool would try to deceive the honorable brotherhood of warriors through false proficiency in edged steel. One look into the deceiving eyes of a weak man by a serious blade-player, and the battle is over. The high art of edged steel is not to be exploited in a sporting arena by those in pursuit of glory, fame, and trophies. Facing the mystical image of knife reality and the personal development of efficient skills requires a deep examination of our own mortality; you either walk the walk or suffer the consequences of being ill-prepared.

A friend and great man of military status once told me, "If you love your family, teach them to use a knife for defense, and no one can touch them." Of course, there are always exceptions, as it is possible for someone to covertly assault and dominate even the best-prepared warrior. However, the enduring fact is that training in edged weapons can cultivate an indomitable spirit. Additionally, that knowledge and skill transforms a simple #2 pencil, fork, or wood sliver into a lethal tool. Thus, his statement was an accurate summation of the power in man's oldest weapon—an inevitable truth in steel and the high art of the blade.

The ability to wield a knife as a defensive weapon has evolved over centuries. Today's knife concepts have been refined through countless cultural influences, yet still preserve a traditional truth: the ability to feed, clothe, and protect man—the warrior—from harm's way.

GIVING THANKS

by Lynne McClure, PhD

---

*Dr. **Lynne McClure** is nationally recognized as a leading expert in managing high-risk behaviors before they escalate to violence. President of McClure Associates, Inc. (www.McClureAssociates.com), in the Phoenix area, she is the author of* Angry Men: Managing Anger in an Unforgiving World; Angry Women: Stop Letting Anger Control Your Life!; Anger & Conflict in the Workplace: Spot the Signs, Avoid the Trauma; *and* Risky Business: Managing Employee Violence in the Workplace. *Her workshop video is called* Managing High-Risk Behaviors. *Dr. McClure has been featured by* CNN NewsStand, U.S. News & World Report, Newsday, *the* Los Angeles Times, *and other prominent media.*

❖

I didn't know it then, but I became what Lt. Col. Dave Grossman calls a sheepdog at age 15, as I recovered from severe head injuries due to a car accident on a bridge in Seattle.

An army medic who happened to drive by at the moment of impact saved my life. He had to break through a crowd of gawking spectators who jeered, "They're already dead," and (in the days before cell phones) convince one of them to find a pay phone down the road and call the police. While waiting for help to come, the medic cut a hole in the throat of my friend, the driver, whose windpipe had been smashed, and he saved her life as well.

Once I was out of the hospital, I read the police report, got the name and phone number of the medic, and went to his house to meet him, his wife, and their new baby. I said I wanted to thank him. He smiled, shrugged, and said, "You don't have to thank me. That's what we're here for, to help each other." I liked what he said but insisted that I wanted to thank him and, in some way, return the love, concern, and kindness he'd given me.

Finally, he said, "Okay, here's how you can pay me back: when *you* see someone who needs help, *help* them."

Neither of us knew it then, but this man—whose name I wish I could remember and whose whereabouts I wish I knew—guided me toward my role as a sheepdog, a protector, an early-warning alert who *wards off* the face of danger.

With the medic's words emblazoned in both my mind and my heart, I began to look at people through a new lens, hear them through a new frequency, and sense them through a stronger intuition. Whenever I encountered someone, I silently asked myself: in a crisis, would he be a "gawker" or a "medic"— a sheep or a sheepdog? I soon added a third option: would he be a perpetrator, the *source* of the crisis? My emerging intuition continued to expand and intensify.

It became clear to me that there were far more sheep—and more perpetrators—than sheepdogs in the world. It was also clear that I was one of the sheepdogs, the warriors. It took longer for me to learn how alone, how unsupported, and how unheard a warrior sometimes can feel—and how the warrior must persist regardless.

My life's work is teaching people how to intervene early— *long before* the employee becomes violent at work, or the spouse, partner, parent, child, or sibling becomes violent at home. As a consultant, I help companies prevent workplace violence. As a volunteer, I help survivors of domestic violence recognize and avoid the potential for further abuse.

After a violent incident occurs in a company, management is eager to bring me in to prevent future events. When an abused woman escapes from the abuser, she is eager to learn how to stop attracting, and being attracted to, abusive partners. Being a warrior is easy under these circumstances, because the people I'm helping are receptive and open. They *know* they need to learn.

But prevention is hard to sell to people who've never experienced violence. In the workplace, too many people let themselves become victims because they can't see the risk until *after* the incident. At home, too many women live with abusers willingly, but not knowingly. And though everyone has heard about workplace violence and domestic violence, most people believe that *those kinds of problems* happen *elsewhere,* not *here.*

One of the most challenging periods I faced as a warrior was in 1995 when I finished writing my first book, *Risky Business: Managing Employee Violence in the Workplace.* Even though my consulting experience had alerted me to the fact that violence was a huge issue looming on the horizon for corporations, few agents or publishers saw any market for workplace violence prevention. Ironically, *EAP Digest* later named *Risky Business* "the best book on workplace-violence prevention." But it took workplace tragedies and huge legal settlements before most companies began to recognize the risk.

As a warrior, I had to learn to trust what I saw and heard, say what I knew to be true, and teach what I could, even when those I tried to protect were not yet ready to listen. My most frustrating situations have been when I've seen the risk escalating, known how to prevent it, but been unable to break through the sheep's denial—and then, after the fact, been called in to prevent the tragedy from happening again. I've had to learn to accept feelings of helplessness and continue in spite of them. I've had to learn to pace myself to match others' levels of commitment to prevention.

Domestic violence also was an issue no one wanted to talk or hear about. I've included this topic in my corporate violence-prevention workshops. My volunteer work with abused women began when, individually, survivors of abuse would talk to me privately and furtively after these workshops. Later, I began to speak as a volunteer to women in domestic violence shelters. My frustrations have been that most survivors blame themselves, and that most of those who manage to escape from abusers end up going back to them. I've worked at developing ways to show the survivors that they were targets, not causes, of the abuse. I've worked at learning how to encourage them to leave and take good care of themselves, permanently. I've had to learn to focus on how I *can* help—and to accept the limits to what I can do.

I've learned a lot since I was 15, yet my goals and sense of purpose remain the same. To me, being a warrior means knowing that evil exists and feeling, deep in my bones, the clarity and "rightness" of protecting people from it.

Being a warrior means knowing what gifts I have, so I can tell which forms of evil I can—and which forms I cannot—protect people from. Being a warrior means that I feel, trust, and know my gifts, and use them when they rise up inside me—instead of "logically" talking myself out of it. Being a warrior means recognizing emergencies while they're brewing, *before* they occur—and taking steps to prevent them even when no one else sees them coming. Being a warrior means getting outside myself and focusing on the needs of the people I'm protecting. Being a warrior means trusting my intuition and doing what I know is right and necessary, regardless of how little support I may have or how much resistance or opposition I may face. Being a warrior means living a life of giving—and giving back. Being a warrior means using everything I have to help, and accepting my own limitations. Being a warrior means knowing what I *can* do—and *doing* it.

Several factors support my desire and ability to be a warrior. At those moments when my gifts and the other person's needs are aligned, my intuitive and primitive mind expands beyond my ordinary self, and I feel connected to the person who's in danger, to everyone on earth, to all the good in the world. When I see the light in people's eyes as they go from unknowing to knowing the risk, I know they are willing and able to prevent or avoid the coming violence. When abuse survivors get in touch with their strengths, I know they are willing and able to empower themselves.

Like all sheepdogs—who love the sheep they protect, whether or not the sheep know it or appreciate it or are even aware of the risk—the medic saved my life because, "That's what we're here for." Each of my actions as a warrior is a form of thanks to him for leading me toward my own role as a fellow sheepdog, warrior, and protector.

WARRIOR LESSONS LEARNED AND UNLEARNED

by Phil Elmore

Phil Elmore is a freelance writer, martial artist, and published author who lives and works in central New York State. His columns and articles have appeared in a variety of virtual and hard-copy publications. As the publisher of The Martialist: The Magazine for Those Who Fight Unfairly *(www.themartialist.com) and a ghost-writer who also pens professional product reviews, Mr. Elmore is active in the martial arts community, both online and in the "real world." His first novel,* Demon Lord, *is available through most online booksellers. He can be reached through his Web site, www.philelmore.com.*

❖

Most martial artists have at least a small library of books devoted to the techniques, the histories, and the philosophies of the world's fighting systems. Some have many shelves groaning under the weight of scores if not hundreds of such volumes. I am no exception. Like many, I came to the martial arts believing I understood them and seeking to learn the mechanical components I knew I lacked. What I did not know, and what has taken me well over a decade to learn, is that the path of the warrior—the journey of the martial artist—is not a quest for physical accomplishment punctuated by the consumption of Asian wisdom and ancient pondering. It does not teach lessons found in a book, no matter how many books are written on the topic. It is not easy, and it is not at all what I thought it to be when I began. It is at once more fulfilling, more sobering, more invigorating, more revealing, and more hopeful than I could have imagined in my educated ignorance.

When I started karate in college, I did so in the same way I did everything in college: within a fog of spectacular ignorance. To be 20 or 21 years old is to be just old and knowledgeable enough to be both arrogant and uninformed. I was arrogant because I thought I knew what I had yet to learn. I was uninformed because I did not know enough to realize that this approach was completely wrong.

It is no coincidence that it was in college that my collection of books began. I bought books on karate technique, yes, but these held only a fraction of the interest inspired by the books on martial philosophy. I read *The Art of War* and the *Japanese Art of War*. I read *The Martial Way*. I read the biographies of famous martial artists who became movie stars and movie stars who became martial artists. I read *The Tao of Jeet Kune Do*. I read and I kept reading—and for years I did not truly understand.

Much as you cannot truly grant *yourself* a nickname, you cannot walk into a room and announce yourself *changed*. You cannot look a crowd or a family member or a spouse in the eye and say with sincerity, "I understand myself now. I pronounce myself different, my journey fulfilled, my quest ended." To be truly transformed is something that occurs without direct knowledge. It is something of which you become aware over time. It is something realized slowly, acceptance dawning and increasing as you examine the mounting evidence of an inner process that, because it must come from within, never really *arrives* until it has already *been*.

Reading my books, fantasizing about scanning rooms of miscreants with my steely gaze, picturing myself shouldering past muggers and thugs and the assorted villainy of life's lesser mortals was an adolescent dream born of my lack of understanding of the true spirit of the warrior. I wasted years moving aimlessly from art to art, desperate to fill my repertoire with techniques, all the while glossing over everything with a thin film of ersatz martial philosophy that simply could not be *ingested* from stacks of paper. When I finally started *learning*, when I finally came to realize the fundamental error of my approach to the martial arts and what I thought they represented, my efforts produced changes in areas of my life that were the last things I could have imagined.

I am becoming a better employee. I am becoming a better husband. I am becoming a better *man*.

I say "becoming" because I can no more pronounce myself *changed* than I can announce myself finally *knowledgeable*. To do so would be to commit the very crime of which I was so guilty for so very long. No, it was only relatively recently that I became aware of the changes wrought in my character and in my soul. Even then, it took others to teach me that I *was* changing. Eventually, I would have seen myself more accurately and experienced that slow realization that my training was producing profound benefits, but there is little that is more memorable than being told by others what you did not know about yourself.

I have always been a sarcastic man, proud of what I consider my acerbic wit. For years, however, I was also a pushover—a passive and angry man who avoided conflict whenever possible and could not bring himself to be assertive even when it was necessary. I was, as a coworker once put it, a "follower of the Glorious Path of Least Resistance"—a wry comment that I actually took as a compliment at the time.

You might be saying to yourself, "But a martial artist *does* avoid conflict when possible. There's nothing inappropriate or passive about that." Well, that is true, up to a point. The difference between a warrior and a simple soldier, or a warrior and an assassin, is that the warrior *stands* for something. The killer is a tool, an implement. He is a mechanism through which violence is done, through which force is delivered. The warrior, by contrast, has *ideals*. The warrior does what is right according to the code to which he subscribes.

What this means is that while the warrior does not relish the thought of doing violence and prefers to solve conflicts without using force, that warrior also knows that there are times when violence is necessary and when force is warranted. The warrior does not shrink from conflict if to do so means to grant sanction to evil. The warrior does not allow another to make victims of those about whom the warrior cares. Something forgotten by many who believe they pursue the warrior ideal is that the warrior does *not* submit passively to being used poorly, either. Self-preservation and *self-respect* demand otherwise.

For years I allowed myself to be bullied at work by bosses and coworkers. If I came into conflict with a fellow employee, rightly or wrongly, I apologized and wanted only to get along peacefully with each person at the office. If a boss treated me shabbily or without proper respect, I accepted this as my superiors' prerogative. If I worked hard on a project and that project was judged less than acceptable, I bore the burden of what I saw as rightful shame and pledged to work harder. I could not say no when given more work. I spent hour after hour of unpaid overtime, working late into the night and arriving at painfully early hours of the morning. I believed, through all this, that I was a good employee—that my efforts were evidence of my earnest desire to serve my employers well.

There came a time that I now realize was the beginning of a real understanding of the path of the warrior. I would like to say this came about because of my diligent, if haphazard, reading of martial arts texts and commentaries, but I would be wrong. No, the first hints of understanding came to me through the efforts of gifted teachers. I began training in a pair of martial arts: an eclectic and personal style whose name translates to "virtuous strength," and the traditional kung-fu style of wing chun. To the teachers of those two arts, I owe a debt I probably will never repay. Their lessons began the changes I only now perceive.

The first lesson was that of *fear*. My eclectic teacher, also a friend, scolded me harshly when I was hesitant to close and engage him in sometimes brutal, nearly full-contact sparring. I outweighed him by an honest 100 pounds and was still hesitant. I *knew* his strikes would shatter my defenses. I *knew* he would be everywhere at once.

"Stop being afraid," he spat at me. "You're not afraid of *me*. You're afraid of *yourself*." He pantomimed nailing one of my feet to the ground. "Now. You will stand your ground. You can rotate on that foot. You can kick with the other foot. But you are *not* to back up. *Do not give ground to me*." That was the beginning. That was when I learned to conquer, however briefly, the fear of myself.

My wing chun teacher, who emphasized in each class the vitally important principles of that traditional art, taught me the second lesson—one I choose to term "space domination" and which others have called "forward drive" or "seizing the initiative." We were taught that when an opponent closes to within kicking distance, he has crossed the boundary of safe personal space and must be *attacked*. "Do not wait," my Sifu told us many times. "If he's too close, *get him.*"

I choose to highlight these two lessons because they are at the heart of the changes of which I am only now becoming aware. They are also fundamental to the differences and the benefits I have seen as a person. To cope with fear and to take the initiative are the heart of confidence and the soul of assertiveness.

I had been training in wing chun for perhaps half a year and in my eclectic art for maybe three times that when a coworker—an unpleasant woman who had never really treated me with respect—began acting skittish around me. She finally commented, to the agreement of a couple of other office personnel, that I had become "much more aggressive." I gathered that she did not find this development comforting. I was confused by her observation.

I spoke with another coworker whose cubicle was located next to mine, someone whose company I truly enjoyed. "Do I seem different at all to you?" I asked, mystified. "Is my personality different?"

"You've definitely become much more assertive in the year that I've known you," she told me. "You don't stand for things that you would have tolerated before. You make nervous the people who used to treat you badly. Haven't you noticed they don't treat you like they used to? It's because they know they can't get away with it."

I thought about that for a long time.

When something is perceptible in your work life it becomes perceptible (immediately or eventually) in your home life as well. To be a spouse and to be a man is, ultimately, to be a warrior. No woman wants as her partner and husband a man who is too weak to do what he must. I had always seen my pursuit of the tools and methods of violence, of the knowledge of the use of force, as my natural role as a *man.* What I did not realize in all the years that I failed to understand the nature of the warrior is that my passivity, my pursuit of the path of least resistance, does not do justice to the demands of a man who has pledged his eternal loyalty and love to his wife. You are more than a man when you are married. You are a *husband,* and your responsibilities increase accordingly.

To be a man and a warrior is to be strong, not necessarily physically, though that never hurts, but mentally and emotionally. The warrior is a source of strength to his wife. He is assertive on her behalf without being overbearing. He is firm without being unyielding. He is confident without being arrogant. He treats her with respect and acts forcefully and without hesitation when she is treated badly by others. He makes his wife proud for good reason and stands up for her and for himself. He does this because he has the confidence and the wisdom that are found scattered in pebbles large and small along the path of the warrior.

I am finally learning.

With the slow realization that my training was changing me for the better came the knowledge of how little I had learned before—and why. I still read the books in my martial arts library, but now I understand to where their philosophies guide me. I am not foolish or arrogant enough to believe I have *arrived.* I am, however, finally armed with the knowledge that I am making the journey in earnest. It is with pleasure and with wonder and with fear—yes, a *healthy* fear—that I ponder the psychological and physical benefits of my training. It is with anticipation and reservations that I walk the path of the warrior. It is with a humility balanced with an appropriate self-respect that I seek the self-*knowledge* such a journey promises.

To be a warrior is to be changed, but that change cannot come from the words of any book. It cannot come from the mind or hands or feet of any teacher. That change can only come, slowly and imperceptibly, from within each of us, creeping up on us, surprising us, and altering us as we work to free ourselves from what we *think* we need to know in order to reach what we truly *have* to know.

It is a lesson at once learned and unlearned.

FIRE, BLOOD, AND PAINT

by Nho Nguyen (as told to Loren W. Christensen)

Nho Nguyen was born in Hue, Vietnam, in 1945. He joined the Army of the Republic of Vietnam (ARVN) in 1969 and served for six years, at times in some of the bloodiest battles of the war. In 1975, the conquering North Vietnamese imprisoned him for six brutal years of forced labor under starvation conditions.

Prior to joining the army, Mr. Nguyen attended and graduated from the Fine Arts National College of Hue, taught art at the Cultural and Art School in Qui Nhon, and worked as a decorator of exhibiting arts in Vietnam.

He resides today in Portland, Oregon, where he is a member of The Sculpture Group and serves as a cofounder of the Vietnamese Artist Association in the Northwest. Mr. Nguyen works as a designer at Portland Signs Studio.

❖

"I like holding a paintbrush," 57-year-old Nho Nguyen says with a shake of his head. "I don't like holding a gun. War is stupid."

War is stupid. He should know. Nho lived smack in the middle of it from 1945 until he and his wife, Hoa Bang, left Vietnam for the United States in 1995. In fact, as his mother was giving birth to him under a shelter trench, without the luxury of medicine or a midwife, and his father was cutting the umbilical cord, the Japanese were dropping bombs on his small village just outside of Hue. "That pushed my mother to be near the angel of death," the slight man says.

As a young boy, he was surrounded by death, and there was always the thumping and trembling earth from distant, and not so distant, artillery and bombs. "I saw many dead bodies before I was even 9 years old," Nho says, rubbing a hand through his thick salt-and-pepper hair. "Sometimes, the Communists would come to the village and cut off the heads of suspected traitors and leave the heads impaled on stakes as a warning to others."

There was nowhere the boy could escape from the horror; he could always see and hear it in the distance and see and smell it in his village. There was nowhere to go but into his mind.

Even before he was 10 years old, Nho had a raw talent for art: drawing, painting, and creating things with his hands. With a handful of colored pencils, he would find a place to sit in an open field and draw—animals, trees, flowers—peaceful images far removed from the constant of death.

Nho does remember a period of quiet. "From 1955 to 1962, we had a little peace," he says with a sad smile. It was a wonderful time when he could go to school and do what kids do in a happy place. Then the smile fades. "But the war started again in 1963." And it would be with him continuously for the next 20 years.

He finished high school and then began attending the Fine Arts National College of Hue in 1964. Always, the war raged around him: the heavy thumping of big guns on the horizon, sporadic small arms fire in the city, and the sudden explosions of terrorist bombs.

Nho loved the colors of Dutch Post-Impressionist painter Vincent Van Gogh and the thick brushwork of French landscape painter Claude Monet. He immersed himself in their work and in his own, painting mostly peaceful landscapes of the Vietnamese countryside. In the process of their creation, he could escape from the sound of war and enter a quiet place, at least for a while. But then there was the cacophony of the 1968 Tet Offensive, a historically horrific time in the Vietnamese war during which there would be no quiet for almost a month.

For several thousand years, the Vietnamese Lunar New Year, Tet, has been a traditional celebration that brings the Vietnamese a sense of happiness, hope, and peace. But in the early-morning hours of January 31, the first day of the Vietnamese New Year, Communist troops and commandos attacked virtually every major town and city in South Vietnam, as well as most of the important American bases and airfields. Nearly everywhere the attacks came as a surprise. Large parts of Saigon suddenly found itself "liberated," and parades of gun-waving Communist soldiers marched through the streets proclaiming the revolution. Some even rounded up citizens they deemed collaborators and government sympathizers for show trials and quick executions.

In Hue, Nho saw the streets of his beautiful city turn to bloody chaos, as over 12,000 Communist soldiers invaded the city and remained there for 28 days, fighting, beating, torturing, and killing. They called it Strategy of Terror. By the end of the month, 119 Americans, 363 ARVN soldiers, and nearly 6,000 Communist soldiers were dead. That was the first count, but there would be more. In the wake of the offensive, 5,800 Hue civilians were found dead or declared missing, though in subsequent months most of the missing would be found in single and mass graves with clear evidence of having been tortured or shot after being bound.

Nho's school, which was in the Imperial Palace of Hue, sustained considerable damage and remained closed for the entire month of the fighting. Still a year off from being a soldier, he did what he could to survive, including painting. After Hue was recaptured from the Communists, there was a demand for paintings of the battle from Vietnamese citizens living in other parts of the country. To make money, to survive, Nho painted images of the damaged Imperial Palace, of mausoleums, old citadels, and old Buddhist temples, and sold them to tourists. Though he didn't like painting images of the war, he found that the process of creating helped him escape to a more peaceful place.

In 1969 he joined the Vietnamese army and, because of his education, was made a second lieutenant. His first assignment was below Saigon in the provinces of Vinh Long and Sa Dec. He had it fairly easy then, doing mostly office work, but that was about to change. In 1972, a move north to Quang Ngai Province brought him to one of the bloodiest battles of the war. The Americans were gone now, and the ARVNs fought desperately for months over a hill they dubbed *Bato*, "Blood Hill," as so many on both sides bled out and died on its soil.

"It was a terrible battle," Nho says, screwing up his weathered face, deepening its lines. "I don't like to think about it now." There were many times, as rockets, mortars, and artillery incessantly pounded his position, that he would hug the dirt walls of the trenches, convinced that he was about to die. Sometimes, during pauses in the onslaught, he would unfold a small photo of his mother that he carried in his pocket and sketch her face with a few pieces of broken pastel chalk. As he concentrated on capturing her great strength and beauty, he knew deep in his heart that she was praying for him at that exact moment, so that should a deadly rocket slam into his position, he was content that at least he would die with her image in his mind.

It was during these times, when his mind and spirit flowed into his art, that there was, for at least a few moments, a cessation of the falling silver rain.

The war ended in 1975, and Nho and all the other officers were immediately put into a Communist prison. Actually, they were forced to build one for themselves in a clearing in the jungle. The prisoners were forced to build shelters, fencing, and make useful utensils out of damaged weapons and tanks. They cleared the forest to plant rice, cassava, corn, yams, vegetables, and beans, though they didn't get to eat much of what they planted. Nho's stomach was never full; often he was close to starvation. There were escape attempts, of course, and the desperate were shot on the spot. Nho wanted to escape, but he never tried because he knew his weakened condition would not have allowed him to get far.

One night a friend of Nho's ate another man's bowl of rice, an unpardonable violation. The barracks exploded into chaos before the guilty prisoner gathered his courage to shuffle forward shamefully and admit that he had eaten it. He was punished immediately with extra work, more than his starving body and ever-weakening psyche could tolerate. Then at night, when his bone-weary fatigue made it nearly impossible to stand, the Communists gathered all the prisoners together to condemn and curse the man for what he had done.

Finally, he broke. One night he came to Nho's bunk and said, "I can no longer endure. I have to die." Nho tried to talk to his friend, to convince him to live, to live for his mother. But soon after, the man placed a note in his bowl of rice and gave it to the one from whom he had stolen. The note was an apology for the theft and gave permission for the man to eat his bowl of rice. The next day, Nho's friend, his mind and body savaged, escaped into the jungle and hanged himself from a tree before the guards could find him.

Nho kept his sanity by "leaving" his surroundings and immersing himself in his art. As when he was a child in his war-torn village, as when he was a young man during the battle of Hue, and just as when he was in the trenches in Quang Ngai as a soldier, Nho again found a peaceful place in the creative process. "My inner energy allowed me to put my mind and heart in my work. The 'outside' got set aside and I was no longer afraid."

He drew pictures of the other prisoners so they could send them home in the bimonthly mail to show their families that they were alive. However, the drawings were confiscated when they depicted prisoners as too malnourished or too sickly, as the Communists didn't want the outside to know of the prisoners' treatment. Sometimes Nho hid his work during inspections for fear the guards would take away what few art supplies he had.

Nho was to stay in prison for six years, nearly 2,200 days of witnessing and experiencing great physical suffering, mental deterioration, and death. Always he drew and painted and created to keep his spirit and mind alive and healthy. A warrior does what needs to be done, what he needs to do to survive. Nho knew that as a platoon leader he needed to stay mentally healthy to guide the other prisoners.

He was released in 1981 and returned to his family. He began working in the art world again, married a schoolteacher, fathered a daughter, and in 1995 he and his family came to the United States, bringing with them a few paintings, brushes, paint, and a single suitcase of clothes. Since his friends and relatives told him that money was easy to make in the United States, Nho and his wife gave all but $50 away to those they left behind.

Today, Nho and his family live in an apartment in Portland, Oregon, where he paints every day. He earns money by designing and painting signs for businesses and by selling his creative work in occasional gallery showings. He worries that his arm, broken in prison and never set, will eventually interfere with his work, and that his eyes might go bad.

The aging warrior never paints images of the war. Mostly he favors the ocean, still life, and people. For a long time his work was dark: brooding colors and seemingly angry strokes. For a while he painted crosses, dark crosses against gloomy skies. One painting depicts multiple crosses, all of them dripping blood. "I'm a Buddhist," he says, "but sometimes I paint crosses. I don't know why. Something inside my head tells me to."

Lately, his paintings have been brighter with lighter colors, with a focus on aestheticism to modernism and abstract, an approach that makes his "heart and brain become more peaceful." He says that painting saves him. "Painting rebirths me in my late 50s."

Perhaps his job, the loving task of raising his daughter, and his work in the community are also pushing the war a little further back into his mind. "I feel happy," he says. "I feel very lucky because I came to America."

Nho Nguyen lived the warrior life for decades, doing what he had to do to survive and to help his men survive. Art, and the creation of it, was part of that process and is what he still does to ward off the darkness, the horror, to bring light and joy to his life.

CHAPTER

3

How Are Warriors a Different Breed?

Studies I have done suggest that the warrior code is primarily bred into our genes; in other words, it is in the nature of the person one normally identifies as a warrior. . . . Researchers have linked the personality trait of craving exciting new experiences to a gene on chromosome 11. This gene helps regulate dopamine, a chemical mediator for pleasure and emotion in the brain. If a person has a longer version of the D4DR gene, he is more likely to be what most people might call courageous or craving excitement, as opposed to timid or reserved.

—Martina Sprague,
from "Are Warriors Born or Made?"

A HIGH SENSE OF DUTY

by Tony L. Jones

Tony L. Jones has more than 14 years of experience in SWAT operations and nuclear weapons security, plus 20 years of concurrent military police/security experience. Much of Jones's experience has been in training and management positions, from shift commander, sniper commander, and firearms instructor to contract officer for the U.S. Marshals Service.

Mr. Jones served in the U.S. Army, Army National Guard, Air National Guard, Air Force Reserve, and Air Force for a total of 20 years. His military service includes everything from fire team leader to military police supervisor to SWAT and emergency response training (ERT) instructor. Mr. Jones participated in Desert Shield, Desert Storm, Task Force Rushmore, Operation Northern Watch, Operation Noble Eagle, Operation Enduring Freedom, and Operation Fundamental Justice. He presently holds the rank of senior master sergeant and is a member of the Air National Guard Senior Noncommissioned Officer (NCO) Corps.

Mr. Jones is the founder of a tactical/security consulting company called Heightened Vigilance. To date, he has provided tactical/security consulting, product evaluations, and tactical/firearms/leadership training to a variety of private and government agencies.

As an author, Mr. Jones has written nine published books: Booby-Trap Identification and Response for Law Enforcement Officers, Court Security: A Guide for Law Enforcement Personnel, Effective Response to School Violence: A Guide for Educators and Law Enforcement Personnel, A Guide to Chemical Agent Use in Police Work, Specialty Police Munitions, Surviving and Operating in Dim-Light or No-Light Conditions, SWAT Leadership and Tactical Planning, SWAT Sniper: Deployment and Control, *and* Tactical Communications for SWAT Teams. *He has also written more than 200 articles that have appeared in a host of periodicals.*

Mr. Jones graduated magna cum laude *from the American Military University with a master's degree in management,* cum

---

laude *from Ohio University with a bachelor's degree in criminal justice,* magna cum laude *from Southern State Community College with an associate's degree in business management, and* magna cum laude *from Air Force Community College with an associate's degree in industrial security.*

❖

A typical definition of the word warrior is "a man engaged or experienced in warfare." This is adequate for an overall broadbrush view but falls well short of explaining why a warrior is a special breed. There are a number of intricate ingredients and concepts that truly make a warrior special. Many people possess a few of these, but the warrior breed possesses an abundance of these delineating qualities. No amount of study or learning will make a man a true warrior; only natural qualities acting as a crucible can make a warrior a special breed.

Let's look at the qualities that make a warrior a different breed. Those that come to my mind are fairness, diligence, sound preparation, discipline, professional skill, honor, readiness to fight, loyalty, self-confidence, consideration, excitement, fulfillment, integrity, ambition, fear, the will to win, and camaraderie. All of these qualities are needed, to some extent, to foster what I call the warrior spirit that in turn makes the warrior a special breed. In other words, the warrior spirit and warrior breed are inextricably intertwined.

Fairness, diligence, sound preparation, discipline, professional skill, honor, readiness to fight, and loyalty all generate a warrior spirit that goes a long way in achieving victory. Have you ever noticed that a warrior takes these characteristics to the grave? Indeed the warrior spirit never seems to grow old once it has taken hold of a person. The question begs asking—are warriors born or trained? I believe parts of the warrior spirit, such as sound preparation, discipline, and professional skill, are learned behaviors, but the qualities of fairness, diligence, readiness to fight, honor, and loyalty are truly found in the core of a person. Training merely energizes these traits and brings them to the surface.

To be a warrior in our present armed forces is exciting and fulfilling. The United States has the best technology and the best-trained, most efficient officers and men in the world. This situation generates self-confidence that in turn generates victory. This is a far cry from the situation that existed when I first entered the military in December 1974, a time when the army was in ruins, the draft had ended, the volunteer armed forces were taking shape (which many people predicted would fail), and many citizens at home ridiculed their own servicemen and women. Despite recognizing all of these problems, the warrior breed still stepped forward and made the volunteer services a success.

Warriors tend to look back on their military service—even the most violent moments—as the culminating experience of their lives. To fight for a reason and in a calculating spirit, otherwise known as the will to win, is something to be cherished. A warrior knows he is always liable to be smashed by superior force but is always prepared to do his best. The true mark of the warrior breed comes into play when the likelihood of defeat is present. Many people are brave when they believe they are going to win, but how many people, other than a true warrior, will continue to fight even when they believe they will likely lose? Those of the warrior breed believe that it is better to die on their feet than to live on their knees.

After the Twin Towers and Pentagon were attacked, many young and able people said, "Let's kick their ass," but few accompanied the warrior in this endeavor. Where were these people after 9-11? Were they angry? They say yes. Were they ready to protect the country? They say yes. Were they ready to become warriors—volunteer to join the armed forces and go to war, leaving their families, friends, and comfortable lives? No, but they were ready to cheer, watch the war on television in the comfort of their homes when it suited them, and continue to live a comfortable, safe existence as long as the warrior met the challenges and horrors of war. The warrior willingly (remember, everyone in the armed forces has volunteered) leaves all of these familiar things at home, choosing to move toward the unknown.

To be entirely honest, the warrior breed often feels a thrill in knowing something is taking place before him that is unknown and terrible. He knows he will be tested but has no conception of the hated word *defeat*. He doesn't know it yet (unless he has experienced war before), but he will be changed forever when he passes his test and becomes an even stronger member of the warrior breed. Indeed, it is common for a warrior to volunteer time and again to go to war.

The warrior has no inclination to do anything other than close with the enemy and soundly defeat him. Thus, he feels more worthy as a man upon returning home. When he is home, he remembers the physical and emotional discomforts of the war zone. However, he is also reminded of what he stands to lose if he fails in his chosen profession. The warrior's knowledge of his profession tends to heighten his courage and stimulate his will to win, which is ever present in the warrior breed. Concerning the will to win, consider how many civilians would willingly move toward the sounds of guns when every human instinct screams to run away? The warrior breed is taught—when all else fails, move to the sounds of the guns to find the enemy, fix the enemy, fight the enemy, and finish the enemy.

There is no tighter bond than that of warriors who have developed into comrades. There is no substitute for the personal sharing of dangers and hardships. Consideration for others is an all-pervading factor in a warrior's life. Warriors are inextricably interrelated: supplementing and strengthening each other, willingly sharing the last drink of water or bit of food with another, taking turns wearing one coat, holding a fellow warrior because he just lost a friend in battle or a loved one at home, or sincerely hurting with another because his wife or girlfriend just sent him the infamous "Dear John" letter. In an instant, a warrior can find himself essential to the life of another, and vice versa. Consider the mutual trust that abounds when one warrior screams out, "Cover me" because he intends to move into harm's way and willingly place his life into the hands of his comrade.

Indeed, many warriors fear letting their "buddies" down more than receiving wounds or even being killed. There is an inherent feeling that comrades (the people the warrior trusts, respects, and loves most) will bear witness for or against a warrior's career in some manner. There can be no closer bond than camaraderie between warriors; it can even surpass family ties. A person who decides to be a liar, a loner, selfish, uncaring, disloyal, phony or a "bluffer," a "goof-off," or a constant screw-up may become successful in the civilian world but will never become a member of the warrior breed.

Are warriors so different from others that they feel no fear? Absolutely not. The warrior fears many things. However, he has the ability to master his fear by falling back on the qualities of the crucible that make the warrior a special breed. I believe the three things he fears most are letting his comrades down, permanent disablement and/or disfigurement (the true horror of war is wounds, not death), and failing his country.

I purposefully structured this discussion into linking camaraderie and fear in order to focus on a common but seldom discussed warrior practice—entering into death pacts. It is very common for warriors to seek out a few trusted comrades before entering into battle and consummate the pact that "If I get disabled, especially paralyzed, and you know it, shoot me dead." The warrior breed solemnly expects this pact to be honored. To some, this may seem cowardly, but to the warrior, it is essential to his soul that he continue to be fit and able to fight.

Let's end this examination of what makes a warrior a different breed by considering the following words: duty, honor, country, service, liberty, and freedom. The "duty, honor, country" motto of the United States Military Academy at West Point is certainly well thought out and represents the core of the warrior spirit. For most warriors there is never a moment spent without feeling a sense of duty. Warriors often feel that exactness in little things is a wonderful source of cheerfulness. Indeed, duty becomes a habit due to the mental byproducts of pride of accomplishment, feelings of strength and boldness, and sense of purpose and energy. The warrior breed does not serve his country for homecoming parades (many never experience these festivities, even today), medals, or other awards. Does this mean the warrior does not value parades, awards, and medals? Absolutely not. Many are ambitious (a valued warrior virtue), but the warrior breed serves out of a sense of duty. There is perhaps no greater professional asset for the warrior than a high sense of duty, and his true happiness lies in discharging his duty.

President John F. Kennedy articulated much of what comprises the mind-set of a warrior during his 1961 inaugural address. Warriors think in terms of service to their country, not in terms of what their country can and should do for them. Warriors are willing to pay any price, bear any burden, meet any hardship, support any friend, and oppose any foe to ensure the survival and success of this country. For a warrior, patriotism represents a steady devotion to the country over time in lieu of the "flash-in-the-pan" patriotism displayed by others in a time of crisis. The warrior breed can condense this concept into four words: country first, self second.

Liberty and freedom are far more than words to a warrior. They equate to responsibility, and that responsibility often requires that he undergo fatigue and hardship in carrying out his duty to protect liberty and freedom. Freedom and liberty generate responsibility, and that responsibility is willingly shouldered by the warrior, who understands that he is charged with protecting the freedom our citizens enjoy today. To the warrior, the concept of dying without having shouldered this responsibility is horrible and is almost the same as living as a coward.

In conclusion, I want to say that trying to explain warriorhood is most daunting. It is as difficult as explaining to a blind person what the color green looks like. My task was to explain whether the warrior is a different breed. My question in turn became: to understand my explanation would someone need to experience the warrior crucible? Only you, the reader, know if I have succeeded in my task. I sincerely hope so.

I have been told that people can identify those who have been in the military just by the way they walk and the way they perform even the most menial task. I would not say this is true for everyone who was or is in the military, but I will say it is true of the warrior. There is a great difference between being a member of the armed forces and participating in actions that fuel the essentials of the warrior spirit.

There is one thing concerning this discussion of the warrior breed that I absolutely cannot ignore and that is the fact that some people think a terrorist is a warrior. It has been said frequently that one man's freedom fighter is another man's terrorist. This may be so, but a freedom fighter is not necessarily a warrior. Furthermore, a terrorist will never be a warrior because of the nature of the target of attack. The warrior breed will never accept the deliberate killing and maiming of innocent noncombatant men, women, and children. Any warrior who has visited the crater that was once the World Trade Center will see terrorists for what they are and will feel a fire in his belly. This fire is the crucible that drives the warrior forward to protect our great nation.

I cannot neglect to mention the citizen who chooses to exercise his freedom of speech by saying, "I am against the war but I am for the troops." No warrior believes this "psycho babble." The war and the warrior are one and the same. The warrior breed expects only one thing from the citizens of the United States and that is to *back the warriors who are fighting and being wounded and killed.* The warrior will not forget those people, such as entertainers, who abuse their role in society by making hurtful statements and expect the warrior to ignore or forget the views they try to force upon others. Remember, the warrior breed is honorable and certainly remembers who comes to the war zones to entertain the troops and who sits at home and berates what the troops are doing. Civilians seem to quickly forget what a favored entertainer says or does, but warriors do not. I know many who will not watch a movie or have anything to do with any endeavor tied to certain entertainers, even as far back as the Vietnam War. This is as it should be, because the warrior backs up his words with conviction and action.

Perhaps the best explanation I can give of the warrior being a special breed comes from a picture I remember seeing. The setting was a parade, and the color guard was coming down the street. The only person standing when the colors came abreast to the crowd was a man, a veteran in a wheelchair. This disabled man felt the warrior spirit and pushed himself to a standing position while everyone else continued to sit.

There can be no doubt that he was an old warrior.

ARE WARRIORS
BORN OR MADE?

by Martina Sprague

Martina Sprague has studied the martial arts for 17 years and holds black belts in kickboxing, street freestyle, and kenpo karate. She has a special interest in the principles of teaching and learning, the physics of martial arts, and the tactics and philosophies of modern wars (Vietnam and newer). She is a certified flight instructor with a BS in aviation from Westminster College in Salt Lake City.

Ms. Sprague has written three books focusing on the principles of physics in the martial arts and one book on the techniques and strategies of competition kickboxing: Fighting Science: The Martial Arts Book of Physics; The Laws of Physics for Martial Artists; The Science of Takedowns, Throws, and Grappling for Self-Defense; *and* The Complete Kickboxing Strategist. *The last three books are available from Turtle Press, www.turtlepress.com. You can reach Ms. Sprague or learn more via her Web site at www.modernfighter.com.*

❖

Studies I have done suggest that the warrior code is primarily bred into our genes; in other words, it is in the nature of the person one normally identifies as a warrior. The warrior is, therefore, literally a different breed.

Being a warrior requires the ability to face a situation squarely and honestly, to step up to the task, and to take action in difficult, dangerous, or unpleasant situations. In his book *The Blank Slate*, Steven Pinker says, "If you have a longer than average version of the D4DR dopamine receptor gene, you are more likely to be a thrill seeker, the kind of person who jumps out of airplanes, climbs up frozen waterfalls, or has sex with strangers." Although I don't believe that jumping out of airplanes, ice climbing, or having sex are necessarily warrior qualities, I do believe that the thrill-seeking nature that leads to the desire to partake in these activities is. I also believe that those who seek these and other thrills are the kinds of people who are most likely to embrace the warrior code.

Researchers have linked the personality trait of craving exciting new experiences to a gene on chromosome 11. This gene helps regulate dopamine, a chemical mediator for pleasure and emotion in the brain. If a person has a longer version of the D4DR gene, he is more likely to be what most people might call courageous or craving excitement, as opposed to timid or reserved. I know I will probably take a lot of guff over this, because it suggests that a person who does not have the required genetic variation cannot become a warrior, no matter how hard he tries. That is, of course, if we agree on the warrior code.

My definition of a warrior is that of a person who has a natural passion about being strong, courageous, intellectual, analytical, and a leader. You might say that the warrior code is this person's calling, because he is not happy unless he can exercise it. Sure, you can acquire warrior qualities through discipline and hard work, but for those who are not naturally passionate about it, it will be a very long haul.

Warriorhood is not a 9-to-5 job; it's a lifestyle. You live by your principles, and you're on duty even when you're off duty. Looking at it this way helps you determine who truly is a warrior. Examples of fake warriors are

- Parents preaching to their children about the dangers of smoking or drinking, but when the children aren't looking they sneak one themselves.
- A martial arts instructor requiring his or her students to bow when stepping into the training hall, but when he is alone, he steps in without bowing.
- A police officer giving you a speeding ticket, but when he is off duty, he speeds or drives without wearing a seat belt.

Integrity is one of the most important warrior qualities. A warrior is clear-sighted and speaks the truth without willfully offending others. He avoids twisting or beautifying for the sake of staying politically correct. He understands that he can't help a bad situation unless he first admits that the situation is bad. The warrior honors his word, maintains his commitment, and realizes the importance of his responsibility to himself and others. Although a warrior speaks the truth, he refrains from speaking at all when he has determined that silence is the better option. The warrior weighs each issue in accordance with his life, times, and circumstances. For example, lying to your friends or to those you have been entrusted to protect is a violation of the warrior code; lying to your enemies is not.

The warrior is committed to his craft and has a combat mind-set. We know when a warrior steps into the room because his presence takes over; we can literally feel that he wants to be there. When a bad situation develops, no matter how unpleasant, the warrior takes charge and does the best he can with what he has. A warrior is a different breed because he has conviction, understands the pleasure/pain dichotomy, and takes pride in his physical and mental strength. He has stamina and an analytical mind.

Warriorhood is action, not good intentions. Rather than stubbornly refusing to give up that which has long ago gone stale, the warrior differentiates between the price and the value. For example, a warrior might quit martial arts training prior to becoming a black belt, despite the fact that he joined the black belt club, if he has determined that it is a path no longer worth pursuing. After a period of evaluation and self-reflection, a warrior might determine that it is inappropriate to go to war for the nation he loves so much, despite his claim of citizenship. These are issues that most people don't address publicly for fear of sounding lazy or unpatriotic. However, being a warrior means that you evaluate a situation, face the issues squarely, and then speak the truth and do what is right and necessary. The warrior understands that no matter what he does there will be consequences, and he has a good sense of how to balance the scale. A warrior is trusted and admired even when he is the carrier of bad news, because he refrains from instilling false hopes in those under his care.

A warrior identifies, thinks through, and defines before getting emotional or jumping on the bandwagon. Words such as courtesy, modesty, self-control, and perseverance are often stated in martial arts class and can be associated with the warrior code. However, the warrior is careful not to repeat these words without giving them sufficient thought. A warrior doesn't take anything literally but rather questions and understands that the world comprises all kinds of people and that sometimes, depending on a person's background and experiences, right can be wrong. The warrior embraces the yin-yang concept and acknowledges differences while allowing them to coexist in harmony. This tolerance requires self-control.

You cannot claim warriorhood. You can force others, through intimidation, threat, or brute force to do what you want them to do, but this is not warriorhood. You don't become a warrior, hero, or courageous person by doing what is your only option. For example, a person is not a warrior simply because he survives a life-threatening illness. A soldier is not a warrior simply because he goes to battle or is injured in battle. There has to be a choice. Warriorhood doesn't happen by accident. You must willfully and consistently choose the warrior path, despite your many other options.

Although warriors may be present in times of war or conflict, warriorhood is not determined by presence or power alone. The warrior fights for something deeper than the glorification of war or the preservation of the warrior tradition. The passionate pursuit of his goal is often more important than arriving. Having the stamina to remain a warrior through all phases of life is closely tied to a person's convictions and ideals, and primarily to his passions.

In accordance with the definition of warrior I have discussed in this essay, it would be false to say that, with enough work, everybody has the potential to become a warrior. How do you know if you have the required genetic variation? If you are naturally thrilled by the warrior code, you are probably suited to be a warrior, without requiring motivation from others. If not, other people's attempts to motivate you are not likely to help in the long run. Warriorhood is not a one-size-fits-all concept. You must be naturally (genetically) predisposed to and thrilled by the warrior code in order to act on it and make it a lifestyle choice.

CHAPTER

4

Why Do They Do It?

The Twin Towers were still a smoldering pile of rubble and body parts when the sensitive second camp began rushing about trying to understand our enemies. After all, we must have done something to provoke the attack. We must have deserved it somehow by the wrong we had done others. That's how nonwarriors think. They never seem to understand that lighting a candle and chanting, "Give peace a chance" is not going to convert bullies and tyrants to the wonders of modern civilization. A warrior knocking their dicks in the dirt—now that grabs their attention.

—Charles W. Sasser,
from "Warriors in the Genes"

WARRIORS IN THE GENES

by Charles W. Sasser

Charles W. Sasser has been a full-time freelance writer/journalist/photographer since 1979. He is a veteran of both the U.S Navy (journalist) and U.S. Army (Special Forces, the Green Berets), a combat veteran and a former combat correspondent wounded in action. He also served 14 years as a police officer (in Miami, Florida, and in Tulsa, Oklahoma, where he was a homicide detective). He has taught at universities, lectured nationwide, and traveled extensively throughout the world. Mr. Sasser's bio is included in Who's Who in America *and* Who's Who in the World. *He is the author of more than 40 published books and 2,500 magazine articles and short stories.*

At various times, Mr. Sasser has solo-canoed across the Yukon, sailed the Caribbean, motorcycled across the North American continent, ridden camels in the Egyptian desert, floated the Amazon River, dived for pirate treasure, ridden horses across Alaska, motorcycled Europe, climbed Mt. Rainier, run with the bulls in Spain, and chased wild mustangs. In 1986, he was a finalist to fly into space with NASA's Journalist in Space project. In 2001, he set a world record by making the first transcontinental flight in an ultralite-powered parachute aircraft. Mr. Sasser has been a professional rodeo clown and bronc rider, professional kickboxer, sky diver, college professor, newspaperman, and anthropologist. . . . He does dinner theater and has starred in numerous plays, including The Odd Couple *and* The Foreigner. *He currently lives on a ranch in Oklahoma, where he pursues his writing career and rears and trains registered quarter horses for rodeo events.*

❖

At barely 18, a tough little hillbilly kid out of the Ozarks, I ran away from home to enlist in the U.S. Navy. Through the sometimes brutal process by which kids are molded into weapons, I rose to become one of America's warrior elite in the U.S. Army Special Forces, a Green Beret soldier. For more than a quarter century, I trained myself and I trained others in the military art and science of warfare. I went to war six times, from Vietnam to Desert Storm. In between, I served in the demilitarized zone (DMZ) in Korea, parachuted into Panama, tested the security of American foreign embassies, shot it out with Latin American Communists, and even slipped back into Vietnam in the 1980s when it was Soviet-occupied. I worked overt and covert operations. I survived plane crashes and bullet wounds.

Why did I do it? Why does any warrior do it? Perhaps it is part of the pride in being a man. Perhaps it's even in the genes.

From the breaking dawn of human history, warriors have been essential to the survival of their people and their clans. A man who could not fight, or who would not fight, fell rather quickly before larger, more aggressive males—or he became food for prowling predators. When a woman mated, she chose a male with the capability and determination to protect her and her offspring. Wimps needed not apply; their gene pools frequently ended rather abruptly. A man was judged by how well he defended his woman, his family, his cave, and his nomadic clan of scavenger hunters.

Society's first heroes were warriors like Odysseus from Homer or David from the Bible, who slew Goliath face-to-face with a slingshot. Now that took balls. Only later, much later, did the sensitive, feminized male emerge, his existence made possible because other males took up the sword in his stead.

As mankind grew more agrarian and "civilized," the warrior breed developed into specialists largely collected into armies. Reasons for fighting expanded into a warrior philosophy that went beyond hearth and home to encompass broad principles of patriotism, pride, honor, duty, and freedom—God, country, and mom's apple pie.

The events of September 11, 2001, and the subsequent War on Terror clearly divided American malehood into its two separate and distinct camps. First were those with deep character and conviction, willing to fight if necessary to protect their homeland, their idealized larger cave. Even though I was 61 years old and had served in the military 29 years, I immediately called in to volunteer once again for active duty, only to be informed I was too old. Let the young ones handle it.

Would I have been afraid to go into combat again? You bet your ass. I was afraid *every* time someone shot at me. Only a fool is never afraid. Yet, a man who is afraid to die for his principles is equally afraid to live for them. There *are* things worth dying for. Call me sappy, but I believe in honor and courage, in pride and duty. I believe in protecting my people and in defending the cave and the clan. It's part of being a man. These are admittedly old-fashioned values in a politically correct age of narcissism and self-centered "entitlement" mentalities. Yet, such values propelled mankind from his cave to cross oceans, settle continents, and plant the first human footprints in space. Besides, warriors are the type of men with whom I prefer to associate.

Like many other paratroopers, I knew a soldier who was terrified every time he had to jump out that awful door into the sky. I asked him why, if he was so afraid, did he keep doing it.

"It scares me half to death," he admitted, "but I do it because I like being around men who *do* do it."

The warrior needs courage, but he also needs an ethical framework of honor in order to be an effective fighter while he remains a human being with a soul.

"The sniper (or the warrior) must feel that he can kill when the time comes," said Maj. Dick Culver, who helped create the U.S. Marine Corps Scout Sniper School at Quantico, Virginia. "He has to have no compunction against killing but must also have compassion. He has to have a conscience, not necessarily be a tremendously religious person, but one who kills wantonly is worthless. You don't want a man who will kill for the sake of killing."

American gestalt was constructed upon the bedrock of a man doing what a man has to do because it is the honorable thing. Something inside a man, something as deep and fundamental as dark caves generations ago, responds to honorable warriors facing odds and overcoming. Popular culture, at least up until recent times, reflects this viewpoint.

Who, for example, can ever forget Gary Cooper in *High Noon* striding into the street alone to take on the bad guys because he had honor and it was his duty? Or John Wayne as crusty old Rooster Cogburn in *True Grit*: "Fill your hands, you sonofabitch!" Such images continue to appeal to the American warrior's sense of honor, fair play, duty, and courage in ways that the current crop of sensitive, guilt-ridden icons never will.

Former President Richard Nixon held a clear understanding of warriors and who they were: "When you have to call on the nation to be strong on such things as drugs, crime, defense, our basic national position, the educated people and the leader class no longer have any character, and you can't count on them." In any crisis, he continued, they "painted their asses white and ran like antelopes." Those you could count on, he said, were "men, not softies . . . two-fisted types."

Terrorists attacking America proved that. While the first camp was composed of warriors prepared to fight, a second camp made up of wimps ran for cover deep inside the cave to tremble behind big, burly men willing to protect them from the bullies of the world. Fearful and timid, they hid behind girly-girl rhetoric that enabled them to bellow like bulls even though they were in fact steers, while at the same time they attacked the warrior mentality of those who made them safe. It was almost like they were looking in their fear for someone to accept their surrender. Better to be a slave, I suppose, and secure than to be a warrior and face danger.

The Twin Towers were still a smoldering pile of rubble and body parts when the sensitive second camp began rushing about trying to *understand* our enemies. After all, we must have done *something* to provoke the attack. We must have *deserved* it somehow by the wrong we had done others. That's how nonwarriors think. They never seem to understand that lighting a candle and chanting, "Give peace a chance" is not going to convert bullies and tyrants to the wonders of modern civilization. A warrior knocking their dicks in the dirt—now *that* grabs their attention.

"Our parents taught us not to hit when we were young, not to hit back, and that's exactly what we're doing," cooed a peacenik. "Violence will only beget more violence."

Wrong. Keep giving your lunch money to the schoolyard bully and he'll keep taking it from you. Punch out his lights and you get to start eating lunch again. Now that's something I understand. My old pappy from the Ozarks always told me that he'd beat me once I got home if I wouldn't fight or if I lost a fight. He also told me he'd beat me if I *started* a fight.

Mad Dog Carson was the commo man on my Special Forces "A" Team, a crusty, rough-spoken man with a clear view of the world. "Once everything turns to shit," he was fond of saying, "all the feminists and sissies will start looking for a strong man to protect them."

A warrior for those times that try men's souls.

It is to the warrior that the nation owes its survival, its identity, and its liberty. Warriors rarely interfere with the fashion industry, Oprah Winfrey, or the flowering idiots in Hollywood. Yet, to such shrinking violets of cowardice, the warrior will always be looked upon as a testosterone-crazed killer—which actually means "braver than we are." But watch what happens, as Mad Dog put it, when "everything turns to shit."

There can be worse reasons for being a warrior, for being willing to fight, than patriotism, pride, honor, duty, and freedom—and for woman, family, cave, and clan. When bullets start to fly, however, a warrior can only hope that the buddy next to him is not some transgender or slip-assed girl fulfilling some social program, who will surrender at the first opportunity.

Women as Warriors

To be effective in self-defense, you cannot just defend—you must attack back. For a female, this is the ultimate reversal: you become the huntress, not the hunted; the predator, not prey. You summon and unleash all your life forces—courage, will, wrath, cunning, physical powers—and use them like secret weapons. Nothing is out of bounds; nothing is unthinkable. There's little to compare this to: you dial up the creature within; you trade in your polite self for your animal-self; you issue the "sic" command and give that beautiful junkyard bitch within carte blanche to go for the throat.

—Melissa Soalt, from
"Fierce Love: The Heart of the Female Warrior"

FIERCE LOVE
THE HEART OF THE FEMALE WARRIOR
by Melissa Soalt

Melissa Soalt, aka Dr. Ruthless, is a Black Belt *magazine Hall of Fame recipient named Woman of the Year 2002 and a columnist for* Self Defense for Women *magazine. A prominent women's self-defense expert and consultant and a former private practice psychotherapist, Ms. Soalt has taught thousands of women how to protect themselves from danger and summon their primal instincts to fight back and survive. She is well known for her no-nonsense attitude and practical, down-n-dirty methods. In 1986 she brought the Model Mugging program—the original full-force, scenario-based, armored attacker training methods—to the East Coast. Her on-site seminars have been conducted at such notable institutions as Harvard University, Polaroid, Hewlett Packard, Reebok International, Procter & Gamble, and the* Miami Herald, *to name a few.*

Ms. Soalt's media credits include ABC's The View, *NBC* Nightly News, *TNN, National Public Radio, and numerous newscasts. She has been cited and featured in more than two dozen publications, including* SELF, Woman's Day, *the* Wall Street Journal, *Germany's* Stern Magazine, Newsweek Japan, *and the* Prague Post. *She cohosted* From Fear to Power, *a self-defense radio show that aired in two media markets, authored a personal safety newspaper column, and has written feature articles for* Black Belt, BUST, *and professional trade publications. She is currently at work on a book.*

Ms. Soalt's best-selling Fierce and Female *videotapes, which focus on rape defense, have been hailed by law enforcement, seasoned fighters, and women's groups alike. A woman on a mission, she seeks to change the face of female fear: from fearful to fearsome.*

To learn more about her methods, services, and Fierce and Female *videos, visit www.dr-ruthless.com.*

Shortly after my *Fierce and Female* videos came out, I ran across a review by a self-defense pro whom I highly respect: "She has more balls than most men I know," he raved. I was flattered, all right, but . . . *balls?*

I have received this comment before and always take it in the complimentary spirit in which it is meant, but it speaks volumes to the association between courage and *manhood,* between courage and *virility,* and just how deeply this association embeds in our language and culture.

This is something I should like to change.

The warrior spirit lies deep within us all. It's a vital, rousing force that can turn the meek into the fearsome. Women, as a tribe, are endowed with their own warrior instincts, insights, and powers, born in the female psyche and biology.

For example, classical warrior texts call for a *dis*passionate mind-set, devoid of emotion: *you must control your fear, control your emotions,* they say. But that, I protest, is part of a male paradigm. While it's true that strong emotions can hijack body and mind—"Don't let your emotions get ahead of your technique," I tell my students—it's precisely the swells of rage, terror, and love itself that fund a woman's fight, fueling her body, enabling her to evoke the warrior spirit—be it to protect herself, loved ones, or the sovereignty of her peoples.

Rage. Terror. Love. Fury. These aren't words you're likely to find in any warrior's code or combat manual. Yet fighting, and the business of being a warrior, is an emotional and primal reality as much as it's a moral and spiritual one.

For 18 years, I've been teaching women how, when all else fails, to shed their civilized skins, unleash their *Savage Beauty,* and attack back—not like playful kittens, like wolverines. (The goal, of course, is to facilitate escape.) But I am also a woman who's been assaulted and fought back. At five feet tall on a good hair day, I can attest: *it's not the size of the woman in the fight; it's the size of the fight in the woman!*

Fighting spirit is a lot like beauty—it's both innate and can be cultivated but is always kindled from the inside out, whereas power is a commodity that can be sourced from many places. And I have siphoned power from violating hands: from rapacious hands that stole pieces of me in the darkness, trying to evict me from my very own body; from the sweaty pulp of my would-be rapist's palm slapping over my mouth as he bashed my head against the wall (I struck back and escaped); from hands that tightened like a noose around my throat, before I spit in my attacker's face and a vicious fight ensued; from the hand that *I* broke that wouldn't take NO for an answer. (That was a dawning recognition: *my body was a tool and instrument of power, and with this tool I too could be dangerous.* A knowing, long before I had any training, that I have since passed to countless women.)

Power is also kindled by fear. I'm talking about primal, animal-level fear. The kind that Ambrose Redmoon, Native American warrior and writer, so aptly described "could pull the flesh off your face"—which I think should be a requirement for anyone teaching self-defense. If you haven't been scared to death you don't qualify, especially when it comes to teaching women, most of whom are already experts in fear, many of whom have fought their very own "War on Terror."

Terror is the mother of all fear. You know it when you feel it. An icy chill rips through your body at warp speed, catapulting you into a Darwinian world of predator and prey. When I unpack my memories, I can still feel the terror I felt when a man shrouded in darkness broke into my home in the dead of night, after first cutting the power and phone lines, then headed for my bed—knife in hand. Fortunately I repelled his advances with a Godzillian yell from Hell. This incident is what led me from martial arts to the down-n-dirty methods that would *become me.*

That memory still haunts like a ghost from time to time. But the terror itself has been absorbed, eaten, you could say, and transformed into fuel in the belly of the beast. Now, when the memory arrives that chill turns cold-blooded—the French call it *sang-froid*—and is seasoned with invective. From the neck up I am ice; from the neck down, I am fire. I imagine tearing into this man using everything at my disposal—my bare-naked body, the walls, furnishings, improvised (and not so improvised) weapons.

So I know a thing or two about this dirty business. This intimacy is no doubt part of what the reviewer perceives in my demeanor and "spirit of entering" and identifies as *balls*. But frankly, I would attribute it to primal rage and fear.

My own stories pale by comparison. As a former psychotherapist, I have companioned survivors of violence and assault into netherworlds of horror where moments can unravel into lifetimes of suffering. I am not the first to say this, but sexual and bodily attacks are microcosms of war leaving heaping, smoking mounds of devastation in their wake. And let me tell you: it ain't a pretty picture. The effluvia of rape and child abuse stinks, and makes you want to sob. So my mettle, you could say, also comes from heartbreak hardened into resolve. And from E-mails alerting me to atrocities against women all over the world; they flash across my computer screen like smoke signals from afar—and not so far. Women being tortured and burned and killed and gang-raped by civilians and soldiers alike; beaten because they were handy when "his" demons struck. This makes my skin crawl, and it incurs my wrath.

We have nice, civilized, air-fluffed terms for this feeling: Righteous rage. Moral indignation. But what I feel is far more primitive: each story fuels my fire and undying reverence for female disobedience, adding another stripe to my war face.

So this essay is really a call to arms that I hope will awaken women's warrior spirit, shatter myths of female defenselessness, and topple some unspoken enemies: the cavernous divide between femininity and aggression (into which many victims have fallen); the insidious New Age notion that *flow* is not compatible with *force*; a culture that rewards women's "looks over competence" and wants women to believe that confidence comes in a roll-on. (Don't even get me started on the farcical term "feminine protection." Protect what—our underwear?)

Oh sure. There's progress. Let's not forget Hollywood, where a woman *can* be a deadly dame, but first she has to give good face and qualify as "babealicious." The mandate is clear: you can act tough, but keep it *pretty, not gritty.*

No creature on Earth other than humans has done such a menacingly fine job of socializing the killer instinct out if its females. It would be a tidy coup if I, as a feminist, could blame all this on the "evils of patriarchy." But it isn't just age-old conservatism or ads boasting, *I live for a great halter top!* that atrophies the female-animal muscle, truncating women from their baser selves. Popular New-Ageism and "moon-to-uterus" spirituality co-conspire in this pacification and would like us to believe that women are innately all-beatific, all-nurturing do-no-harmers with nary a virulent, aggressive, or power-loving bone; that we are always the embodiment of the "peaceful warrior goddess," always ennobling our higher, holier selves while disavowing our dark side and bestial potential. (Frankly, this doesn't sound like any woman I know. Can the notion of men as all malevolent be far behind?)

We hear a lot about higher callings, the yearning to connect with forces greater than oneself, and about the power of returning to one's roots. This is precisely the gift of self-defense—it returns women to native powers buried beneath fear and the rubble of socialization, and it bestows saving graces—not from heaven above, but from below—from our *lower* center of gravity curiously located near the site of the womb. (More reasons why self-defense is a *womanly* art!)

Self-defense is not a sophisticate: it's raw; it's primal. It involves a descent into a subterranean strata of your being, far below the topsoil of the nice lady cammo. Here lies a respite from the ubiquitous hum of civility: the meaty thuds, the heated rush, the bellowing sounds all part of its primitive appeal. There's magic too: learning to fight back locates women back in time, long before plastic bosoms, bikini waxing, and "feminine" deodorants, returning us to an earlier Self. Each thwacking blow, each bellicose yell peels back a layer of the modern-day veneer until, stripped to our essence, we uncover what anthropologist Michele Rosaldo has called "The image of ourselves undressed," the stuff we are made of at the core—a vibrant and formidable mélange of Beauty and Beast, I attest. And it can knock a man out.

To be effective in self-defense, you cannot just defend—you must *attack back*. For a female, this is the ultimate reversal: you become the huntress, not the hunted; the predator, not prey. You summon and unleash all your life forces—courage, will, wrath, cunning, physical powers—and use them like secret weapons. Nothing is out of bounds, nothing is unthinkable. There's little to compare this to: you dial up the creature within; you trade in your polite self for your animal-self; you issue the "sic" command and give that beautiful junkyard bitch within carte blanche to go for the throat.

I know this part of myself intimately—as all women should —and could no more disown this savage endowment than I could amputate a limb. Like my maternal nature, it's bedrock, or maybe it's this simple: survival, like romance, has captured my heart.

Yet I speak of this love affair with some trepidation. In spite of a culture gone warrior-chic and the alarming fact the CDC (Centers for Disease Control) has identified sexual assault and violence as one of the greatest health concerns of the 21st century, my enthusiasm for "going animal" and teaching women how to morph their bodies into weapons of destruction makes some folks nervous. Maybe it's the glint in my eye, but when I tell choice stories—like the one about the cocktail waitress who nailed her attacker's foot to freshly laid tar with her stiletto heel—or when I gush about my Afghan knife and confess that at night you might find me in the darkness slicing the air as if across a man's forearm, then neck—I am often flashed a look of disdain. The concern is that I have abandoned Venus for Mars; that my flight into the hardness of warriorhood represents a radical departure from the fleshy pink interior of femininity. That the Beast Girl's cravings are an anomaly of nature.

Nonsense! Somewhere along the line, we lost life's original instructions. What could be more natural, more in tune with Mother Nature than knowing how to bash back and *not* become prey or fodder for a scumbag's amusement? But the concern is telling, and betrays an unspoken fear: that the tools of aggression/forceful resistance/use of force are coming to a female near you.

And it should. I think about my student Sheila, who suffers brain seizures, a result of having been boxed in the head by her attacker. "Why didn't anyone ever teach me what to do?" she laments. These are haunting words that resound in every women's self-defense class.

If I were Warrior Queen for a day, I would issue a decree that all women become too dangerous to attack.

No one would ever ask a man, "Hey there, manly man, what possessed you to learn to protect yourself from all manner of scum?" What a silly question that would be! In a man's world, self-defense is deemed natural; it comes with beer and nachos and having a penis, whereas women are encouraged to rely on "good guys" to protect them from "bad guys"—a fundamentally flawed (not to mention disempowering) strategy because women are typically alone when violence strikes. Plus that good guy/bad guy line can get blurry, *fast*.

The underlying belief is that we aren't made of the right stuff; that women are the weaker sex; that *she'll only get hurt worse,* blah blah blah. What a screwball argument! *Of course* fighting back carries risks. And, yes, you might get hurt. Count on it, visualize it, become accustomed to the idea, I urge women, as though being raped, beaten, or slaughtered doesn't constitute injury? Not possessing explosive counterattack and escape skills—the first few seconds are often the most critical—and hoping to be rescued by a savior in uniform blue, or simply hoping . . . is far more injurious to women than fighting back. Strategies aside, this archaic attitude reinforces the age-old pas de deux: men are the protectors; women are the protectees. In other words, *you, a wussy female, are helpless against attack. Got it?*

Tell that to the Chicago woman who, in 2001, bit off her would-be rapist's balls. Or the Boston coed who feigned unconsciousness then sliced her rapist's face with a razor from her purse. Or my student who cracked her attacker's head against the bumper of her car and made pulp out of his accomplice's groin. Or "Kathleen," who chomped her knife-wielding rapist's finger down to the bone during a vicious attack. (Her story is recounted in Sanford Strong's book, *Strong on Defense.*) "I was so enraged that I went primal. Just because I'm a woman doesn't mean I can't fight like an animal," she vigorously declared.

Like I said, estrogen doesn't exactly make us sissies. Female ferocity is hard-wired, as old as the womb itself. And this fighting capacity goes far beyond *self*-defense.

As I write this, I am surrounded by copious accounts of women warriors from every era and corner of the globe—from ancient warrior queens to modern-day guerrilla fighters. While their stories often go untold, the list is as long as the world is wide: from Sri Lanka's Tamil Tigers, a renowned and deadly fighting unit, to anti-Nazi Resistance fighters; from the "Russian Battalion of Death" to petite martial nuns; from South American revolutionaries holed up in jungles to American frontierswomen homesteading with child in one arm and shotgun in the other. Armed with their love and their fury—and weapons, and explosives, and combat skills—women have *always* been fighters, willing to fight to the death to protect their brood, their land, and the sovereignty of their peoples.

These accounts lend veracity to Margaret Mead's observation that "When women disengage completely from their traditional role, they become more ruthless and savage than men." When pressed to fight, she observed, "the aroused female . . . displays no built-in chivalry."

Female militancy is almost always fueled by oppression and atrocities. "Women are reacting to their victimization with a matter-of-fact military vengefulness," wrote Naomi Wolf in her feminist tome *Fire with Fire* when discussing Balkan women who have taken up arms. One woman she cites joined the fighting "because of the mistreatment, the killing, and the rape. When I am on the front lines, I don't see any difference between the men and the women," she states. Another woman Wolf cites, a Sarajevan doctor, remarks how a third of the women she treated for rape "waited to have their gynecological problem resolved and then went out and picked up a gun."

But it's the words of Marisa Masu, an Italian Resistance fighter from World War II, that I find most sobering:

> At the time it was clear that each Nazi I killed, each bomb I helped to explode, shortened the length of the war and saved the lives of all women and children. . . . I never asked myself if the soldier or SS man I killed had a wife or children. I never thought about it.

Her words point to disturbing truths about survival—how the unfathomable becomes fathomable; the unthinkable becomes doable; and the forces of dark and light, creation and destruction, the maternal and killing instincts are not opposites but merely a few degrees of separation apart.

I learned this lesson 28 years ago while on my maiden voyage into the world—I was living in Israel at the time—when a fierce killer instinct summoned my hand onto a machete, leaving me ready and willing to slice-n-dice a man had he continued to close in and not opted to flee. A seed inside of me popped open a chink in my armor, and a whiff of something ancient passed through me. I knew in a heartbeat—I could kill in self-defense. This potential is in our blood, and perhaps our souls, and it could save women's lives.

And that is what I beseech.

I don't mean to suggest that fighting back is the solution to violence against women, or that it's always effective. But when you boil it down, the answer to why men violate women, or each other, may be simpler than we think: they do it because they *can*.

I too long for a more equitable world, and I abhor and oppose war and the horrors it wreaks. But until women reclaim the warrior spirit and know that we too can be dangerous creatures, and not just the endangered ones, we will never be safe or whole. As long as men are the sole agents of violence and women are the casualties of their actions, the spoils of war, the victims on the pointy end of male aggression, there will never be a balance of power between the sexes. Women will remain relegated to a subordinate status, too powerless or too fearful to resist the dominance and brutalities of others, limited by social contract and restraint in the ways in which we can express our own ferocities, yearnings, and fighting spirit.

Perhaps a more immediate reason to internalize warring women's "play for keeps" attitude is this: whether a woman is fighting for her homeland or fending off a thug or rapist, it amounts to combat, requiring the same martial mind-set and unfettered willingness to attack back, to fight for one's life. This calls for a brutish mind-set, enabling you to bring your weapons to bear, to survive the brutalities, and to take the hits. This is why, when learning to fight back, the sound that must erupt from a woman's body is not a shrilling plea for help, but a bellicose war cry. Because it is.

In my world, it's understood: the sanctity of love, the sovereignty of body and soul sometimes require acts of aggression, and the tools of violence are encoded in flesh.

The face of the warrior belongs to us all.

6

Why Warriors Are Needed

For every predator who has been righteously deprived of his freedom for the crimes he has committed, there are now all his potential victims who have the freedom to live their lives without becoming his prey. The average citizen does not think about this much and rarely appreciates or understands this gift that law enforcement gives him.

—Alexis Artwohl, PhD
from "Enjoy Your Freedom? Thank a Cop"

ENJOY YOUR FREEDOM?
THANK A COP

by Alexis Artwohl, PhD

Alexis Artwohl, PhD, is a law enforcement trainer and consultant. She writes for a variety of law enforcement publications and is coauthor with Loren W. Christensen of the best-selling book Deadly Force Encounters: What Cops Need to Know to Mentally and Physically Prepare for and Survive a Gunfight. *Dr. Artwohl can be reached via her Web site at www.alexisartwohl.com.*

❖

Democratic Ethical Warriors are a major part of the foundation on which democracy is built. Without them we would descend into terrifying chaos and brutalization by tyrants.
—Dr. Alexis Artwohl

One of my favorite bumper stickers is this: *Enjoy your freedom? Thank a vet.* Truer words were never spoken. Warriors in the military purchased our freedom in the Revolutionary War and paid interest on it in the War of 1812. They freed the slaves and held our nation together in the Civil War. They have gone to defend the United States and other countries from brutal totalitarian aggressors in two world wars, the Cold War, the Korean War, the Vietnam War, the Gulf War, and now the War on Terror. Without warriors willing to put their lives on the line, our nation would never have existed, much less survived.

WHAT MAKES A WARRIOR GREAT?

There are many qualities that make a great warrior: personality, talent, courage, training, dedication, and others. When we think of the great military heroes in history, certain names always rise to the top, such as Alexander the Great, Julius Caesar, Napoleon, and Hannibal. However, for the purposes of this discussion, I would like to consider one of the great military heroes for our modern age: George Washington. Washington was not a great military genius like the others. However, he made a choice that would have astounded these other military geniuses, and thus he gave birth to the hope of freedom for a nation and a world. He was offered supreme power, and he *turned it down*. After the war, there were those who still did not believe that this new idea of a representative democracy could really work, and they urged Washington to be, for all intents and purposes, the new king of America. He declined their invitation. He did, however, agree to become the first president of a government *for the people, by the people, with liberty and justice FOR ALL.*

THE DEMOCRATIC ETHICAL WARRIOR IN THE MILITARY

Our founding fathers, supported by the military warrior who led the birth of our democratic nation, wisely realized that, human nature being what it is, it is far too dangerous for ultimate power to reside in the hands of any one person or group of people. Yes, George was a great guy and he would have been a kind, benevolent, and ethical king, but what about the next king who assumed power? What if he was a power-mad asshole?

How many power-mad assholes have slaughtered millions and caused untold human suffering to puff up their own egos and get all the goodies and glory for themselves and their minions? Some of these were military geniuses whose battles are still studied in modern war colleges. Sure, they may have been successful warriors, but their ethics did not meet the modern standards we must adhere to if we are to achieve stability, peace, and freedom on our war-weary planet. Washington, in his infinite wisdom, rejected the idea of giving all the power to him and instead endorsed, along with our other founding fathers, the tripartite system of government, wherein the executive, judicial, and legislative branches must share the power and be accountable to each other and the people who elected them. That way no one can grab too much power, because, sooner or later, assholes will inevitably come along and abuse it unless the system automatically keeps them in check. Washington's greatness was most eminently embodied in his willingness to *give up personal power* to ensure the future freedom of the people he had fought for. He was not just the father of our country, he is the *role model* for all Democratic Ethical Warriors, the new spiritual and ethical standard to which all warriors must aspire if we are to avoid the abuses of the past.

I ENJOY MY FREEDOM,
AND I THANK ALL YOU VETS

This sharing of power by all citizens, including all warriors, in a democratic country can be messy, inefficient, and noisy at times. However, Winston Churchill summed it up best when he said, "Democracy is the worst form of government in the world; except for all the other forms." Our nation is far from perfect, but our successes as a democratic society have turned us, in an amazingly short time, into a nation that provides individual freedom and a standard of living that few other countries enjoy.

As a military brat, I grew up living in foreign lands. These were great experiences, and I enjoyed the countries I lived in, but especially as a woman, this experience of seeing the world outside the United States has made me forever grateful for the freedoms I enjoy here that were purchased so dearly by our warriors. In many areas of the world, women and children are second-class citizens—sometimes virtual slaves. However, the fundamental principles of democracy have allowed the United States to move beyond this profound injustice. Yes, there are still strides to be made, but as a woman, I thank all the warriors who fought to preserve democracy so it could mature and make me a full-fledged citizen.

Today's Democratic Ethical Warriors not only support and protect women as fellow citizens, they also welcome them into the Ranks of Warriorhood at home and abroad so they can make their own contribution to keep our precious freedoms intact. America's Democratic Ethical Warriors are members of the most powerful military machine the world has ever seen, yet they do not control our government, instigate coups, grab power, or oppress the citizens they could easily overcome. We are truly fortunate to have them protecting us from foreign threats and from themselves.

WARRIOR COPS

While the military defends democratic freedoms primarily from foreign threats, law enforcement defends the citizens from internal threats. There is only one reason we have law enforcement officers who are armed and authorized to use deadly force if necessary: human predators, which include murderers, rapists, child abusers, gangbangers, domestic violence devotees, terrorists, professional criminals, cop killers, and a host of other violent, sociopathic, and deranged individuals who are only too willing to take everything from us, including our lives, just because they can. If it were not for these predators, we would not need armed police officers authorized to use force, even deadly force. If there were no predators, we would still need traffic enforcers, animal control officers, firefighters, emergency medical personnel, and the whole range of other emergency services personnel to respond to plane crashes, natural disasters, and the whole range of other FUBAR things that can go wrong in this world.

But the one reason we have armed cops on duty 24/7 is because we do have predators, and we count on cops to protect us when the predators pick us out of the herd as their next victim. When these predators make their next vicious move, who needs to confront them? Officer Friendly? Officer Social Worker? Officer DARE? No. Although these valuable and useful roles appropriately occupy the vast majority of police officer behavior, when the violent predator is ready to spring, only Officer Warrior will save the victims, and the victims are sometimes the officers themselves.

When I first started training police officers and talked about the officer as warrior, I was shocked when some police personnel would tell me, "We don't like to use the word 'warrior.' We think it's inappropriate and will encourage officers to use too much force." That still happens, and I still totally disagree with them. This denial of the warrior role is dangerous, destructive, and only contributes to use-of-force problems. But do not get me started on that, as that is a whole other article.

COPS AS DEFENDERS OF OUR FREEDOMS

Police officers have the scary power to deprive us of our freedom and even our lives if the situation calls for it. So how is it that they defend it?

Freedom from Predators

For every predator who has been righteously deprived of his freedom for the crimes he has committed, there are now all his potential victims who have the freedom to live their lives without becoming his prey. The average citizen does not think about this much and rarely appreciates or understands this gift that law enforcement gives them. He too is in denial of the vital role Officer Warrior plays in helping to ensure a peaceful life free of violence and perpetual fear. The idea of vicious predators and warrior officers engaging in a life-and-death battle in your neighborhood is too scary for most people to acknowledge or think about.

Some "experts" on crime claim that police activities do not reduce crime and point to other socioeconomic factors as the primary causes of violent crime. I think that is total baloney. Yes, it is true that crime is a complex problem with many socioeconomic causes that need to be addressed. However, even if all those socioeconomic problems were to get fixed, the human population would forever have a certain percentage who are just assholes, and only Democratic Ethical Warriors can stop them. If you do not believe this, try this mind experiment: Imagine that an evil genie appears on the six o'clock news tonight and announces that at midnight all law enforcement personnel will suddenly disappear, never to return. Then at midnight, this actually happens. By half past midnight the predators would be gleefully roaming the streets, and all decent citizens would be cowering in their homes hoping not to be their next victims. Within a short time, America would look like those sad, lawless countries where roaming bands of thugs ride around in their "technicals," dominating the landscape and abusing the citizens at will.

Once in a group debriefing done after an officer was killed in the line of duty by a predator, officers were justifiably complaining how hard it was for them at times to go out and risk their lives for the civilians who have no appreciation or understanding for what they do. One of the SWAT officers in the group was a professional and dedicated warrior who had answered for himself that critical, spiritual question every warrior must ask: what does it mean to *me* to be a warrior? His comment was this: "I know that our fellow citizens—even my family, friends, and neighbors—have no clue how dangerous the streets can be and all that we go through to keep them safe. But you know what? Their cluelessness actually makes me feel *good* because that means *I'm doing my job*. They don't have to think about predators because I take care of that for them. I do it because I can and it needs to be done. I don't expect their understanding or appreciation. I only need that from myself and my fellow warriors." This dedication to service, because it needs to be done, not for glory, personal power, or riches, characterizes the Democratic Ethical Warrior. Yes, recognition and appreciation are sure nice, but that is not what it is all about. It is about something bigger than you.

My stepson, Scott Butzer, is a new young warrior firefighter who recently went to New York and attended the 9-11 memorial service. He described being overwhelmed by the awesome spiritual sense of being part of something bigger than himself, the sacred call to service and potential sacrifice in his role as protector of his community. He already gets it. It is something that only other warriors can understand, as he found out when he tried to explain it to his friends who have not been called to service. His lifelong friends did not get it, but my stepson felt an instant connection with all other public service warriors at that moment when the warrior spirit showed him what his call to service really meant.

Freedom from Oppression

Sometimes officers will arrest a suspect who is an immigrant (legal or otherwise) and are surprised when the suspect freaks out from mortal terror of the officers themselves. Why are these suspects so terrified of the police? Because in many countries the police are the scary people who come to take you away in the middle of the night for no probable cause, never to be seen again. That is it. You are gone. No attorney, no phone call, no civil rights or legal protections, no trial, no appeal, just gone and presumed dead. The police officers who do this are not held accountable for their behavior. In fact, it is their job. They have free rein to oppress, brutalize, and kill citizens until the next dictator comes along and either kills them or hires them to join his own new police force, which will begin eliminating the next round of citizens who are not deemed politically correct by the current regime.

However, in our democracy police officers are sworn to *serve and protect their community.* Not the latest dictator. Not even the latest elected politician. Their community. Democratic Ethical Warriors are held accountable by the community, by each other, and by their own personal warrior code of ethics. Our democratic system will not let any one person or group of people grab too much power, including the police.

Have there been abuses at times? Sadly, yes. But police misbehavior in our country is considered to be an unacceptable aberration by those within the profession as well as by the citizens who expect law enforcement to protect them against the predators. The vast majority of today's officers are Democratic Ethical Warriors who see themselves as true protectors and defenders of the clueless citizens under their care. They follow in the tradition of our first great warrior, George Washington. They may be powerful individuals with great warrior skills, but they know that power belongs to the community, not to them. They are only borrowing it to serve and protect the community, then pass it on to the next generation of warriors when it is their time to retire. They have nothing but scorn and contempt for aberrant cops who brutalize citizens and act like bullies, and they are increasingly willing to report these abuses and hold other cops accountable. We are truly blessed that we can conduct our lives without the constant fear of cops showing up in the middle of the night to help us do a magic disappearing act.

COPS AND THE MEDIA

Research confirms that Americans are lucky to have a competent and professional police force that does not routinely oppress the citizens its officers are sworn to serve and protect. However, from listening to the liberal media and the ranting of the professional cop bashers, you would not think this is true. From watching cop movies and TV shows, you would think cops are trigger-happy barbarians who shoot every other suspect they encounter. Ask the average citizen this: what percentage of all police calls for service result in the use of any kind of force?" You will often get answers like "Twenty percent," "Fifty percent," or "Most of the time." However, research done by the International Association of Chiefs of Police shows that *less than one percent* of all police calls for service across the United States results in any use of force, much less deadly force. Of course, Democratic Ethical Warriors quietly going about their job of serving their community and resolving the vast majority of threats without any use of force is boring. It does not sell tickets or attract viewers.

What might happen after the tiny percentage of times police are forced to use force, especially deadly force, by uncooperative suspects who are literally calling the shots? The professional cop bashers sometimes come out of the woodwork, howling that police are brutal, racist thugs who routinely shoot and beat innocent people for no reason. That is always sure to get them a sound bite on TV that might further their political careers.

Investigative journalist Heather Mac Donald wondered if this was true and wrote a book on her findings titled *Are Cops Racist? How the War Against the Police Harms Black Americans.* Her conclusion: law enforcement as a profession is *not* racist and is *not* brutal; racial profiling is a myth, and the minority suspects who get arrested and/or shot are engaging in criminal behavior; and the police are just doing their job.

She takes this one step further and points out that cop bashing has gotten so bad that some cops and agencies are now reluctant to hold minority predators fully accountable for their behavior. Due to concerns that police attempts to proactively pursue and arrest minority predators will be seen as "politically incorrect," arrest rates have gone down and violent crime has gone up, especially in the minority communities, since minority predators prey primarily upon minority victims.

The cop bashers, instead of helping the minority communities avoid the alleged constant abuses of so-called brutal cops, are instead harming these communities by obstructing the work of Democratic Ethical Warriors and encouraging the predators to be even bolder in their criminal activities. Kudos to Mac Donald and other responsible members of the media who are open-minded and courageous enough to find out what is really true and report it.

This is not to gloss over the real problem of the small percentage of bad cops, including racist cops, who do abuse their power. All professions have their bad apples. Police misconduct must always be taken seriously, and the cops who violate the "serve and protect" code of the Democratic Ethical Warrior must be held strictly accountable.

DEMOCRATIC ETHICAL WARRIORS ABROAD

As I write this article, my husband, retired Assistant Chief Dave Butzer, is on a nine-week mission in Kosovo to teach community policing to the local police. He had no idea what to expect when he got over there. What has astounded him the most is the very positive reception he has gotten from the local citizens. Clearly identified as an American, he is touched to have many of them wave, smile, and say, "Hello, American!" and even thank him for being there. They don't speak English, but they have learned enough to say that. They actually like him as an American and as an American cop. He said that after 27 years working in a liberal city where he and his fellow officers were frequently portrayed in a negative light by the media and rarely shown any appreciation from the clueless citizens they protected, it is wonderful to experience this recognition and appreciation of his role as a Democratic Ethical Warrior. After years of brutal repression, secret police, and warfare, the citizens of Kosovo are happy to have Americans there as protectors and role models. Unlike too many of us here in America, they do not take freedom and democracy for granted.

Before he went, we were discussing his training mission to Kosovo with community policing expert Nancy McPherson. She had done community policing consulting overseas years before. She said that although she and her team went over with a curriculum to teach the nuts and bolts of community policing, they never got to it. Instead, they spent all their time simply talking about human rights. This concept, so fundamental to our country and our Constitution, was sufficiently foreign to them that the nuts and bolts of applying it were way beyond where they were. They were still struggling to make a philosophical leap that we made 200 years ago.

Sgt. Rocky Warren, a police warrior colleague, recently sent me an E-mail rejoicing in the safe return of his son from military duty in Iraq. He said, "Sean is doing well and is very proud of what they accomplished in Iraq. Despite the biased garbage you hear in the media (which frustrates his Marines to no end), the citizens in Iraq love them. The Iraqis often give a thumbs-up sign and shout, 'Bush good! Saddam donkey' whenever they see the Marines. Women and children especially walk along with the Marines on patrol wherever they go."

I believe we are at an interesting point in global history where the world is facing a choice: continue with the usual cycle of despots, dictators, and the "I'm much better than you are" ethnic hatred, or embrace the principles of freedom, democracy, and respect for diversity that characterize our imperfect but dynamically successful society. As usual, Democratic Ethical Warriors in the military and law enforcement are already leading the charge to protect the citizens of the world and let them have the choice of which way they want to go. Some pundits scornfully call this "American imperialism." I call it giving people who have known only brutal repression and no civil rights a choice. The despots and terrorists will continue to prey on them until Democratic Ethical Warriors from all democratic nations step in between the citizens and the predators and say, "Enough."

The exporting of the democracy, freedoms, and civil rights that Americans and other democratic nations enjoy to the oppressed citizens in less fortunate countries is a process that will not be completed in our lifetimes. All the despots, dictators, oppressive monarchies, terrorists, and other power mongers will not easily give up their personal power. They are no George Washingtons. But thanks to Democratic Ethical Warriors, there is hope that one day people in all nations can drive around with bumper stickers that read, *Enjoy your freedom? Thank a vet. Thank a cop.*

WARRIORS IN THE SILENT SHADOWS
NINJA BODYGUARDS FOR ASIAN ROYALTY

by Stephen K. Hayes

The 1998 Black Belt Yearbook *refers to* **Stephen K. Hayes** *as a "legend in the martial arts."*

Mr. Hayes began his martial arts career as a teenager in Ohio in the 1960s. In 1985, he was elected to the prestigious Black Belt Hall of Fame *for introducing the legendary Japanese ninja martial arts to the Western world. In 1993, Grandmaster Masaaki Hatsumi of Chiba, Japan, awarded him the extremely rare honor of 10th degree black belt. In 1997, Mr. Hayes founded the martial art of To-Shin Do.*

In 1991, Mr. Hayes went through formal ordination to become a teacher in the 1,200-year-old Japanese esoteric meditation tradition.

He regularly served as personal protection escort and security advisor in the 1990s for Nobel Peace Prize winner the Dalai Lama of Tibet.

Mr. Hayes is the author of 19 books that have sold more than a million copies; many of his volumes have been published in a variety of languages around the world. He has been featured in publications ranging from Black Belt *to* Playboy *to* Inside Kung-Fu *to* Tricycle Buddhist Review, *and his biography appears in the international edition of* Who's Who.

A 1971 graduate of Miami University of Oxford, Ohio, Mr. Hayes majored in theater and, during his years in Japan, acted in a variety of Japanese television and film projects. Most notable to American audiences was his role in the NBC samurai epic Shogun.

Mr. Hayes spends much of the year traveling the world as a teacher, seminar leader, and lecturer. He is chairman of the board of SKH Quest Centers, dedicated to promoting the benefits of self-development training through martial arts and meditation in a network of licensed affiliate schools around the world.

His Web site is www.skhquest.com.

What is violence and what is nonviolence? We can't make a clear demarcation between violence and nonviolence on a superficial basis, since it is related with motivation. Out of sincere motivation, certain verbal actions, as well as physical actions, may look more wrathful, more violent, harsher, but in essence, because these activities come out of a sincere motivation of compassion or sense of caring, they are essentially nonviolent. On the other hand, with negative motivation, trying to cheat, trying to exploit, trying to deceive, and using nice words—with a big artificial smile and with a gift—might look like a friendly gesture, but because of the motivation, it is the worst kind of violence. So I feel that in certain cases violence can be said to be a manifestation or expression of compassion.

—His Holiness the Dalai Lama of Tibet

It was not my original intention to end up as a bodyguard for the Dalai Lama of Tibet, divine king to more than 6 million Tibetan people, spiritual inspiration to millions around the world, and Nobel Peace Prize winner. Life just somehow took me to that role as one of the steps on my own personal path of the warrior. What I had always dreamed of being was a ninja.

When I first began my apprenticeship in Japan in the home of Togakure-ryu ninjutsu grandmaster Masaaki Hatsumi, I felt I was fulfilling a childhood destiny. At that time, I had been training in a form of karate for 10 years. I even ran my own martial arts school. However, I was beginning to feel more and more closed in by the limits of the system I was practicing. I had never thought of myself as a sportsman, and yet my involvement in the martial arts world kept pushing me closer to a career as a competitor or coach. I did not want that at all. In a final, desperate lunge for the depths of the martial truth I had been seeking since my youth, I left America and moved to rural Japan, where I hoped to be accepted as a student of the ancient legacy of Japan's ninja night warriors.

In the days of ancient feudal Japan, the ninja families of the Iga and Koga regions were legendary for their skills at the craft of "invisible warfare." Relying on extensive underground networks of contacts and specially developed physical skills of climbing, gaining undetected access to secured places, and individual combat techniques, the ninja families played a major role in the shaping of feudal Japanese history and culture.

Of particular importance in the history of feudal Japan was the connection that existed between the ninja, the esoteric Vajrayana Buddhist temples, and various groups of the spiritual ascetics known as *yamabushi* (mountain seekers of power). The ninja often relied on esoteric Buddhist models of the workings of universal natural laws as means of successfully overcoming even the fiercest of adversaries. Even today, the modern practitioners of the traditional combat methods of Iga and Koga refer to many of their training kata "model fights" by means of names derived from cryptic Buddhist references. Perhaps most famous in the history of feudal Japan was the common enemy shared by the ninja families of Iga and the Tendai sect esoteric Buddhist temples of Mt. Hiei northeast of Kyoto; both were the targets of massive invasions by the cruel and powerful shogun Oda Nobunaga. Hundreds of years later, ironically enough, due to massive Muslim invasion purges throughout India and China over the centuries, the only two places on earth remote and unreachable enough for the Vajrayana esoteric Buddhist teachings to survive the eradication at the hands of the conquerors were Japan and Tibet.

The Dalai Lama of Tibet now lives in exile as a guest of the government of India. He travels the world promoting spiritual intelligence demonstrated as compassion and speaking out on the political plight of the Tibetan people forced to live under Chinese occupation rule since 1950. As an exiled leader, he is vilified by the Communist Chinese government as a counter-revolutionary influence. Because of pressure from the Chinese government, supported by much of the American business community seeking lucrative trade opportunities in China, the

Dalai Lama is not recognized by the U.S. government as a head of state, which would qualify him for Secret Service protection during U.S. visits. For years, the Dalai Lama's government in exile had to rely on private sources of protection for their leader during his trips outside of India, and my background and connections to the Dalai Lama's family took me into the role of protector escort for him in the 1990s. Recently, the U.S. government has extended Department of State Dignitary Security Services protection to the Dalai Lama when he is on U.S. territory, and I was able to retire to a position of assisting with liaison duties coordinating the Dalai Lama's Tibetan administration and the State Department agents assigned to provide higher-level protection.

I first met His Holiness the Dalai Lama of Tibet during a Himalayan trip in 1986, a few years before the Tiananmen Square massacre in Beijing and just a few months before the demonstrations in Lhasa, Tibet, which were quelled by the Chinese military police. The Dalai Lama had wanted to speak with me about the conditions I had witnessed during my trek through Tibet and over the Himalayas. After that first encounter, I had several "chance" meetings with the Dalai Lama over the next three years.

During the 1990s, I had the privilege of serving as a personal protection agent during North American visits by the exiled Tibetan ruler. By providing protection to this worthy world figure, I had the opportunity to exercise the most authentic quality of warriorship. The Japanese word *samurai* is derived from the Japanese word *saburau*, which means "to serve." When we examine this most important definition, we can see that the noble warrior is not one who causes wars, but rather one who serves the highest of ideals when the specter of violence threatens.

The most appropriate physical security specialist for a public figure such as the Dalai Lama is one who appears to blend in to the entourage most of the time and yet can stand out when it seems necessary. The highly benevolent nature of the Dalai Lama's message of awareness and compassion makes it totally inappropriate to have him surrounded by tough or cruel-looking guards. For that reason, an agent trained in the martial art of Japan's ninja invisible warriors seems perfect. In the case of certain entertainment world celebrities, there might be some point to hiring a team of huge, beefy heavies in mirror sunglasses. One must really wonder, however, whether such overstated muscle is more an attention grabber for career-advancing publicity than an honest attempt at legitimate security.

Despite the Dalai Lama's personal demeanor of humility, spirituality, and compassionate concern for all, he is nonetheless the exiled temporal ruler of Tibet. He functions as the primary symbol of hope for the independence of the Tibetan people. This makes him an extremely embarrassing annoyance to the Chinese government that invaded and occupied Tibet in the early 1950s under the pretext of "liberating" Tibet. He is also a high-profile spokesperson for the rationality and validity of the Buddhist path of life. This makes him a possible target for religious fundamentalist extremists who oppose what they see as a threat to their cultural control from proponents of New Age views. For these reasons, plus the fact that he is an international dignitary who draws thousands of admirers to each of his appearances, strictly managed security is mandatory for his safety.

The job of a security agent is to provide the means for as smooth, convenient, and productive a day for the principal as possible. First on the list of responsibilities is the protection agent's ability to make everything as seamless as possible for the one being served. This means being aware of everything from arranging for elevator doors to open at just the right moment to knowing what is ahead on the schedule and when to make sudden changes to anticipating the protectee's personal needs before they are even requested. If I do my job well, I am preventing danger, rather than having to fight against it when it arises unexpectedly.

In many cases, it is helpful for the security agent to have a personal network of acquaintances who can be of help in getting past restrictions that would hinder ordinary people in their daily activities. In this respect, the ancient legacy of Japan's historical ninja networks provides a very appropriate model for us today. It was crucial to the ninja family's survival to lay the groundwork to facilitate the defeat of an enemy long before actual warfare broke out. This establishment of a reliable undercover intelligence-gathering network was known as *to-iri no jutsu*, or the "art of entering from a remote vantage point." In the Japanese language, *to* of *to-iri* can refer to remoteness in both timing and distance, indicating wise preparation for future danger. To-iri no jutsu tactics were the guidelines for sending ninja agents into a potential enemy's region before war broke out. Once in place, the ninja were then able to set up their network and establish the means for eventually weakening and overcoming the enemy from within.

Beyond all this preparation for the prevention of danger is the area of actual physical protection that most people would associate with the work of a person called a "bodyguard." As a personal physical security agent in the service of the Dalai Lama of Tibet, my role is to provide three fundamental types of protection.

PROTECTION FROM PHYSICAL DANGER

The first and perhaps most obvious is bodily protection. I walk alongside the Dalai Lama, always within arm's reach. Put most bluntly, my job is to keep anyone wishing to harm the Dalai Lama from gaining access to him. It is especially important for martial artists to note that the job is not to *fight and defeat an enemy*, but to prevent that person from harming the man I have made a commitment to protect. If a dangerous person manages to get close enough to the Dalai Lama, my team's responsibility is to get the Dalai Lama out of harm's way and get the assailant restrained and out of the picture as quickly and unobtrusively as possible. Often this means intercepting and unbalancing the intruder in such a way as to cause him to have to fight against losing control of his momentum and balance. I want to prevent him from being able to focus on fighting me as an identifiable adversary. I do not have the time, space, or desire to engage a possible killer in some sort of boxing or wrestling contest to see who is the "tougher guy" or who has the "best technique." My tactics are to unbalance and disarm the invader in such a way as to render him incapable of continuing an attack. Since I am protecting a world figure known for his views on compassion as a means of encouraging world peace, most often this means using techniques that are neither flashy nor dramatic. We are definitely not talking about the kinds of flamboyant things audiences cheer for in a martial arts movie. More often than not, such a scenario would mean not finishing or "winning" the fight. I am flanked by badge-carrying armed local and federal agents who are authorized to arrest and detain anyone I throw their way as an attacker attempting to do harm to the Dalai Lama. I would intercept anyone who managed to get by them, and then restrain that attacker for the agents who would make the actual arrest in a locale where I do not have arrest powers.

The second-to-last thing I want is to get into some sort of visibly violent clash in which an agent of the Tibetan Buddhist king and holy man is seen pounding and kicking a screaming person into unconsciousness on the floor. Of course, the absolute last thing we want is to have the Dalai Lama harmed, so it must be said that nothing is ever really ruled out.

PROTECTION FROM
PERSONAL EMBARRASSMENT

The second, and perhaps not so obvious, form of protection consists of preventing the Dalai Lama from having to face embarrassing situations. The source of such embarrassment could be anything from a zealous fan who breaks onto stage during a presentation to a pushy interviewer who oversteps boundaries of propriety to unknown men or women who pretend to have special relationships with the Dalai Lama as a means of slipping past the security net. Awkwardly, preventing most such situations involves strictly split-second judgment calls on my part. It is necessary to use my sensitivity to the potential for danger as my sole basis for deciding to admit a person to the room or physically make him or her leave the area. It is also often a part of my responsibility to check the Dalai Lama's rooms before his return to his residence, just in case there is anyone hidden away who could cause an embarrassing scene.

It is crucial to be able to move someone against his or her will without causing undue damage or attracting undue attention. Such action requires extremely subtle techniques, again nothing at all like what you would see in some martial arts movie about bodyguards. Our martial art contains several methods of getting an attacker off balance and thereby robbing him of his ability to deliver a damaging attack. My team is very sensitive to the fact that it would be most compromising to the Dalai Lama's message of compassion to have his bodyguard hitting or wrenching some person out of the scene. It would be even worse if it turns out that the person does indeed have the right to be where he or she claims to be.

EMERGENCY MEDICAL ASSISTANCE

Third, my job is to be prepared for any emergency medical situations that might arise and to have at hand trained medical technicians ready to jump into action. This runs the gamut from being able to make quick decisions in response to unexpected symptoms such as fainting, falling, or choking to such extremes as moving the principal in cases of drastic injury, such as auto or plane wrecks or gunfire.

Other instructors of the ninja martial arts work with our Dalai Lama protection detail as well. Though I have provided protective services out of personal dedication and admiration for the Dalai Lama, some of my students are full-time professionals in the world of dignitary protection.

Jean-Pierre Seibel, a black belt in the ninja martial arts and a now-retired professional dignitary protection agent, offered his skills and knowledge to the Tibetan exile government of the Dalai Lama for several years. "Being able to head off trouble before it starts is what being a bodyguard is all about," comments Jean-Pierre. "Ninjutsu is the tool that allowed me to do that. The ninja's emphasis on foresight, strategy, and personal preparedness are great skills for a protection agent, or any career that demands resourcefulness. Dignitary protection was just a natural extension of my ninja training, and my personal way of expressing and living my warrior art of ninjutsu. It is not only the physical training. In fact it was the *saimin-jutsu* mind channeling skills that allowed me to get started in this industry that is very difficult to get started in."

Carol Ceramicoli is a black belt, former professional dignitary protection agent, and officer survival trainer of U.S. federal agents. "The experience with His Holiness the Dalai Lama's security detail reinforced what I had learned in my years of training in the ninja martial arts system as taught by Stephen K. Hayes and Jean-Pierre Seibel. I was faced with moments of physical danger, as well as emotionally and spiritually challenging situations where I had to be polite, diplomatic, authoritative, and even threatening—all at the same time. I used every aspect of my ninja training, from energy channeling to physical protection to intelligence gathering. And, of course, the honor of working for His Holiness is a treasure in itself. He is a most inspiring person, and his teachings strengthened my warrior training."

Ninjutsu black belt holder Frank Luce is employed by the U.S. Treasury Department as a special agent and is an officer survival trainer as well. "During the Dalai Lama security detail, I gained a lesson not often taught in usual martial arts schools. I learned how essential to survival it is to be able to work with a team and not as a lone individual. An important lesson was not to underestimate the importance of our non-physical training. I used the mind and energy training much more than the physical combat techniques. Sensing danger, maintaining heightened awareness, and being able to channel energy when I found myself growing tense or tired were just a few of the techniques I employed throughout the detail. Of course, it was also a good learning experience to put my physical ninjutsu skills to work in keeping overzealous fans and potential threats from coming near the Dalai Lama. I employed simple and subtle techniques like lowering my weight and using strategic body movement to keep people at bay. Another good experience was the strong feeling of connection with our 900-year-old ninja lineage. I looked around and saw my teachers and fellow students, and I could picture the ninja of feudal days protecting the shogun in ancient Japan. The legacy continues."

Ninjutsu black belt Dianna Walker has served on several Dalai Lama protection teams. "Being on the protection detail is very humbling, very powerful, and a very challenging experience all at the same time. The years of training with Stephen K. Hayes have provided the foundation for dealing with all aspects of a protection detail, not just the physical but the mental as well. Every detail, no matter how small, matters, and each decision you make can be the difference in the outcome of your role as protector. Serving one such as His Holiness the Dalai Lama of Tibet left me with experiences that I will treasure for a lifetime."

Jeff Davis is a retired police detective sergeant with 30 years of law enforcement experience and a black belt in ninjutsu. "As a member of the protective detail for His Holiness the Dalai Lama, maintaining energy and focus for long hours under varying conditions is essential, particularly true during the Kalachakra ceremonies, which covered a two-week period. Long days and short nights were the rule. Being able to clearly anticipate a potential problem and avoid it is the key to a successful protective detail."

Black belt Steve Pavlovic has headed up several protection details for the ninja bodyguard team. "The training I received over the years from Mr. Hayes has been invaluable. Not just the physical skills but the mental aspects as well—ability to sense danger, ability to identify people and things that are out of place, to make split-second decisions that are necessary when dealing with an ever-changing environment, to be able to use my presence alone to help provide a controlling and calming effect during tense situations."

Black belt agent Todd Norcross observes, "There is the

question, would you give your life to protect another person from harm? To be a true protector the answer must be yes. If we would shield our baby or loved one from harm, then why not the person who advances the lives of many, such as the Dalai Lama? The minute we hesitate it is too late."

Warrior Leaders

The warrior leader can multiply his own positive impact by continually seeking out and teaming up with other warrior leaders. The warrior leader never works alone when it is possible to join forces with others of skill and commitment.
—Chief Michal Dorn,
from "Warrior Career Survival Skills"

WARRIOR CAREER SURVIVAL SKILLS

by Chief Michal Dorn

Michal Dorn is one of the nation's best-known, respected, and highly credentialed school safety experts. He currently serves as a lead program administrator in a state homeland security antiterrorism unit. He served as the lead technical expert for the nation's largest state government school safety center for four years and as the chief of police for the Bibb County Public School System for 10 years of his 20-year law enforcement career. He also serves as the executive director of Safe Havens International, Inc., a nonprofit safety center.

Mr. Dorn is a prolific writer, having authored and coauthored 19 books. His book School Law Enforcement Partnerships: A Guide to Police Work in Schools *was the first ever published on the topic, and his* Weakfish: Bullying through the Eyes of a Child *is considered by many to be the most powerful and provocative book on the timely topic of bullying. He also writes books for Jane's Information Group, a leader in public safety, military, and school safety publications. Mr. Dorn writes columns for six nationally published magazines, coauthors Web courses, and has appeared in 11 training videos and DVDs, which are in use by more than 50,000 school systems and law enforcement agencies in 20 countries. The Federal Bureau of Investigation (FBI); Secret Service; Bureau of Alcohol, Tobacco, Firearms and Explosives (BATF); Transportation Security Administration (TSA); Federal Emergency Management Agency (FEMA); Israel Police; and British intelligence and security services have used his first video,* Weapons in Schools. *He is also a highly sought-after speaker and trainer and regularly keynotes state, national, and international professional conferences.*

Mr. Dorn has bachelor's and master's degrees from Mercer University, is a graduate of the FBI National Academy 181st session, and has completed more than 19 months of law enforcement and emergency management training. He received 14 days of intensive antiterrorism and counterterrorism training in Israel by the Israel Police, Israel Prison System, Israeli Defense Forces, and the Mossad.

Techniques Mr. Dorn developed are now standard in most American schools and have been used successfully to thwart several dozen planned school shootings and bombings. Visit his Web site at www.safehavensinternational.org.

❖

The premise of this essay is that too often those who are ahead of the curve by way of the warrior mind-set are not understood by those who are not as astute. Some exceptional military, law enforcement, public safety, risk management safety, and security officials, as well as dedicated citizens, have found their career opportunities stifled because they recognized trends and risks ahead of their time. In other instances, warriors have found themselves fighting a corporate or government culture that is resistant to progressive and forward thinking. This essay provides advice for those who want to remain successful in their careers while effecting positive change in their organizations and communities.

THE OSTRICH EFFECT

Illicit drug activity, youth gangs, school violence, and terrorism have all been allowed to become much greater problems for our society than could otherwise have been the case. Urban, suburban, and even some of the most rural communities in America have awakened too late to chronic problems. Rampant drug problems have developed in many locales because community leaders felt that somehow their piece of the American dream would be exempt from the scourges of heroin, crack cocaine, crystal methamphetamine, and other deadly poisons.

Some experts contend that youth gangs have left their mark in our country since before its inception. Gangs called "highwaymen" plagued colonists before the 1700s, and in the ensuing years a host of other groups emerged, finally exploding dramatically in the late 20th century. Over the past few decades, school violence has skyrocketed in town after town, following a pattern of denial. Many contend that we have lost control of order in our classrooms, acquiescing to outmoded beliefs like "boys will be boys." Fear of school violence has dramatically changed the face of American education. Many parents have responded to what they perceive as an unsafe and undisciplined environment by home schooling their children in unprecedented numbers. Failing to heed the warnings of terrorism experts, we as a nation accepted lax airline security and lack of support for adequate intelligence efforts for many years. This allowed terrorists to easily exploit one of many Achilles' heels when they used our own commercial airlines system to wreak devastation on our country on September 11, 2001. Unfortunately, we, like a host of other nations, have allowed many bad things to happen to countless good citizens because of the tendency to wish these types of problems away. Like the proverbial ostrich that thrusts its head in the sand rather than deal directly with the threat of the lion, mankind sometimes chooses the easy way out in the short term, only to pay the price in terrible ways later.

But there is hope. There have been and will be successes as a select few—the warrior leaders—push for change. The warrior leader who feels compelled to read a book such as this one does so not only to better prepare himself for such threats but also to venture bravely forward to wage war on the vulnerabilities that allow such human tragedies to occur. Like the salmon that refuses to give up against insurmountable odds in order to propagate its species, the warrior who aspires to lead others can avert much tragedy. He can do this by using not only his knowledge as a warrior in a tactical sense, but his skill and savvy to achieve lasting change in a strategic sense. The warrior leader must overcome certain common hurdles that can be as daunting as the lone aggressor with a gun in an alley at 2 A.M. and, in a career sense, just as deadly and final. He must learn to use his instincts, talent, and patience to overcome resistance to change in a society that sometimes rewards political correctness over technical competence and pragmatic realism.

WHY CHANGE BEFORE
"IT" ACTUALLY HAPPENS?

One of our nation's worst mass murders occurred when two highly intelligent but disturbed young men pent with rage killed their classmates and teachers at Columbine High School in Littleton, Colorado. What makes the situation an even greater tragedy is the fact that techniques developed by school district police officers and mental health workers in the Bibb County, Georgia, Public School System could have averted the tragedy. Bibb County School Police had been training tens of thousands of their colleagues across the country in the techniques.

Atrocities of this type have been occurring in public as well as private schools in the United States on rare but regular occasions for decades. Unfortunately, many communities have been slow to address the unlikely but very real possibility that an event of extreme school violence could occur in their own region. There is no such denial of the potential for other types of tragedies—be they related to natural disasters, accidents, or acts of violent people—in other settings. We must identify, address, and root out all risks that endanger our citizens in any setting, be they young or old. Life and a peaceful existence are far too precious commodities to sit back and roll the dice, hoping they will never fall the wrong way. The most important job of the warrior leader is to make those critical assessments and effect change before, not after, a horrendous wake-up call occurs.

THE "WE HAVE ALWAYS DONE IT THAT WAY"
MENTALITY AND HOW TO BREAK IT

For years, astute law enforcement officers questioned the deaths of their colleagues that occurred when criminals outgunned them. And during this time, these warriors with vision asked a simple question: "Why are we equipped with revolvers that are clearly inferior to semiautomatic pistols in a gunfight?" Out-of-touch senior officers around the country all replied the same way: "We have always carried revolvers." This failure to adapt to changing conditions cost the lives of many fine law enforcement officers, men and women who left behind not only colleagues, but spouses, parents, and children who loved them. I distinctly recall the chief executive officer of an agency lamenting that it was unfair that his officers were outgunned because their killer was armed with a semiautomatic pistol with superior firepower to their service revolvers. My first thought was that they were killed using the very revolvers that he had supplied them with, inferior weapons to equip dedicated professionals who must regularly face danger. His choice to allow his staff to venture underequipped into the most difficult situations that officers can face likely played a role in their inability to survive the confrontation. Warrior leaders never lose sight of the tasks they send those who follow them to fulfill.

SELLING YOUR CONCEPTS ON THEIR TERMS

A key strategy of the successful warrior leader is to learn to continually sell the concepts he knows to be important from the perspective of others. As one example, for years there has been a dire need for American law enforcement officers to be equipped with shoulder-fired carbines. For many years, the police handgun has been a weapon of convenience, designed not to offend a public that does not wish to see its officers wearing submachine guns or other offensive weapons. It is lightweight, more comfortable to carry for a long shift, and unobtrusive. The handgun also happens to be the least accurate weapon available in the hands of a well-trained officer and the worst possible firearm to have in most gunfights. Long ago, the law enforcement community began issuing police model shotguns to be secured in the police vehicle for extreme situations, but many in the field began questioning the wisdom of this choice, since the shotgun has distinct disadvantages, such as heavy recoil and increased danger of stray buckshot striking innocent bystanders. While there is still a need for the police shotgun for some tactical situations, the police carbine can fill a significant void in law enforcement.

But warrior leaders who try to improve the situation may find themselves facing hostility from different directions. Some may argue that they are trying to equip their officers with powerful new weapons that will pose a danger to citizens. Others, with fiscal responsibilities, may object to the expense of the new weapons, ammunition, and training. A skilled warrior leader can often overcome these objections by viewing the problem from these viewpoints and realizing that they are actually in agreement with his objectives. Rather than trying to focus on the points that seem most powerful to him, he may have better results by emphasizing the needs of the people or groups he wishes to convince. For example, when faced with the position relating to expense in the above example, pointing out the benefits of greatly reduced civil liability might be effective.

DEFINE ACCEPTABLE LOSSES

Will Evans, Director of Safety Education for Markell Insurance Company, is one of the nation's top safety experts. He often helps clients and trainees sharpen their focus by urging them to define their acceptable losses when balancing prevention efforts with the effort and expense required. In a business, acceptable losses might include loss of property, loss of income, and costs of repairs for property crimes. In a school, the concept becomes a compelling way to view safety as we are forced to consider whether the lives of children and educators are within our parameters of acceptable losses. The concept of acceptable losses can be a means to help the warrior leader prioritize what he is responsible for protecting when faced with limited resources. In the world of antiterrorism, defining acceptable losses can help with the daunting task of deciding where to focus our efforts when there are so many potential targets in a target-rich environment like the United States. The warrior leader can also use the concept of acceptable losses as a convincing means to redirect those whose priorities are not in line with the potential for danger.

BE SHARP, STAY SHARP TO WIN

The warrior leader must concentrate his efforts on remaining sharp in his fields of expertise. To lead others to the fullest potential, extreme technical competence is a must. A good military commander must first be an excellent soldier. Excellent leadership skills are not enough in today's highly technical professional world. Once the warrior leader becomes sharp, he must maintain this edge by continually seeking additional knowledge, remaining current on issues and occurrences in his field, and looking forward to identify emerging trends based on fact, rather than an endless stream of "what ifs."

PRESS ON

The warrior leader must develop a high level of perseverance to maintain the ability to effect lasting change. Effecting significant change requires continual effort and the inner ability to press onward when others would quit. Whether the warrior leader is a member of the fire service, law enforcement, military, or emergency management community, or a concerned citizen who wants to take his role in spurring local officials to act, he must possess the ability to press on when it seems fruitless. The quality of thoughtful tenacity can help the warrior leader push change through when the going gets tough.

MAINTAIN THE EDGE ONCE YOU GET IT

There often comes a point where a truly effective warrior leader gains a reputation as a sharp and reliable expert in his field. This edge can become dull if the warrior leader does not capitalize on his successes. Without becoming boastful, the effective warrior leader ensures that others understand his sheer competency. It is also important that he remember to credit others who have worked hard to effect positive change. To become truly effective, he must use past successes to demonstrate that he should be trusted in his continual efforts to effect positive change. The warrior leader must, in effect, become proficient at marketing his philosophies as well as his competence in order to achieve his full potential.

LEARN TO COLLABORATE EFFECTIVELY

This book includes the thoughts of some of the nation's most skilled and respected experts in the fields they represent. By now, the reader is aware that the combined efforts, expertise, and philosophies of the authoring team provide greater insight than would be possible had any one member of the team acting alone written the book. The warrior leader can multiply his positive impact by continually seeking out and teaming up with other warrior leaders. The warrior leader never works alone when it is possible to join forces with others of skill and commitment.

There have been countless times in history when the need for the warrior leader was great. There has probably never been a point in history when so few in our complex world could do so much harm to so many. This means that there has never been a time when your abilities as a warrior leader could do so much good. Law enforcement officers and public safety officials are drilled with the concept that they cannot help others if they do not take reasonable actions to ensure their own safety first. In this same spirit, the warrior leader must maintain the presence of mind to retain the stability of his position of leadership so he can continue to influence others for greater good.

Training

> *When warriors train they always imagine using those skills in combat to ensure that they win the confrontation; others simply go through the motions. At the firing range, others simply see a paper target in which they need to get a certain number of holes to qualify. Warriors, however, imagine that someone is attempting to kill them, attempting to take them away from their family. Warriors prepare to succeed in armed combat while others simply prepare to qualify.*
>
> —Brian Willis,
> from "The Warrior Pyramid"

MUSES FROM A WARRIOR TRAINER

by Sgt. Rocky Warren

Rocky Warren is a U.S. Army veteran, former SWAT operator, and law enforcement veteran of more than 28 years, having worked as a military policeman, sheriff's deputy, detective, jail supervisor, and patrol sergeant. He has received two Bronze Medals of Valor.

Mr. Warren's complete biography is included with his essay "The Heroic Set of Shoulders" in Chapter 1.

❖

IT'S FINALLY PAYDAY . . .

I watched John and Dennis standing in front of the audience. John was talking to every one of his coworkers, peers, and supervisors who could possibly be present tonight. John Poretti and Dennis Walsh had each just received a letter of commendation from Placer County Sheriff Ed Bonner.

I remembered when I first heard about this case. "Hey! Did you hear that Dennis and John got into an officer-involved shooting last night?" My initial alarm largely wore off when I found out that neither of our deputies had been injured. Dennis had been attacked from four feet away by a mentally disturbed person wielding a large fillet knife. When I talked to both of the deputies later, I found out the suspect had come very close to killing Dennis. Closer than anyone in the public could know.

The situation was difficult for all involved. The suspect hadn't survived, but he hadn't intended for our deputies to survive either. Despite the best efforts by other deputies on scene to administer CPR and first aid, the suspect hadn't made it.

My teaching partner, Dave Rose, and I were standing at our table in the middle of the large ballroom gathering. Dennis and

John were still standing up front after the presentation of their award plaques, and, in an unusual move, John stepped up and took over the microphone. Up until this time, no one receiving an award had been allowed to make a statement. John didn't ask permission; he just stepped over and spoke up.

My eyes misted over when John thanked Dave and me for the training program we'd initiated and the tactics we taught that allowed them to survive the attack. They'd stopped a deadly threat using our contact-and-cover training. They defended each other and won the right to continue to live and breathe when it very easily could have ended otherwise.

Those of us in the audience gave John and Dennis a well-deserved standing ovation for their awards and for their heroism. They had met a felon armed with the weapon of his choice, who chose the ground, the force level, and the exact instant at which he wanted to start the violence. The suspect had tried to kill a uniformed patrol deputy. Our two deputies acted properly. The stab wound into the chest of Dennis's ballistic vest trauma plate proved that the criminal had nearly achieved his aims. The blade of the fillet knife, bent at a 45-degree angle from striking Dennis's ballistic vest, showed just how lethal the intent behind the attack really was.

John and Dennis accepted the applause and walked back toward their waiting families. As I sat down in my chair, I leaned over to Dave and said, "You know, we get a check every two weeks and it's never enough, especially for the beating we take as use-of-force instructors. But tonight? What John just said? Tonight is payday, pal."

Dave heartily agreed.

Nationally, nearly 200 law enforcement officers are killed every year, an average of one every 50 hours. The cost of law enforcement in our country is very high, and it's bound to go even higher given the current problems in the world. Yet, when it comes time for the next duty shift, and despite ever-present danger, uncertainty, and lousy work conditions, just as many working police will "hit the streets" as did the last time roll call was held. It's no miracle. It's just plain, old-fashioned courage.

Deputy Dennis Walsh and Deputy John Poretti received a Commendation Plaque, Silver Medals of Valor, and, later, Silver Stars from the National Police Hall of Fame. By their actions, they also earned the right to live the rest of their lives.

THIS NEXT GENERATION

I climbed into the pickup, and Chris put it into gear and then slowly backed out of the driveway. We chatted quietly as he headed toward a rural back road. I was surprised at the fact that this slim, determined 18-year-old had beaten an issue I'd never been able to scratch—although I must admit that since September 11, 2001, there have been plenty of changes made.

A couple days previous, Chris had telephoned and asked me to train him on firearms. He had his high school senior project coming up and, having completed the government portion of it, wanted me to train him with a handgun to my law enforcement agency's qualification standard. I'd cautioned that several other people had tried to get firearms approval from the high school and been denied permission to do the project but said he was more than welcome to try for it. Chris had a secret weapon. He was already enlisted and on the delayed-entry program of the U.S. Army Rangers. We were both surprised when the school granted permission for me to train him and have it count for credit on his senior project.

Chris and I arrived at the rural, muddy clearing that served as a firearms range. The young man went to the rear, opened the tailgate, unlocked a box, and proceeded to belt on a handgun with impressive economy of motion. No excitement, no fear. It was all safety and caution, and pure business. I removed my rifle from the case, cleared it, and benched it for later use.

Anyone watching us wouldn't have known the background. I've been an instructor and trainer for almost 20 years and a military veteran and peace officer for even longer. Chris's first assignment on his project was to write a three- to five-page, single-spaced essay titled "The Ethics and Responsibility of Firearms." He had to rewrite the essay four times before I was satisfied that he understood. Proposition: "When you own and carry a firearm, in whatever capacity, you are responsible for its ethical use as well as the life and welfare of every person around you." Until Chris understood that and could explain and defend that proposition and its implications, he'd never touch a gun.

Chris started out slowly over the span of days, eventually qualifying and shooting for record. We had some time left on his project, and he wanted to go beyond it. I decided we'd do some high-speed, low-drag rifle training that would give him a jump-start on what they were going to give him in Ranger training. My military and SWAT background allowed me to train him up to my standards.

Chris was diligent, and when we moved into the tactical end of the training he really buckled down: tactical movement, communication, failure drills, and remedial action drills, the entire gamut of tactical topics. I'm happy to say Chris was a great student, which has nothing to do with my teaching or me. He was willing to listen, willing to work, and worked to apply what he learned. He did extremely well.

I did similar training for my son before he went into the Marines, though there wasn't quite as much time. He enlisted and left home fairly quickly.

Tonight, February 2, 2003, I sit at home wishing I could shed 30 or even 20 years. My son, Chris, and several of my friends' sons are in the military and in combat. This old warhorse and others of my generation are left to wait and hope for our young warriors to do well, to protect and defend our God-given but human-preserved rights, and then to come home.

FAST FORWARD TO JULY 25, 2003

Chris has come home after fighting in Operation Iraqi Freedom, and I'm invited to breakfast with the family on his first morning. I feel as if I've been adopted into the family. When I arrive, I'm met and hugged by Chris's father, mother, and the young warrior himself. Wiping away tears, we all move into the house, and Chris promptly disappears for a minute. He comes out of his bedroom and hands me a large, high-quality switchblade knife. He looks me full in the face and says, "That's the first time you saved my life." My eyes half fill with that pesky water again, as I bluster, "Really? Tell me a story, kid."

During the initial clearing of Baghdad, Chris's squad was engaged in what the army calls military operations in urban terrain, or MOUT. Chris was clearing a building where they were taking enemy prisoners. The threat and tension level on this operation was very high. He and his backup entered a room where they confronted a Republican Guard in full uniform just inside the door. The enemy soldier was armed with the knife I now held in my hand. Chris and the enemy soldier were three feet apart. Following his training, Chris neutralized the tactical position the enemy soldier took and was able to stop him. He took the bared blade from the enemy soldier's hand and continued with the room-clearing mission.

Later, during a patrol mission on a Baghdad city street, Chris's unit had been hit with a classic ambush. Rocket-propelled grenades (RPGs) hit the front and rear HUMVEEs in an attempt to lock the troops into a trap on a narrow street. Despite receiving heavy fire from rooftops and windows, Chris, separated from his unit by smoke and explosions, fired on the move and rescued one down and wounded comrade. Then, reunited with and aided by the rest of his squad, he organized the rescue of two more wounded soldiers. All of the wounded survived.

His mother and father have thanked me for training Chris many times. They do so again during today's breakfast. Their son has made it home and is able to sit with us and live his life—all because of his courage and valor. If I contributed to his safe return home, that is enough for me. The rewards Chris got—his combat infantry badge and a presidential unit citation, as well as the credit for saved lives—belong to him.

The warriors of the older generation are those who raised their children in the right ways—who taught them values, ethics, and hard work, rather than operating on a sliding scale of morality. Thank you to the parents who gave their children a conscience and the ability to engage in pragmatic, critical thinking.

Like the generation before them and those even further back, those young warriors went into harm's way—and it won't be the last time. But it's their turn. They acquitted themselves with bravery and honor and with valor and compassion.

At one point during our time together, Chris asked me, "How can I ever repay you?" I had the answer all ready for him. "Chris, someday it's going to be your turn to teach, to let someone else know what you know. Tell them the truth. You can repay me by paying it forward."

After all, they're the best of us. When it comes their turn, they'll pass it on. They're admirable and magnificent, and we owe all of our veterans so very much.

This Next Generation.

HOW SHOULD A
WARRIOR TRAIN?

by Dave Grossi

Dave Grossi is a retired police lieutenant from upstate New York. For 12 years, he was the lead instructor for the Calibre Press, Inc., Street Survival Seminars. A combat veteran of Vietnam, he is a graduate of the FBI National Academy, holds a bachelor's degree in police administration, and was the first police trainer in the world to receive the Certified Law Enforcement Trainer (CLET) designation from the American Society of Law Enforcement Trainers (ASLET). Mr. Grossi holds instructor credentials in more than a dozen force-related disciplines, including firearms, impact weapons, chemical agents, weapon-retention techniques, electronic restraint systems, handcuffing, and edged weapons.

Mr. Grossi is the recipient of more than 20 awards and commendations for outstanding service, including a Heroism Citation from the Rochester (New York) Chamber of Commerce, the Special Award of Honor from the International Narcotic Enforcement Officers Association for his work as an undercover narcotics investigator, and numerous other honors in the field of law enforcement training. He has testified extensively across the United States and Canada as an expert witness on behalf of police officers and agencies regarding use-of-force issues. He may be reached via E-mail at GrossiDave@aol.com.

❖

Warriors, by definition, are fighters. As such, they must train with the understanding that at any given time they might have to fight for their lives or the lives of their partners, or to defend the lives of innocent third parties. So how should warriors train? Where is the emphasis? On their equipment? Their firearms skills? Their physical conditioning? How about tactics? Or mental conditioning?

The answer is *all of the above*. A warrior cannot afford to ignore any points on the Survival Star.

THE SURVIVAL STAR

Those of us old enough to recall the Survival Star from the early Calibre Press, Inc., Street Survival Seminars will remember that *physical fitness, mental conditioning, tactics, firearms skills, and equipment* all held equal positions on that star. The Survival Star concept was developed years ago by Trooper Shayne Slovacek of the Oklahoma Highway Patrol. A true warrior recognizes that the old three-sided survival pyramid of just *shooting skills, tactics,* and *mental conditioning* lacked two essential areas. Being a good shot, possessing an awareness of your surroundings, and having the right mind-set are no longer enough to survive today's mean streets and even meaner courtrooms, where a lot of our battles are now taking place. It takes more. A warrior has to train with the understanding that his battle could demand extraordinary skills in any one of those areas represented by the five points of the Survival Star. Let's examine each of those five points in taking a look at how a warrior should train.

PHYSICAL TRAINING

To survive as a warrior, you have to get into and stay in top physical condition at all times. However, if most warriors were 100 percent honest with themselves, they'd probably admit that physical fitness isn't their top priority. You can probably count on one hand the number of agencies in your state that require annual physical fitness evaluations (or even medical examinations) for their in-service officers. If that's the case in your department, you, as a warrior, have to take responsibility for your own physical conditioning and training. Regular physical exams after age 40 (for both men and women warriors) and a fitness program that includes both aerobic (endurance) and anaerobic (strength) training, coupled with a sensible nutritional program, are a great place to start.

Train for what you may be required to do at any given time. Here's an example. FBI Supervisory Special Agent Gordon McNeil was the team leader on that fateful day that he, along with Special Agents Ed Mirales, Jerry Dove, and Ben Grogan encountered robbery suspects in Miami, Florida. Special Agent McNeil, very early in the gunfight, took a .223-caliber round fired from an AR-15 rifle directly in the neck. What should have been an incapacitating hit didn't stop McNeil from continuing the firefight. What prevented this high-velocity round from penetrating further to his spine was the tremendous buildup of muscle mass in his neck from years of power lifting. Peak physical conditioning resulted in peak performance that day.

MENTAL CONDITIONING

My friend and fellow police trainer Sam Barber likes to say, "The body can't go where the mind hasn't been." The mind and body are not separate entities, and today's warrior trains and conditions both for battle. They are a *team*, just like you and your on-the-job warrior partner are a team. And they function best as a team. Remember the basic concepts of mental conditioning that you learned back in your basic academy, and understand that they are as valid today as they were back then. Police equipment, such as batons, chemical agents, and firearms, may have evolved over the years. Indeed, wooden sticks have been replaced by side-handle and expandable batons. Mace has been replaced with OC. Revolvers are rarely seen nowadays, replaced by high-capacity semiautomatic pistols. But the tried-and-true concepts of *positive self-talk, crisis rehearsal,* and *autogenic breathing* work just as well now, in the 21st century, as they did back in the late 1980s when they were introduced.

Positive self-talk means you constantly reinforce in your own mind that you have the skills you need to successfully confront and overcome today's challenges. But remember, you've got to back it up. If you just engage in positive mental dialogue without backing it up by mastering the skills, tactics, and techniques you need to physically win any street confrontation, you're simply indulging yourself in an empty pep talk.

Crisis rehearsal might be defined as advanced positive self-talk. Here you substitute those verbal messages with mental imaging to plan the appropriate response to those threats you're conjuring up in your mind. So when a real crisis occurs you've got those planned and practiced responses all ready to go.

Finally, *autogenic breathing*. SWAT and ERT team members and competitive shooters have practiced this tried, true, and proven technique for years. Deep, slow, and rhythmic breaths, inhaling through your nose, holding your breath for a 3- to 4-second count, and then exhaling slowly and steadily out your mouth will have an instant calming effect on your body. It slows your heart rate, lowers your pulse and blood pressure, and may actually help you think better.

TACTICS

A warrior trains constantly from a tactical standpoint. A true warrior looks at every call, every response, and every situation as an arena or a classroom to perfect and hone his or her tactical skills. Every low-risk vehicle stop is an opportunity to perfect your observations and communication skills. Every unknown 911 call is a chance to practice "if/then" thinking. Every silent alarm dispatch is an opportunity to fine-tune your invisible deployment skills. And even those slow or "down" times during your shift allow for some crisis rehearsal. Today's warrior constantly looks for opportunities to practice his street tactics to the point of mastery. A professional warrior never stops learning and exploring new and updated tactics for building searches, high-risk vehicle stops, or one-on-one field interviews.

FIREARMS SKILLS

A warrior knows how to use his or her equipment skillfully, properly, and carefully. When called upon to respond with deadly force, a warrior makes that decision only after a careful but quick evaluation of the facts: What is this subject's intent? What are his words and especially his actions telling about his intent? What type of weapon am I facing? What kind of delivery system does my opponent possess? Also, the trained warrior analyzes options and is sure of his or her target and background. A true warrior never looks for a window of opportunity to use his or her firearm needlessly, but he will not hesitate to resort to deadly force should it become necessary. And a professional warrior is confident in his or her skill with a firearm if and when it does become necessary to use deadly force.

EQUIPMENT

A warrior must be skilled with all of his equipment, and he trains constantly with every tool in his tactical toolbox. If your agency does not (or will not) provide less-lethal force training, then you as a true warrior must seek that training on your own. Don't settle for the standard department-issued drugstore D-cell flashlight. Light control (as both illumination and distraction) is an officer-safety issue. Go out and invest in a new Stinger or Maglite flashlight, or drop the hint to your spouse or significant other that what you'd really like is a LaserMax pulsating laser sight for your Glock .40 caliber this Christmas. Or how about investing in a Hindi Baton Cap for your birthday? Sure, your vest gets hot after 8 to 10 hours during a day shift in July or August, but the true warrior knows that his or her body armor is vital equipment.

Equipment is a fundamental point of the Survival Star for today's warrior, and being skilled with that equipment is just as important as having it. Physical skills (defensive tactics), impact weapons (baton), chemical agents (OC), restraint systems (tactical handcuffing), and verbal defusing techniques (dialogue) must be as familiar to you as your sidearm or long gun. A warrior understands that he or she must also be proficient with equipment that is not force-related. Your driving or negotiating skills with your gas-powered vehicle (or other conveyance), be it a Ford Crown Vic, a Trek mountain bike, a

Harley-Davidson Electra-Glide, a Kushman scooter, or even an appaloosa, could be crucial to your survival.

SUMMARY

Well, that's it, fellow warriors. You've just received a refresher course in "Warriorship Training 101." Now it's up to you to put what you've just read to use. If you needed a jump start to head over to the gym or dojo to get back in top physical shape, let this essay be it. If you needed some words of encouragement to get off your butt and spend some off-duty time at the range to fine-tune your firearms skills, then I hope this essay provided them. And if you've been thinking about attending a course on ground fighting, tactical handcuffing, or laser sight training, or paying for an officer survival seminar on your own, then I hope I've pushed you in that direction, too.

A wise man once told me, "Old warriors never die . . . they just live on in their words." It is my sincere hope that these few words from this old warrior will live on in you.

Stay safe!

THE WARRIOR PYRAMID

by Brian Willis

Brian Willis has been a full-time police officer with the Calgary Police Service (a Canadian agency of 1,500 officers) since 1979 and is currently a sergeant in the training section. Mr. Willis is also the president of Winning Mind Training, Inc., a training and consulting company specializing in mental preparation skills for warriors, trainers, coaches, and athletes. Mr. Willis holds a Certificate in Adult Learning from the University of Calgary and is certified in hypnosis and neurolinguistic programming. He is also certified as an instructor or instructor trainer in subject control tactics, officer safety, emergency vehicle operations, rapid intervention, and crowd management.

Mr. Willis has given presentations on mental preparation and conditioning at numerous international law enforcement conferences and has had articles on the topic published in law enforcement periodicals in Canada and the United States. He serves as an advisory board member for the International Law Enforcement Educators and Trainers Association (ILEETA) and Police Marksman *magazine and is a member of ASLET, the International Association of Law Enforcement Firearms Instructors (IALEFI), the National Tactical Officers' Association (NTOA), and the National Guild of Hypnotists.*

Mr. Willis has trained officers from federal, provincial, state, and municipal law enforcement agencies from across North America as well as military personnel, corrections officers, competitive shooters, martial artists, and athletes and coaches from a variety of sports to harness the power of the mind. He continues to work as a mental preparation coach for a number of amateur and professional athletes.

❖

To be a warrior is to learn to be genuine in every moment of your life.
—Albert Einstein

The Warrior Pyramid is a concept that was developed to assist those who have chosen the path of a warrior to better understand what is required for total preparation for this honorable calling in law enforcement, military service, corrections, and other warrior professions. Pyramids bring to mind images of powerful structures that have been around for thousands of years and have withstood the test of time due to their structural integrity. That structural integrity comes from all four sides being evenly developed. A three-sided pyramid would always leave itself open to the forces of nature and become vulnerable.

The blocks used to build the pyramid must be strong to ensure the overall strength and integrity of the structure. Those blocks represent the learning that takes place during a warrior's lifetime. Some represent formal training sessions, others represent informal or self-directed training, and the rest represent lessons learned in battle. This work will examine briefly the four sides of the pyramid and then focus on the side that truly sets the warrior apart from others—mental preparation and conditioning. This is the one side that is *completely* within the individual warrior's span of control.

First, however, let us examine the mortar that binds the blocks together, as it plays a critical role in the structural integrity of the pyramid and is the start of mental preparation and conditioning—commitment. Commitment binds together all of the building blocks of skills and tactics for warriors. Bound together, these blocks have tremendous strength to weather any storm and withstand the test of time. Without commitment, the blocks stand in isolation and are more likely to break down or be lost in that moment of truth. The question then becomes this: commitment to what?

Winning—Sir Winston Churchill said, "Victory at all costs, victory in spite of all terror, victory however long and hard the road may be; for without victory there is no survival." Warriors understand that winning is always the goal and the only acceptable option in any confrontation. Now, winning takes many forms. It can range from the use of effective communication skills to gain the voluntary compliance of an enemy or subject to the use of lethal force to win a confrontation by taking the life of the enemy. It can be setting and accomplishing short- and long-term goals in training, combat, or any aspect of a warrior's life.

Training—William Jennings Bryan once said, "Destiny is not a matter of chance, it is a matter of choice; it is not a thing to be waited for, it is a thing to be achieved." Warriors understand this about destiny and make a personal commitment to continually train their mind and body. They understand that all they ever need to train is themselves and a commitment to train. Training partners, training equipment, training courses, and training facilities are all "nice to haves," not "need to haves." Warriors know how to improvise and create all these things. They also understand that they can always train in their mind. Others make excuses and abdicate the responsibility for training to their agency or organization; they are not willing to commit their personal time and money to train. Here is the unfortunate reality for those with this type of thinking: There has never been, and never will be, an agency killed or injured in combat. It is police officers, corrections officers, and soldiers who get killed and injured in the line of duty, not agencies. Although there is an onus on agencies to provide training to their personnel, those on the front lines must make a personal commitment to train, since they are the ones who go into harm's way.

Family—In *The Gates of Fire,* author Steven Pressfield wrote, "Spartans excuse without penalty the warrior who loses his helmet or breastplate in battle but punish with loss of citizenship rights the man who discards his shield. Because the warrior carries a breastplate and helmet for his own protection but his shield is for the protection of the whole line." Warriors understand the importance of family and make a commitment to them that they will always be the priority. Family includes parents, siblings, children, significant others, and close friends. Family also refers to their brother and sister warriors with whom they train and go into battle. In order to fulfill this commitment, they must also fulfill the commitments to training and winning.

THE FOUR SIDES

As mentioned previously, the structural integrity of a pyramid relies on the even development of all four sides. The four interdependent sides of the Warrior Pyramid are skills, tactics, fitness, and mental preparation and conditioning.

Skills—Warriors must develop a level of competency in the skill sets necessary for their job. This includes verbal and non-verbal communication, empty-hand skills, skills with all their weapons systems, and vehicle operation skills.

Tactics—Once warriors develop a degree of proficiency in all skill areas, they must then develop an understanding of the tactical and operational application of those skills. Tactics includes the ability to use empty-hand skills in close-quarters battle and multiple-assailant confrontations, edged-weapon proficiency, weapon-retention, disarms, and ground fighting. It also comprises downed officer rescues, rapid intervention, cover and movement, building clearing, vehicle stops, and vehicle assaults. The list of tactics necessary will depend on the types of missions the warrior will be tasked with throughout his career.

Fitness—Warriors must develop a strong foundation of aerobic and anaerobic fitness. They must then develop a level of combat fitness. Combat fitness refers to training the body and its energy systems in preparation for the high-intensity, short-duration confrontations that warriors often find themselves in. In addition to strength and endurance, warriors must develop explosive speed and power in preparation for these combative events.

Mental preparation and conditioning—It has been said that "the mind of a warrior is what sets him apart from others in the midst of battle." What is it about the mind of a warrior that allows him to perform at higher levels in the middle of combat? In the military, as well as in law enforcement, everyone goes through the same basic training. Yet in the field people perform at different levels. Some excel under pressure and consistently perform at the highest levels, while others are frozen with fear or overcome with anxiety. Even among the top performers there are a select few who rise to the top and lead the others. This is not a new problem; it has been around as long as men have engaged in battle. In 500 BC, Heraclitus identified this issue when he wrote to his commander, "Of every 100 men, 10 should not even be here, 80 are nothing more than targets. Nine of them are the real fighters. We are lucky to have them, they the battle make. Ah, but the one. One of them is a warrior and he will bring the others back."

WHAT SETS THE WARRIOR APART?

What is it then that determines how people will perform in the heat of battle? Of all those who serve in the warrior profession, what is it that separates the nine who are the real fighters from those who are nothing more than targets? And what is it about "the one"—the warrior? If it is the mind of a true warrior that sets him apart from others in the midst of battle and in all aspects of life, then what is different about the way he trains and prepares his mind?

Some would suggest that since everyone in basic training receives the same mental preparation and conditioning, these components are not the deciding factors. The difference, they would argue, lies in the area of control. The training cadre has control over physical skills training. They determine what drills will be conducted, how many repetitions of any given skill will be performed, what information will be presented during the academic sessions, and what exercises the students will participate in. What they do not control is what goes on inside the mind of the individual soldier or officer. The most powerful weapon this warrior possesses is his mind. Yet it cannot be inspected by the trainers. It does not come with an owner's manual or a manufacturer's guarantee. Inside the privacy of the mind lies the key to unlocking the warrior spirit and the blueprint of a true warrior. Let us examine the aspects of mental preparation and conditioning that separate warriors from others in the midst of battle.

The Winning Mind

This is the law. The only purpose of fighting is to win. There is no possible victory in defense. The sword is more important than the shield, and skill is more important than either. The next weapon is the brain. All else is supplemental.

—John Steinbeck,
*The Acts of King Arthur
and His Noble Knights*

Warriors possess the winning mind and know that the only purpose for fighting is to win. They are confident in their skills and abilities, they are committed to their mission, and they are physically and mentally prepared to do whatever is reasonable and necessary to accomplish that goal. They have worked past the childhood philosophy that it is not whether you win or lose that is important, but rather how you play the game. Warriors understand that neither training nor combat are games, and winning is important. Their training allows them to understand that every situation is winnable. This is not to suggest that they have the "superman syndrome" and think they are impervious to harm, but rather that they understand that in combat there will always be unexpected elements. Warriors train hard for the unexpected, so when it happens it is neither hard nor unexpected. Warriors think offense, not defense. In combat they become the predator and use cunning, skill, ferocity, speed, strength, power, cover, movement, and team tactics to be successful. They commit to winning, not survival. They understand that survival for many people is defensive in nature and that if they win, they will also survive.

Imagination

Imagination is more important than knowledge. Knowledge is limited. Imagination encircles the world.

—Albert Einstein

Imagination is a powerful component of the subconscious mind that works continuously to shape our beliefs and expectations, yet for most people it lingers untapped below the level of consciousness. A warrior's imagination is focused on success. We discussed previously the importance of training. Warriors train the way they want to fight. They train with imagination and emotion, knowing that only then will they fight the way they train.

What does it mean to train with imagination and emotion, and why is it so important? When warriors train they always imagine using those skills in combat to ensure that they win the confrontation; others simply go through the motions. At the firing range, others simply see a paper target in which they need to get a certain number of holes to qualify. Warriors, however, imagine that someone is attempting to kill them, attempting to take them away from their family. Warriors prepare to succeed in armed combat while others simply prepare to qualify.

In the combatives room, warriors imagine their training partner is an actual attacker who is attempting to hurt or kill them and take them away from their family. Others simply go through the motions, seeing only their buddy, and they go easy on each other so neither of them looks bad or gets injured. Even in training, warriors always keep fighting until they have won. If they do something that is less desirable, they fix it and make it more desirable. If they get slashed, stabbed, or shot in training, they fight through it, becoming even more aggressive in defeating the threat, knowing that they may get injured in combat and still have to win. Others simply go through the motions. They stop when they do something less desirable and harangue themselves for screwing up. When they get shot or stabbed, they stop and say, "I'm dead. I would have been killed by that." Warriors, on the other hand, understand that if you are dead, you don't know it. If you are alive, you keep fighting. Warriors always imagine themselves winning confrontations using all their skills, tactics, and knowledge. Outside of the training arena warriors harness the power of imagery, which allows them to focus and direct the imagination.

In Takashi Matsouka's book *The Cloud of Sparrows,* he talks of a warrior who is denied access to his firearms to physically practice for an inevitable confrontation, so the man must train in his mind:

> The only place he could be sure of privacy was his own mind. So that's where he practiced. Draw. Cock the hammer on the upswing. Sight the heart. Squeeze the trigger. Cock the hammer on the recoil. Sight the heart. Squeeze the trigger. There was an advantage to this. His mind was a portable room; he could practice anywhere he was, anytime.

Humility

> *A warrior is on permanent guard against the roughness of human behavior. A warrior is magical and ruthless, a maverick with the most refined taste and manners, whose worldly task is to sharpen, yet disguise, his cutting edge so that no one would be able to suspect his ruthlessness.*
> —Carlos Castaneda, *The Power of Silence*

There is much confusion about the true warrior spirit within the warrior professions. There are many who think that being a warrior is about machismo, about bravado. They think being a warrior is about racing to all the hot calls, or starting fights to show others how tough they are. They think it is about taking unnecessary risks for the glory or the accolades. True warriors, however, understand that one of the many virtues of a warrior is humility. Warriors do not need to start fights to show others how tough they are. They are confident in their skills and tactics. They understand that there is a time to fight and a time to walk away. When they fight, they fight to win. They fight with tenacity and ferocity. When they walk away, they walk away with their heads held high. They walk away with pride and honor because it is a choice. Because of that humility, warriors also have an aura of professionalism that they bring to every conflict.

❖

Regardless of whether you believe warriors are born or made, the Warrior Pyramid provides a framework for the development and preparation of all warriors. As you continue on your journey through life working toward being "the one," the warrior who will bring the others home, let this serve as a guide for you. Continue to ask yourself, "What condition is my pyramid in?"

THE HEART BEHIND THE TECHNIQUE

by Jerry VanCook

Writer and training expert **Jerry VanCook** *is best known in law enforcement circles for his extended deployments as an undercover officer. The lessons learned from these assignments became the basis for his book* Going Undercover, *published by Lauric Press, which has been regarded as the definitive work on this subject. Mr. VanCook has also been featured on the Law Enforcement Training Network (LETN) and The Learning Channel's* "World's Most Dangerous Undercover Stings" *for his expertise in this area.*

Mr. VanCook is a longtime martial artist and has studied aikido, Thai boxing, kung-fu, and kali. He holds instructor ranks in Okinawan karate and a 7th-degree black belt (shichidon) *in Bei-Koku aibujutsu. He is a Bowie knife instructor and an NRA-certified firearms instructor. He is also the author of* Real World Self-Defense, *published by Paladin Press.*

Mr. VanCook's broad background also includes recent graduation from the Peruvian Air Force Jungle Operations and Survival School. He is a contributing editor to Tactical Knives Magazine, *has published more than 40 novels, and has the distinction of being involved in a firefight with a career criminal that was carried live on Oklahoma television.*

❖

Traditional martial arts instructors, as well as those who teach practical self-defense and close-quarters combat, spend hours, days, weeks, and sometimes years instilling technique in their students. Those same students spend hours, days, weeks, and years practicing those techniques. They become quite proficient.

So why, when they are finally attacked and face the "real thing" on the streets, do so many of these well-trained students fall short of the mark? Why do so many men and women, who perform quite admirably in the dojo or gym, seem to suddenly forget everything they've learned when an actual attack finally occurs?

What happens to them?

An oversimplified answer would be that "things are just *different*" when it's for real rather than practice. There are physiological and psychological changes that occur in the defender's body and brain, and, unless he has experienced such changes beforehand and understands how to put them to positive use, they become tremendous liabilities. Sure, his instructors have told him, and he himself knows in his heart, that a real fight is going to be different than a training session. But, again, unless he has actually experienced this in the past, he rarely has any idea how *vastly different* it's going to be.

Physiological changes include, among other things, an elevated heart rate and varying degrees of fine motor skill loss. Efforts that barely increased breathing in the training hall suddenly leave the fighter winded and exhausted. Legs and arms may feel as if their weight has increased tenfold, and fingers that easily and proficiently manipulated training weapons suddenly become stiff and clumsy when they try to wrap themselves around their real counterparts. But even though these physical problems are very real, they are brought on by the brain's acknowledging that *this time it's for all the marbles.* In other words, instead of shrugging it off and trying again as you do when you make a mistake in practice, this time if you screw up you're going to get seriously hurt or die. It's like the old story about the 20-foot two-by-four: If you lay it flat on the ground, it's easy to keep your balance as you walk along its length. But suspend the same two-by-four between two 30-story buildings, and walking across it like a circus performer on a tightrope becomes a whole different story.

There are as many specific reasons for failure under "real world" pressure as there are well-trained fighters who fail. But over the last 30-some years, I've found that the great majority of these reasons fall somewhere under one of three general categories. So I'd like to briefly explore these subdivisions, these "failures of the will," so to speak; take a look at what causes them; and make a few suggestions about how they might be overcome.

First, and perhaps the most common reason for defeat in people who are quite well prepared to defend themselves *physically,* is a lack of confidence. This can be a lack of confidence in the student's own abilities, in the specific techniques he has learned, or in the instructor who has taught them. There's a nagging little voice in the back of some people's minds that keeps telling them they simply don't have the courage to act under true life-and-death circumstances. This little voice keeps saying, "You're really a coward at heart, you know, and if anything serious ever actually does happen, you're going to freeze." Another little voice sometimes says, "You know this stuff you're practicing only works because your partner is *cooperating,* and if he quit cooperating he could beat your brains in while you try to perform such complex actions." Last, but not least, is a third nagging voice that taunts, either consciously or unconsciously, "Your instructor is full of crap, and the only actual fighting experience he's ever had is dancing around a dojo in his pajamas."

Regardless of whether or not the lack of confidence is in you, your technique, or your teacher, the best cure is actual street experience. But few people are in a position to go out and get such experience without doing jail time. (Besides, if you are the *instigator* of violence you become part of the problem rather than the solution.) A partial solution—and the best for those not involved in some profession such as law enforcement, where street experience is part of the job—is a lot of deep soul searching and visualization. If you are imaginative enough to visualize specific, realistic violent situations, and experience the fear and other confusion that almost always accompany them, you can instill in yourself at least some of the courage it will take to push yourself through those negative emotions. When doing so, never forget that courage is not the absence of fear; it is the ability to act in spite of it.

Realistic combat instructors call this "mind-set," and for most people, it takes far longer to develop than do the physical techniques of self-defense. The socially responsible student must not only come to terms with his own fear but also the fact that hurting, or even killing, another human being may be necessary to ensure his own survival. For most men and women, this is distasteful. Consider the fact that it takes only seconds to teach a beginning self-defense student to perform an eye strike. But most beginners exhibit at least some degree of revulsion at the thought of actually driving their fingers into the eye sockets of another human being, and few leave the gym after that initial lesson with a mental state that would allow them to carry out such a technique effectively. To arrive at that point, the student must take it upon himself to sift through the morality and legality of possibly blinding someone in order to escape injury himself. This not only takes time but also requires an often-painful commitment to reality. Many people are unable, or unwilling, to undertake such a raw and hard-boiled, yet pragmatic view of the world. They are far more comfortable lying to themselves and pretending that the controlled atmosphere of their dojo—where the limits on violence fall far short of what one might encounter on the street—is, in itself, reality. Such self-deception, however, sets them up for serious injury should they ever encounter the true ferocity of which some attackers are capable.

A lack of confidence in the techniques being taught often comes from the very thing that creates a false confidence in other students—performing them at half speed and/or within the other safety restraints. Keep in mind that the focus on safety has become ever more stringent over the last 30 years as our society progressively became a nation of "sewers." (Yes, the double meaning is intended.) Litigation today is always lurking in the shadows, and this has caused many teachers to alter their curriculum. This creates an atmosphere that is even more unrealistic than ever in relation to facing true violence. In short, such schools have become so safe on the mats that their students are no longer safe on the sidewalks.

Finding training partners who are willing to take risks can go a long way toward instilling "real-world" confidence. These partners should *resist,* rather than collaborate with, your efforts. You may indeed wind up with a few bumps and bruises, as we did in the old days when common sense, rather than lawyers ruled the world, but these small injuries can help you avoid more serious damage down the road. They can also help you decide which techniques are better suited to art or sport than survival. And this, in turn, will assist you in determining whether or not your instructor is actually teaching you a legitimate system of reality-based fighting. If practical self-defense is your goal, and your instructor is wasting your time with unrealistic techniques, it's time to dump his Disneyland butt and find a new teacher.

A second common reason for failure to perform in actual engagements is the fear of punishment for doing so. Over and over today we hear stories about people who exercised their Constitutional (not to mention God-given) right to self-defense and ended up in prison. The reality of this problem is that it actually does happen sometimes. Our criminal justice system is far from perfect, and good men and women are sometimes arrested when they should instead be heralded as heroes. Having this in the back of the mind when the moment of truth arrives can cause defenders to hesitate, and, *regardless of skill level*, this hesitation can lead to destruction. Again, a great deal of soul-searching is called for here. The old adage "better tried by 12 than carried by six" must be fully understood. If possible, you should defend yourself in a manner that ensures survival from both the assailant and a justice system that is not always just. But if you must err, err on the side of staying alive.

Last, but certainly not least of the reasons skilled students fail in the street are feelings of *guilt.* This can be broken down into both *direct* and *indirect* guilt, but both are brought on by a conscious or unconscious belief that the defender actually deserves punishment. Direct guilt involves the belief, regardless of how erroneous it may be, that the recipient of an unwarranted attack is at least partially responsible for the grave situation in which he suddenly finds himself. Thoughts such as, "I was warned not to come here," or "I should never have worn this expensive jewelry" may fly through the mind to sabotage defensive efforts. Perhaps the most obvious example of *direct guilt* undermining the ability to exercise productive self-defense can be found in the following story.

Years ago, I had a friend we'll call "Dave." Dave was very tough, very well-trained, and, through his job as a police officer, a very experienced street fighter. He was also, for the most part, a very fine and moral human being. But he was not a *perfect* human being, any more than any of us is, and through a series of almost unbelievably bad decisions, thinly veiled rationalizations, and poor judgment, Dave found himself involved with a married woman. They met on the sly and believed no one but they knew about the affair. As is always the case in such situations, however, eventually *everyone* knew about it, and in due time the woman's husband found out, too.

I also knew the husband, whom we'll call "Tom." Tom was a happy-go-lucky little fellow who crunched numbers for a living. He spent his days wearing a coat and tie and his free time on the golf course. I doubt he had ever even been in a grade school fistfight. Tom was a nice guy, too, but as you might guess, he was not pleased when he learned about Dave and his wife. So he drove to Dave's house, rang the doorbell, and began screaming at Dave to come out.

I visited Dave a few days later in the hospital, and asked him what had happened. "I don't really know," he told me. "Tom didn't know how to fight at all. He just started flailing his arms at me. I blocked him a few times. Then it was like I suddenly lost all ability to fight back. My heart just wasn't in it, and before I knew it I was on the ground getting my head and ribs kicked in." Dave shrugged, shook his head, and I'll never forget the next words that came out of his mouth: "I guess I deserved it."

Think about this story. Dave had *everything* going for him, Tom had *nothing* going for him, but Tom still put Dave in the hospital. Why? Dave answered that question himself when he said, "My heart wasn't in it" and "I guess I deserved it." Dave felt guilty about the affair with Tom's wife, and that guilt stripped him of the *will* so necessary to defend himself.

In addition to direct guilt, *indirect* guilt can also ravage the will. Perhaps you just left your job after skimming the cash register, and now you find yourself surrounded by street punks who want to steal what *you stole*. One thing has nothing to do with the other, and you don't deserve a beating. (What you deserve is to get fired, or fined by a judge, or imprisoned.) But your subconscious does not always make such subtle distinctions. Sometimes all it knows is that you deserve punishment, and here's a chance for you to get it. You may find yourself in the same shape Dave was in, wondering why you didn't make much of an attempt to fight back.

The answer to guilt—either direct or indirect—is to feel good about yourself and what you're doing in your life. Do your best to treat others as you want to be treated (didn't somebody else say that?), and when you violate that rule, as we all do, make your amends as quickly, and as well, as you can. To the best of your ability, keep a clear conscience so you don't set yourself up for failure as punishment.

I have known many terrific fighters over the years. Some were highly trained; others had trained themselves. Some knew literally thousands of techniques; others only one or two. But what they all had in common was a clear mind when it came to defending themselves. And if I need someone to back me up, I'll choose the man with the clear mind over the 99th-degree black belt whose mind isn't right every time.

You see, no matter how much you train, no matter how talented you are or how proficient you become at defending yourself, your body will never perform any action until the brain *tells it to do so.*

Fear

> When we are frightened, our options multiply enormously. Ideas we might never have entertained are suddenly considered. In that willingness to do things differently resides the opportunity—the privilege—to change our lives in ways we might not have in the absence of fear.
>
> —Gavin de Becker,
> from "Fear, Fear Everywhere"

FEAR, FEAR EVERYWHERE

by Gavin de Becker

Best-selling author **Gavin de Becker** *is the nation's leading expert on the prediction and management of violence. His work has earned him three presidential appointments and a position on a congressional committee. Mr. De Becker was twice appointed to the president's advisory board at the U.S. Department of Justice, and he served two terms on the governor's advisory board at the California Department of Mental Health.*

His 75-member consulting firm advises government agencies, universities, police departments, corporations, and media figures on the assessment of threats and hazards. Gavin de Becker & Associates maintains the world's largest library of threat and obsessive communications, consisting of more than 350,000 pieces of material.

Mr. de Becker is the author of the first best-selling book written about threat assessment. The Gift of Fear *spent four months on the New York Times Best-Seller List and is now published in 13 languages. His second book,* Protecting the Gift, *explored the safety of children and was the number-one parenting book of 1999. His current book,* Fear Less: Real Truth about Risk, Safety, and Security in a Time of Terrorism, *appeared on the New York Times Best-Seller List in its first week. The entire proceeds from* Fear Less *go to Victory Over Violence, the charity he cofounded to provide direct support to battered women's shelters.*

Mr. de Becker is the designer of the MOSAIC (Method for Objectively Selecting Areas of Inquiry Consistently) threat assessment systems used to screen threats to justices of the U.S. Supreme Court, members of Congress, senior officials of the CIA, and U.S. Marshals; he codesigned the MOSAIC system currently used for assessing all threats to federal judges and prosecutors.

Mr. de Becker has shared his philosophies about prevention of violence in several appearances on The Oprah Winfrey Show, 60 Minutes, Larry King Live, *and* 20/20. *His work has also been featured in* Time *and* Newsweek, *among many other magazines.*

Mr. de Becker is a senior fellow at UCLA's School of Public Policy and Social Research and a senior advisor to the Rand Corporation on public safety and justice matters.

❖

During my career, I've sat across the table and seen fear in the eyes of public figures, assassins, death-row inmates, soldiers, rape victims, battered women, and police officers. I've discussed fear with a president who was shot at, with another who was hit, with the widow of one who was killed, with an athlete who was stabbed at a sporting event, and with children who grew up surrounded by violence. The fear I've seen has worn a thousand faces, but when unmasked it is the same as yours and mine—and since September 11, we've all seen it at some point in most of the people we've encountered.

Just as we can find compassion for those who hate us and for those who serve in government, so too can we find compassion for ourselves. It is just fine that we felt fear, just fine that we canceled some plans, just fine that we didn't know what to do or how to react to a terrible trauma that still seems unreal. Our nation has been terrorized. What we lost at the start of this war was our peace of mind, and it is time to take back the beachhead.

Before we do, there may be some benefit in consciously feeling our fear for just one more moment, because fear can carry us closer to the truth of who we are. When we are frightened, our options multiply enormously. Ideas we might never have entertained are suddenly considered. In that willingness to do things differently resides the opportunity—the privilege—to change our lives in ways we might not have in the absence of fear. Anyone who has beaten cancer or heart disease sees the world differently today than at the moment the doctor sat him or her down, drew a long breath, and spoke the words that started a new life. You may know such a person. You may be such a person.

For our county, at the exact moment we lost so many lives, we all began new ones. We are changed and changing still, and just as with a person, a nation can become more extraordinary or can slip back into its old ways.

On September 11, many Americans had to give up their belief that we were invulnerable; that day marked the death of denial. Now I want to discuss the denial of death. Ernest Becker wrote a Pulitzer Prize-winning book by that title, and a copy of *Denial of Death* lay unopened at my bedside for two years. You could call this denial of denial of death. That I delayed reading that wonderful book was doubly ironic given that my work has always required me to look at the possibility of death, even the architecture of death. Millions of Americans have had to do the same thing since September 11, and many have accepted death and risk in ways they never had before.

This is the same as accepting life, for life is risk; life is a venture full of promise. Politicians and the media encourage us to go to war with death, to live encamped in a thousand precautions, to be ever mindful of the newest frightening study and the latest life-extending health tip, ever alert to a thousand unlikely risks—as if all this makes any difference whatsoever to death. If death is the enemy, here's the most statistically correct answer to our fears: drive carefully, eat a low-fat diet, don't smoke, and exercise regularly. But I think we are looking for something more profound to emerge from our experience.

At core, unwarranted fear is the fear of death. It frightened us that the 9-11 hijackers acted in spite of that natural fear, and there is great power in that ability. We, too, gain that power when we act in spite of our fear of death. All those who try to frighten us might benefit from recalling this truth: everybody dies, but not everybody lives.

September 11 is our reminder to live—to live as fully as possible, and to live with less fear of one another than we used to.

September 11 is our reminder that we are nowhere near the limits of our compassion.

September 11 is our reminder to go to Disney World, to fly across the country on a surprise visit to loved ones, to go to New York and help "the city that never sleeps" sleep more soundly in the comfort of our support.

September 11 can be our annual reminder to do it now, whatever it is; say it now, whatever it is.

Oh for a way to wake the dead;
So much undone, so much unsaid.

This passage from a poem that was written by my father after the death of his father always makes me feel sadness about things I didn't express to some people in my life. At the same time, the poem gives me hope, for when I read "Oh for a way to wake the dead," I sometimes think, *Oh for a way to wake the living!*

That happened for many people on September 11, such that today it seems Americans are living more consciously than ever before, connected to one another more than at any time in our history. We have felt the sting of terrible violence, and the kindness unleashed is ours for the keeping—if we stay awake. To do anything less than fully embrace the stunning opportunity we hold out to one another would be like waking up to a room full of smoke, opening the windows to let it out, and then going back to sleep.

Those who hate us hope we do just that, for then pain and loss and fear would be the lasting results of our experience of terrorism. But thus far we've made another choice—a choice to see hazard only in those storm clouds where it exists, and to fly more freely in the clear skies between them. Our triumph over terror honors the thousands of people who died on September 11, and makes us heroes in a war we have already won.

FEAR AND WARRIOR
MIND-SET IN
THE SQUARE CIRCLE

by Wim Demeere

Wim Demeere began training in the martial arts at age 14, studying the grappling arts of judo and jujitsu for several years before turning to the kick/punch arts of traditional kung-fu and full-contact fighting. Over the years he has studied a broad range of other fighting styles, including muay Thai, kali, pentjak silat, and shootfighting. Since the late 1990s, he has been studying combat t'ai-chi ch'uan.

Mr. Demeere's competitive years saw him win four national titles and a bronze medal at the 1995 World Wushu Championships. In 2001, he became the national coach of the Belgian wushu fighting team.

A full-time personal trainer in his native country of Belgium, Mr. Demeere instructs both business executives and athletes in nutrition, strength and endurance, and a variety of martial art styles. He has managed a corporate wellness center and regularly gives lectures and workshops in the corporate world.

Mr. Demeere coauthored two books with Loren W. Christensen: The Fighter's Body: An Owner's Manual *and* Timing in the Fighting Arts: Your Guide to Winning in the Ring and Surviving on the Streets *(Turtle Press). They are working on another book for Turtle Press, as yet untitled, on the subject of timing in the fighting arts.*

You can contact Mr. Demeere through his Web site at www.grindingshop.com.

❖

When Loren Christensen first asked me to write a piece for this book, I had two immediate responses: first, I felt honored to be considered, and then I declined the offer, as I had never considered myself a warrior.

In my mother tongue, Dutch, the word "warrior" is translated as "fighter of a primitive tribe." Though we Belgians are certainly not the most refined or cultured people on the planet, I'd hardly say we are "primitive," let alone a tribe. I much prefer the definition given by some English dictionaries, namely, "a person engaged in, experienced in, or devoted to war." Though I served in the military, I never experienced war and, therefore, felt unqualified to work on this project. Loren and I discussed it further, and after he talked about how a warrior is not just a "man of war" but also one who, among other things, has a particular state of mind, a warrior mind, I agreed to do it.

As I started writing, I thought a lot about what Loren said, about the dictionary definition, and how my role as a full-contact fighter fit into all of this. Yes, men and women in the military who step up to go into harm's way to defend their country are most certainly warriors. They go prepared for the ultimate sacrifice of giving up their own lives so others can live. And so do police officers, firefighters, rescue workers, and many other people who choose high-risk professions. One task they all have in common is that of facing danger so others can survive, a truly altruistic and noble act.

Except for working as a bouncer (which is arguably a job where you try to keep others safe), I have never done anything similar to these fine warriors. But I have sought out danger for other reasons, and in so doing, I have looked into the cold eyes of those wanting to remove my head, and I have known many times the distinct taste of fear.

From age 18 to 25, the primary focus of my life was a Chinese full-contact fighting sport called sanda, or sanshou. It is a combination of kickboxing and stand-up grappling, performed on a platform or in a ring. Knockouts and injuries are common, which makes the clash spectacular from the audience's point of view and extraordinarily intense for the fighters.

I began competing on a national level, winning the gold several times in my weight class. This made it possible to join the national team and compete internationally, where I faced fighters who were considered the best in the world. Moving up from the local scene to meet these elite athletes was a frightening progression, to say the least. Though I knew intellectually that these men would be highly skilled and fierce, standing face to face with one of them was entirely different from what I imagined the experience would be. Billy Joel said it most aptly in one of his songs: "Just like a boxer in a title fight, you got to walk in that ring all alone." *All alone.* That is, except for the other guy who wants to kick your head all the way to the 10th row.

You choose to step into the arena knowing there will be an opponent waiting there, one who has trained just as hard as you and one you must assume is of equal or greater skill. The sole purpose of his being there, and his only focus, is to *beat* you, in every definition of the word. You might suffer a few cuts and bruises, you might end up injured or knocked out, you might have to go to the hospital or, as happens a few times a year, you might not make it out alive. How it turns out is all up to you because, as Joel sings, once the referee says, "Fight!" you are "in that ring all alone."

It's a time that is at once alluring and frightening. *You* are the one punching and kicking your opponent into defeat, not your coach, sparring partners, and others who helped you prepare for that moment. If you prevail, there is no one else to take credit for the victory, which is an awesome and indescribable experience.

All alone. Although there is always that sense of being all by yourself in the ring in every fight, never is it more pronounced than the first time you go up against a fighter who is better than you. No matter how good you are, eventually there is going to be someone better, and you are going to have to face him. It's a gut-wrenching and, for some, ego-shattering fear that drapes over you like a body cast as you realize suddenly that your best is simply not good enough. To make matters worse, you cannot forfeit the match. Oh, you could, but you would have to live in the Valley of Shame for the rest of your life. No, you must stay. You trained hard to get there, and you cannot justify throwing in the towel without at least giving it a shot. Never is there a time that the ring is a more lonely and terrifying place.

Making the experience even more surreal is the roar of the crowd—for or against you—as you step into the center of the ring. Some fighters fear performing badly and being ridiculed by the crowd; most fighters fear embarrassment more than they do injury. Fortunately, this was never much of an issue for me. Usually, however, it felt as if I was standing there alone with the whole world watching to see how I would do. Beyond any fear I may have felt, I perceived this as an incentive to perform better. Though I felt the crowd's eyes on me, it never bothered me, and their cheers and occasional booing didn't even register in my mind, as I was always too busy fighting.

There are two major components to competition: training and the actual fight. For me, the training was the more enjoyable. I loved lifting weights until my muscles ached, punching and kicking the handheld pads and heavy bag until I could barely stand, sprinting on the track to develop greater explosiveness, and doing a variety of other drills and exercises to get in peak condition. I especially loved the challenge of solo training, with only myself to keep me motivated to push harder and harder.

Often I had to dig deep to find ways to keep going when my body screamed for me to stop or when getting up in the morning meant walking with baby steps because of the soreness. Sometimes I did it with goals. When practicing on the heavy bag, I'd set a target number of repetitions to do per technique. Whenever I failed to execute a technique correctly, I added two more repetitions—one to make up for the bad one and another to make sure I got it right. I didn't allow myself to stop until I finished the predetermined number of kicks and punches. When I learned that I could overcome pain and exhaustion, it motivated me to try harder, to push the limits just a little farther.

To this day, that mind-set is still with me, though I no longer compete. Trying to improve my skills, my physical condition, and my understanding is what keeps me fascinated with the martial arts after training in them for more than half my life.

Some people say this is part of the warrior spirit. I just call it training as hard as you can.

So physically preparing to compete was a joy, though the mental preparation was difficult. It was all about making a conscious decision to go against someone to try to hurt him, knowing he would try his best to hurt me. I wasn't being mugged on the street or assaulted in a bar. There was no wrong or right, no good guy or bad guy; we both chose to be there for the sole purpose of using controlled violence on each other to inflict pain.

As a heavyweight, I was most often the strongest fighter in the gym, though many fighters were more skilled than I. When I started out, I occasionally injured lighter training partners because what felt like medium-powered hits to me felt like a full-on blast to them. So out of concern that I would severely injure my fellow classmates, I learned to control my techniques. Though my lighter training partners appreciated my efforts, it created problems for me in the ring because I became too conditioned to holding back my power. Instead of punching and kicking as hard as I could, I tried to win on points by outsmarting my opponents. I would continue to do this until a fighter committed an accidental foul against me or deliberately used a prohibited technique.

Once someone kicked me in the groin or used a forbidden joint lock, though, it literally felt as if a volcano had erupted inside my brain. Some observers would tell me that they could literally see a change sweep over me, especially the look in my eyes, as I experienced an intense, violent desire and justification to hurt, even knock out, my opponent, to make him pay for his unsportsmanlike behavior. After experiencing this a few times, I knew I had to make a change in both my physical training and my mental preparation. As I was now facing fighters on the international scene, men with knockout power in every technique, I could no longer afford to hold back. So I spent countless hours on mental programming, working on learning to invoke and then control a powerful mind-set. I watched footage of my fights, mentally reliving each one, imagining going full power where I had held back.

My next step was to program my mind and practice deep meditation. I imagined highly detailed fights, each with a different opponent. I "fought" them like a demon, not letting up until they had been beaten unconscious. Though in my mental imagery I was a merciless animal, I made sure I was always in control of my physical actions. Since being out of control is a sure way to lose a fight, it was critical that my mental training included extreme aggression that was in harmony with the right mind-set to control it.

I tried a technique purportedly taught to KGB recruits. They were told to go to a zoo and study the stares of the tigers and panthers. Sound silly? No matter how much of a warrior you are, when you look into the eyes of a 600-pound Siberian tiger that can kill you with a casual swipe of its claws and deflesh you in a matter of seconds, warriorhood takes on a different perspective. The tiger is a natural warrior. It doesn't think about its savagery; it goes purely on instinct. It kills without remorse and then just goes back to whatever it was doing before. Looking into the eyes of these magnificent killers can give you a different perspective on the warrior mind-set. You realize quickly that there are worse things than being beaten by a human opponent. Having to face a Siberian tiger in his cage at dinnertime is one of them.

In time, it became easier to enter the right mind-set, which led to the final stage—that of implementing a trigger. Throughout the years, I experimented with several ways to do this but eventually ended up with a simple ritual not unlike what many fighters do instinctively right before they start their match. I would bang my gloves together, then bang them against my forehead, and finally thrust them toward my opponent. As I did this in training, I would consciously recall the fighting mind-set I had experienced when meditating, the mind-set I experienced when watching my own tapes, and what I experienced when watching the ferocious cats in the zoo.

In the beginning it would take several minutes to make the connection between the physical ritual and the warlike mind-set. But in time and with arduous practice, the ritual ignited a trigger; that is, it called up at will that violent yet controlled fighting spirit deep inside of me. The moment was no longer about having fun and tagging my opponent to score points. Now I was singularly focused on hurting him, beating him to the floor. The ritual became a powerful device to focus on the task and to help me to regain focus in between rounds after I'd taken a brief moment to rest. I was to learn that this simple mind/body triggering method also helped me control another aspect of competing: fear.

Though few competitors admit it, virtually all experience fear, and I am most certainly no exception. It might not be considered macho to admit this, but I don't feel there is reason for shame or denial. Fighting is dangerous, whether on the street or in the ring; there is always the risk of serious injury or death. Only those who don't understand this have no fear. Ignorance is bliss.

Fear can give you all the energy you need, unless it controls you. In every event I competed in, I was afraid. My stomach twisted into knots, I had to go to the bathroom dozens of times, I felt faint, and I felt weak in the knees. At first, I was ashamed of this reaction, fearing that I might be a coward, but after a while I better understood the nature of fighting, including the psychological and physical reactions. It really clicked in after a two-time world champion told me, "You know, the other guy feels exactly like you do. So it doesn't matter."

His words were simple and logical, and they immediately helped me to accept fear as an inevitable part of competing. However afraid I was, once I triggered my fighting mind-set with my glove-ritual, it all disappeared. I became so focused on the opponent that I literally didn't have time to be scared, and, because I needed all my resources for the fight itself, I didn't have any energy for fear anyway.

Physical training, meditation, philosophy, and activation of my trigger all came together in the three most important fights of my career, each against a three-time sanshou world champion, a Russian man called Djaparov. Every time we met, our fight turned into a brawl, as technique went out the window.

Though he had only a limited set of moves, he was a brutally tough fighter and performed what he knew very well.

Our first fight was in Moscow, the capital of his home country. He had won his first world title recently and was fighting in front of a friendly crowd, which made him feel immensely confident against an unknown Belgian guy. I had just won the Belgian nationals a week before and was suffering from a leg injury. We looked into each other's eyes before the opening bell, and I saw that, like the Siberian tiger, he fully expected to devour his enemy. I just wanted to stay in one piece.

Three seconds into the first round, I surprised him with a quick roundhouse kick to the head. It caught him by surprise and broke his concentration for the rest of the fight. Though he still fought well, he seemed unable to focus, and I went on to win on points. As I limped off stage, I saw his coach angrily slapping him in the face with a towel for losing in front of his own people, and against a nobody.

For me, fighting the Russian was all about surviving, about overcoming my leg injury, and about not giving up. Due to my injury I couldn't find my rhythm, although I managed to stop him from finding his, too.

We met again a year later. This time when we locked eyes, I saw a lust for revenge for the humiliation he had suffered. His eyes were so intense and full of fighting spirit that they forced me to look away. For some reason my head wasn't in the right place for that second fight, and I was probably defeated at the very instant I looked away.

His first move was to pick me up and slam me to the floor and then dive on top of me. As I landed, I felt air forced out of my lungs and my muscles tearing. Knowing I was facing a better man, I very much wanted to quit, but I got up and gave it my best. It wasn't good enough, though, and he won the match.

Our last fight was the most intense. It was to be my last world championship, and I wanted to go out in style—and in a way, I did. We fixed our gazes on each other again, but this time, I was prepared. I stared right back at him, thinking, "You're not going to beat me. You may win, but you won't beat me." Our eyes remained unwavering—we both knew that neither of us would give up.

We fought for three rounds, one big brawl, neither of us taking time to breathe or think strategically. We both just wanted to deal one big, final blow to end it right then and there. His was a full-power right cross into my face. Mine was a throw, straight out of the movies, which launched him out of the ring. And so it went on until the final bell rang and he was declared the winner.

Though I lost the fight, I achieved my goal: He didn't really beat me. I took his best shots, the ones I had no answer for during our second encounter, and I kept on fighting. We both went farther than we had ever gone before, digging deeply into our warrior spirit for the energy and the mind-set to hold on.

Though he won the fight technically, my victory lay not in a medal or title: I was the one still standing when it was over. He fainted and fell down three times on his way to the changing room.

I made it back on my own two feet.

HARNESSING FEAR AS A SOURCE OF POWER

An interview with Bill Kipp by Loren W. Christensen

Bill Kipp is a leading expert on scenario-based adrenal stress response training for self-defense, having logged more than 30,000 instructional full-contact fights in his unique Bulletman body armor. Mr. Kipp served in the elite 3rd Marine Recon teams specializing in counterterrorism and security testing at top-secret military installations. While traveling worldwide as a Recon team leader, he cross-trained in clandestine operations with elite special forces units from Korea, Thailand, and New Zealand, among others. With more than 30 years in the martial arts, Mr. Kipp also worked as a movie stuntman, bouncer, and bodyguard to support his training while living in Asia for a time. He is the founder of Model Mugging of Colorado, FAST Defense (an instructor-training program in padded-assailant adrenal stress response training), and Power Solutions for Life, a highly innovative corporate conflict resolution program. Mr. Kipp has created adult and children's self-defense courses for the National Association of Professional Martial Artists (NAPMA) and is the program designer and chief instructor for Rocky Mountain Combat Applications Training (RMCAT). He currently travels worldwide training instructors to lead adrenal stress response seminars.

Mr. Kipp has authored three videos: The ABCs of Self Defense, FAST Solutions for Life *(available at www.fastdefense.com), and* The Missing Link: Self-Protection Through Awareness, Avoidance, and De-Escalation *(available at www.paladin-press.com). He can be reached at Billkipp@aol.com.*

Loren W. Christensen's biography is available at the back of this book.

❖

LWC: Is fear a good thing for a warrior?
BK: Fear is one our greatest God-given tools. Without it

our species wouldn't have survived to this day. Fear is an inevitable and important survival response for anyone experiencing any sort of intense situation. But without proper training, fear can be a warrior's biggest enemy, causing an internal freeze or flight response in the heat of battle. Unfortunately, most modern-day warrior training dances around the topic of fear. Adding fuel to the fire, many warriors are taught by society that fear is unacceptable and "unmanly." This mistaken belief causes greater confusion when the evil villain fear inevitably raises its head in times of duress. In the ensuing internal struggle with the fear, the would-be warrior in essence takes himself out of the fight by losing focus on the external problem that's causing the fear. Rather than assessing the situation and responding accordingly, he is caught in cognitive dissonance where the fear takes control of the body, mind, and emotions, often with disastrous results. With proper training, the warrior can learn to control and focus fear, giving him a tremendous edge over the untrained warrior who succumbs to the negative effects of fear. The well-trained warrior feels the fear and works with it, using this powerful biochemical and emotional force to his benefit as necessary.

LWC: Many soldiers, cops, boxers, and martial artists say they use fear as fuel. How so?

BK: Fear and adrenaline are the great equalizers. We have all heard stories about normal individuals performing amazing feats of strength and power from an adrenaline rush that was induced by intense fear: women lifting cars to save youngsters pinned underneath, navy sailors tossing 500-pound bombs off the burning flight deck of a ship, and so on. Many an average person off the street has been granted the label "warrior" because of valiant actions taken when he managed to turn the often-debilitating effects of fear into superhuman strength and courage.

The adage "It's not the size of the dog in the fight but the size of the fight in the dog" speaks the truth. Seasoned veteran soldiers, cops, and fighters know that fear is an inevitable component of their lives. They have learned (usually through the school of hard knocks) how to accept the presence of fear and work within it to find the correct and congruent response to a given situation. Sometimes that response is to stay calm and relaxed, and other times it's to fire up and fight for your life. Certainly the warrior who can harness fear as an incredible source of power will almost always prevail over the warrior who struggles with fear, regardless of their formal training or the number of stripes on their black belt. When the proverbial crap hits the fan, the discerning warrior wants to have all that power available as jet fuel for the fight!

LWC: What is going on with a person who charges forward, no matter how dangerous the adversary and no matter what the circumstances. Does he have fear?

BK: Typically such a person is either crazed with fear-induced adrenaline, causing him to act totally outside his normal realm of behavior, or he is genuinely insane. A small percentage of people fall into the latter category, and they don't necessarily warrant the badge of warrior for their actions. But someone who does respond valiantly under extreme fear really is a hero.

Think about a mama bear that fights to protect her cubs being threatened by a predator. She is responding from a strong emotional urge to protect those she loves, and thus she is reacting from fear. The fear is what dictates the defense and what makes her a serious force to be reckoned with. Even larger and stronger male bears will not mess with mama bear when she is crazed with fear and emotional power that will rip apart anyone or anything that gets in her way.

The same is true for humans. A rational, calm person will not go charging forth into a foray without some sort of emotional spark to fire his fear into such extreme action. The soldier whose squad mates are being mowed down by an enemy machine gun and the cop whose partner is being attacked by a gang are just two examples of scenarios in which people have harnessed the power of fear to overcome impossible odds and achieve victory. Invariably, these warriors are responding from what we call the "low-road brain," which houses the emotional and survival centers of the brain, as opposed to the "high-road brain," where conscious, deliberate thought processes occur. Fear very quickly triggers the transfer of brain function from high road to low road. These warriors in full-hero mode are reacting from extreme fear that induces the adrenaline and endorphin body response necessary to pull off these amazing endeavors.

LWC: Why will people look away when a man is browbeating his wife in public or a mother is beating her child at the supermarket? Case in point: I was a in a grocery recently and noticed a 300-pound woman in line behind me with her jammed-full grocery cart, in which perched her two-year-old child. Every time the child reached for a colorful carton in the cart, her mother slapped her face and yelled at her. I told the woman that if she struck her child one more time I was going to knock her on her big, fat butt. The people around me applauded, but not one other person had come forward. Were they afraid?

BK: The bystanders' lack of response exemplifies a classic low-road brain phenomenon. They were triggered into the adrenal rush by fear and responded with the typical emotional freeze. You, on the other hand, reacted with the appropriate response due to your extensive training and life experience. Simply put, people respond to stressful situations as they have been trained to do. Since most people are never formally trained to deal with fear, they tend to react with emotional, knee-jerk responses that either get them into trouble or at least do little to solve the problem. Additionally, the knee-jerk responses they had in past fearful experiences where they froze are hardwired into the low brain as recurring reactions to future stressful events.

The number-one fear in our society is interpersonal conflict. Just being in proximity to personal conflict is enough to trigger most people into the low brain, even if they are not involved. Most people never learn how to deal with conflict effectively, and many have had negative and even traumatic experiences where they failed to do so. These experiences have been stored in the low brain as conditioned coping mechanisms, whether they worked in the past or not. Such people will typically freeze up and feel helpless to fend for themselves or anyone else in need of support and backup. This classic example juxtaposes the bystanders' fear, which controlled their better judgment and prevented them from responding appropriately, and your trained ability to maintain high-road brain function and take the correct action in the chaos of the moment.

LWC: Does fear come and go? When I was on the police department, I recall that in most cases I would be completely calm and collected when responding to a hot call, but there were other times when I got the same type of call that I would be tense and anxious.

BK: Different people are emotionally triggered by different events, words, gestures, and so on, as well as by past experiences and beliefs. In your case, there could have been any number of variables at play. It could be that some detail in a particular call was a stress trigger for you that was not present in other calls. It could be that you were somewhat triggered by other factors when the stress of a particular call put you over the edge into intense anxiety. A great lifetime exercise is to constantly inventory our personal and societal triggers.

For example, a gang of a particular ethnic group attacked me many years ago. The situation was terrifying for me, even though it turned out okay. Decades later, I still have a tendency to overreact when I relate to people of that ethnic persuasion. I am not a racist by any means, yet I have hardwiring that can be triggered by certain people and events. Just being aware of this hardwiring enables me to stop and take a few deep breaths if I should feel triggered, rather than spin out in an emotional, knee-jerk response that stems from something that happened many years ago and has no bearing on this new situation.

Other examples of personal triggers are the threat of injury to children or other loved ones; the middle finger and other gestures, specific words, or comments; and even various types of eye contact. Triggers can come from societal conditioning as well. We are strongly influenced by movies, peer pressure, and a slew of other cultural messages that often feed us destructive behavioral patterns. For women, the message that they should always be nice and not make a scene might be a trigger. For men, it might be the message that they should never back down or show fear. The more we are aware of what triggers us, the less likely we are to respond in emotional, knee-jerk ways that can get us into trouble and even killed. This awareness extends to then using the adrenal fear rush skillfully when appropriate.

LWC: Let's say a warrior has a good handle on his fear. He manages it well to help him think more clearly and to move with finesse, power, and speed. Except today. For whatever reason, he has lost it. Say the warrior is either a martial artist facing an extremely tough opponent, a cop who has to kick in a door where there is an armed person on the other side, or a soldier moving down an eerily quiet street where there is an enemy in hiding. What can this warrior do quickly to get his fear-management skills back?

BK: In the 16-plus years that I have focused on adrenaline stress training, I have used a few different mechanisms to condition the ability to fire up the fear-into-power response at will. The best I've found is selecting a word or sound that can be used to trigger the adrenaline. Just as a police K-9 trainer will condition the dog to take action in response to certain command words, so we can train ourselves. Such training must employ the mind, emotions, and body to anchor new survival responses that are effective and dependable. Just as a person can be hardwired to be a victim by a single bad experience, he can be reprogrammed to be a victor in a very short timeframe—and respond as such for years and even decades to come when under duress. I have a specific word I use in my head that instantly triggers me to be ready for anything. This doesn't mean I go berserk right off the bat. The sensation is like opening an internal water faucet and feeling the adrenaline flood through me like warm water. I'm conscious and deliberate in my actions, and if need be that energy is immediately available without my even thinking about it.

The process of anchoring new, positive triggers is most effective when done during a fatigued state because it will sink deeper into the low brain, which is the part of the brain that's working when you're under extreme duress. So ideally, such training should be done at a point when you are physically and mentally tapped out. Should you then have to deal with a situation you just don't feel up for in the future, you will have that experience and conditioned response to draw from to fire you up for action. As I always tell my students, the bad guys never come at you when you've just had three double cappuccinos and walked out of a Bruce Lee movie! It's always when you are least up for it. This is where adrenal fear conditioning is most important.

LWC: How important is stress training for the soldier, cop, and martial artist? I'm referring to training where a real situation is replicated as closely as possible.

BK: I consider it to be the most important training of all. Without it, all other training may be inaccessible in a real situation. Most training is cerebral and involves the high-road brain. Although very important, it often discounts the reality of the adrenal fear rush, which quickly engages the low-road brain. There is no definitive way for these two different brain parts to communicate, so the vast majority of high-road brain training is not accessible in the heat of battle. Therefore, whatever conditioning is in the low-road brain will dictate the action taken by the officer, soldier, and so on. Without formal training, a person will respond with whatever coping mechanisms he has learned to use throughout the course of his life. It's a real hit-or-miss situation, and more often than not it's a miss. These misses are the result of unconscious, emotional knee-jerk responses. People die every day because of them. But proper training imparts tactics and techniques that can be learned in both the high- and low-road brain that will allow a conscious assessment of the situation and provide the appropriate response to deal with it, even in the most chaotic scenario.

The techniques taught in fear adrenal stress response training are often misinterpreted as flipping the switch and going ballistic on your opponent. The truth is that graduates of such training are much less likely to overreact emotionally and go off inappropriately or underreact and freeze up. Herein lies the beauty of this training concept: it empowers you to find the appropriate response to the given situation, no matter where it occurs or at what level. It's a great way to defend yourself, your community, your country, and your loved ones, and one hell of a great way to live life!

CONTROLLING FEAR AND FACING DANGER

by Dave Grossi

Dave Grossi is a retired police lieutenant from upstate New York. For 12 years, he was the lead instructor for the Calibre Press, Inc., Street Survival Seminars. A combat veteran of Vietnam, he is a graduate of the FBI National Academy, holds a bachelor's degree in police administration, and was the first police trainer in the world to receive the Certified Law Enforcement Trainer (CLET) designation from ASLET. He holds instructor credentials in more than a dozen force-related disciplines, including firearms, impact weapons, chemical agents, weapon-retention techniques, electronic restraint systems, handcuffing, and edged weapons.

Mr. Grossi's complete biography is included with his essay "How Should a Warrior Train?" in Chapter 8.

❖

Gen. Douglas MacArthur said, "If bravery is a quality which knows not fear, then I have never seen a brave man. For the courageous man is the man who, in spite of his fear, forces himself to carry on." These words hang on the walls of more than a few police academies. No one is forced to enter law enforcement as a profession. I've never met someone who was "drafted" into police work. The warrior's lot is one that is served through a "calling." The hand of a higher being has touched the shoulder of all who bear the title "warrior."

Do warriors experience fear? You bet they do. The only difference is a warrior is trained to overcome that fear and forge ahead. He fights through it . . . and gets the job done. The untrained fall victim to it.

Volumes have been written on the fight-flight response and what happens to the body during moments of high stress. Basic academy curriculum and in-service training programs are replete with chapters on the Human Adaptation Theory, the survival mechanism, and emergency reaction and response. So this article won't attempt to plow old ground with the same material. However, what I would like to discuss is how today's warrior can realistically deal with that fear, how he controls those emotions in the face of overwhelming danger and still performs at peak level during high-stress moments.

We all know what adrenaline does to fine motor skills, and most seasoned warriors have experienced perceptual distortions. But how can today's street warrior effectively control and manage that gut-wrenching, heart-pounding fear that all too often rears its ugly head in the face of overwhelming danger? Here are some practical suggestions that can be practiced often, implemented quickly, and passed on easily.

The first step in controlling fear is to *admit that you're afraid*. Now, as ironic as that sounds, admitting that you're afraid doesn't mean that you can't cope with the danger. Not at all. It's just a simple acknowledgment of what you're experiencing. You just admit to yourself that you're afraid. Acknowledging that fear may actually allow you to think better, work through the danger methodically, and respond according to your training. A warrior acknowledges his fear, accepts the danger he is facing, and moves on.

Next, *avoid dwelling on that danger* or the chance of failure. If your mind is constantly preoccupied with feeling fear or facing danger, it cannot focus on success or winning. A warrior accepts that he is afraid, then begins to formulate his plan for combating the problem. A warrior understands that the mind and body are not separate entities. They work better as a team. To begin to control your mind, you first have *to take control of your body*. Warriors understand the importance of autogenic breathing: deep, slow, rhythmic breaths, inhaling through your nose, holding your breath for a full three to four seconds, and then exhaling completely and steadily through your mouth. This will have an immediate calming effect on your body and, in turn, help to clear your mind. Plus, it slows the heart rate, lowers your pulse rate and blood pressure, and may help you think better.

Next, you want to *get your mind focused* on getting through this dangerous call safely. After you've calmed your mind and body, your next task is to focus on what you need to do to complete this dangerous assignment, whether it's a building search, a high-risk vehicle stop, a search warrant execution, or a "prowler now" call. Kevin Costner, in playing the lead role as an aging major league baseball pitcher in the movie *For Love of the Game*, called it "clearing the mechanism." It is a total and complete mental focus on what you need to do in order to survive. In other words, it's going over tactics in your mind, anticipating danger, establishing contingency plans for movement, identifying cover or concealment, calling for backup, and being aware of potential escape routes.

These are the thoughts that must take priority in your mind.

A warrior *expects the unexpected,* and, when faced with a dangerous or fearful situation, he constantly reinforces the fact that he has the ability and the skills needed to deal with unknown or unexpected situations. A warrior does not let panic overtake "if/then" thinking. He has conditioned his mind and body to work as one. A predetermined plan of action has been ingrained in his thinking: "If such and such happens, then I'll do so and so."

A warrior also knows how to *turn fear into a motivator.* In the opening paragraph of this article, I quoted that old warrior, General MacArthur. He said, "The courageous man is the man who, in spite of his fear, forces himself to carry on." The warrior has trained and conditioned himself to turn that fear, that face of danger, into a motivator to forge on. I'm not talking about "tombstone courage" here or "damn the torpedoes, full speed ahead." What I'm suggesting is that you harness that fear, that anger at being placed into a dangerous or deadly situation, and use it as a motivator to succeed. Direct all your energy to getting through this call safely, and believe in your heart that no one can stop you.

Finally, a warrior *accepts that there is a certain element of fate involved* in every call. As we all know, sometimes bad things do happen to good people and, as the events of September 11, 2001, prove, life is not always fair. A warrior accepts these facts as he faces danger head-on, but not recklessly, and he acknowledges them with a positive attitude, coupled with training and good, sound tactics, and with an understanding that he has the necessary tools to survive—and he will do just that!

Let me conclude with some tips that my mentor and friend Chuck Remsberg suggested in his acclaimed text *Street Survival: Tactics for Armed Encounters*. And please allow me to paraphrase his advice. While the words may be dated, the message is as true today as it was when Chuck penned them back in 1980. They are words I lived by when I was working the street and, indeed, still use in my classes, because even after two decades, they're still relevant.

The first thing a warrior understands is that the public safety profession, be it law enforcement, corrections, parole, probation, or private security, is a dangerous job. It takes guts to be a cop today. It also demands your constant vigilance.

Next, the people you'll deal with over the course of your career have different attitudes, different backgrounds, a different set of values, and different motivations for what they do, and their willingness to take you on may be driven and/or guided by a philosophy quite different from anything you've ever been exposed to.

Third, understand that there are probably numerous legal, moral, and psychological implications of your warrior mind-set that must be resolved now . . . before you ever become engaged in a confrontation.

Fourth, because you've chosen to become a warrior, it may become necessary at any given time to use deadly force to save your life, the life or your warrior partner, or the life of a third person. Know it. Accept it. Prepare for it . . . now.

Fifth, practice to the point of mastery with all your tools. Become proficient with all your weapons, and that includes your body and your brain. Train under stress in as realistic an environment as possible to simulate those situations you may find yourself in. This will help you condition your warrior's mind-set.

And lastly, with proper mental preparedness, planning, and peak physical conditioning, you can avoid the mistakes of those less fortunate who have walked the warrior's path before you, and you'll be in a position to successfully conclude most dangerous encounters.

Also in this text, you'll read my thoughts in an article called, "How a Warrior Should Train." I sincerely hope that these two articles, when taken collectively with all of the other essays in this text, will help you thrive and survive throughout your entire law enforcement career. Until then, let me just say, warriors, stay safe!

Politics and the Warrior

So the question is, "How many GIs are you going to sacrifice to avoid how many dead babies?" Is it worth losing ten GIs to avoid one dead baby? Is one for one okay? One dead GI for a hundred dead babies?

—Jim Morris,
from "Baby Killers"

CHIMPS WITH NUKES

by Jim Morris

Jim Morris served three tours with Special Forces (the Green Berets) in Vietnam. Both the second and third were cut short by serious wounds. He was retired of wounds in the grade of major. Mr. Morris is author of the story from which the film Operation Dumbo Drop *was made, was technical advisor for that film, and has written and produced numerous documentary television episodes about the Green Berets and the Vietnam War. Mr. Morris is also author of three nonfiction books and four novels, including the best-selling* War Story. *As a book editor for Berkley and Dell, he edited more than 200 books, both fiction and nonfiction, most on military and adventure themes. As a contributing editor for* Soldier Of Fortune *magazine, he covered eight guerrilla wars during the early 1980s. Mr. Morris currently appears on MSNBC as commentator on special operations. "Chimps with Nukes" was written just before the United States invaded Iraq.*

❖

In Jared Diamond's book *The Third Chimpanzee*, he points out that we share about 98 percent of our DNA with chimpanzees, which is not much greater than the difference between chimps and bonobo pygmy chimps. He also postulates that human behavior is merely an elaboration of basic primate behavior. Bands of chimps hold a territory, and the young males instinctively patrol its boundaries, keeping watch for leopards and the young males of adjacent bands who sneak in and steal bananas. When that happens, they beat them up or kill them if they can.

I've found that a great deal of puzzling human behavior becomes perfectly clear if one thinks of our species as chimps with nukes.

All of our statecraft and "military science" is an elaboration on the theme of stealing and protecting bananas. We just do these things more intelligently than chimps, which is where the real danger lies. A behavior pattern that results in a dead chimp may make sense. One that results in a dead planet does not.

There is probably no one of average or better intelligence who does not believe that war, the way we wage it now, is insane. Yet we keep doing it, blaming each other, captive of our primate genes.

This essay is not an argument for or against war. Winston Churchill was right that slavery is worse than war. Dishonor is worse than war. Lots of things are worse than war. What it's an argument for is leaders who know this firsthand.

Harry Truman fought in France in World War I. Kennedy, Johnson, Nixon, all took the oath and wore the uniform. Even Reagan did that, though he only made training films in Hollywood as a captain in the Signal Corps.

FDR didn't serve, of course. He was wheelchair bound. But his son Elliott served as second in command of a Marine raider battalion. There is no more hairy assignment than that. From a geopolitical standpoint it makes no sense to have the son of the head of state subject to capture by the enemy. Young Roosevelt undoubtedly wanted to be in the war, but if his father allowed it, this must have been, at least partially, to make an egalitarian statement to the country. Vietnam was not a popular war. Getting out of it replaced baseball as the national pastime in the early '70s. Though his father had served in World War II, George Bush skated in the Texas Air National Guard. Cheney, Wolfowitz, and Pearle had deferments. Only Rumsfeld was a navy pilot—prior to Vietnam.

These are not bad men. But if you haven't seen your best friend's face turn to red goo before your eyes or watched a child die because you made a simple mistake throwing steel around at supersonic speed after three days without sleep, well, if you haven't done that, then, by definition, when it comes to war, you don't know what you're talking about.

In March of 1964 I was the "senior advisor" of a patrol of four Americans and a platoon of Jarai Montagnard tribesmen. We were out hunting for the entire population of a Jarai village, whom the Vietcong had kidnapped to use as slave labor in the jungle. It was a small patrol, put together quickly. Frankly, we knew that the chances of finding the village were almost nil, but we had to make a good-faith effort or risk losing support from the other villages.

We had mounted the patrol so quickly that there was no interpreter available. I was "advising" the Montagnard "commander" with hand and arm signals and about a 150 words of survival French I had learned on Okinawa. Ksor Yul, the platoon leader, also remembered some French from his service in the Indochina War. Some of them were the same words. Oddly, this worked well enough. We couldn't discuss philosophy, but we could patrol. About noon of the second day we crossed the Li Piao River, Ayunapa in Jarai, and moved parallel to it, hidden in the bush. Most of the Central Highlands was dense jungle, but this was open and parklike. Then my left flank guy signaled that he had spotted something. It was three Bahnar tribesmen, young boys working in a rice field by the river. I wanted to ask them if they had seen our VC and their group of villagers. We moved around them in the jungle, surrounding them on three sides, with the river on the fourth. The river was three feet deep and more than a hundred across. No one but a fool would try to escape across it under such circumstances. A fool or a kid. The boys broke for the river. I charged after them, into the water wearing 40 pounds of gear and clothes, which soaked and dragged me back. It was like running in a nightmare. My Americans fired warning shots. We had taught our Jarai a lot, but not about warning shots. They had been at war with the Bahnar, on and off, for about 900 years. They shot to kill. I screamed, *"No g'pow! No g'pow!"* (*g'pow* being Jarai for gun). Probably the only thing that saved two of the boys was that my troops had to shoot wide to avoid hitting me. But they hit one of them, and blood ran down his back as he ran. The other two scampered over the bank and into the jungle on the other side, but this kid wavered and fell by the river.

He was bleeding from a head wound. We bandaged it, but that didn't stop the bleeding. I didn't have an American medic, but we pulled a can of blood expander out of our Montagnard medic's pack. He had filled it with aspirin.

Then a sniper opened up from across the river. I took a squad, moved back into the jungle again, crossed the river out of sight around a bend, and moved through the jungle toward the sniper. None of my squad would take the point, so I did. I knew the sniper, if we found him, would have the first shot. I have great confidence in my marksmanship. If he missed me on the first round I'd kill him before he got off a second. That's a big if, and I was more scared than I've ever been. But the sniper had bugged out. I crossed the river for the fourth time. When I reached the bank, I stood and watched the boy die. And I watched him die in my dreams every night for the next 10 years. I will probably see him die on the day I do, and I will still grieve for him. I bear responsibility for his death, and I never knew his name. In war, every digit of every casualty figure has a story like that attached to it, and every one is a tragedy for a family and for the comrades of the dead. We have objectivized language in the military. Dead babies are "collateral damage." Dead teenagers, last May's bright and hopeful high school grads, are "friendly" or "enemy casualties." There's a reason for the language. As long as you can think like that you can keep fighting. But in the dark of the night for all the long years that follow, they're just dead kids, and the tears that you've managed to postpone come at strange and inappropriate times.

But our leaders will not have these troubles with their dreams. Somehow this country is now run by people who think they're too good to fight for it.

This was dramatically brought home to me a few years ago when I was an editor in New York publishing. I learned that the editor-in-chief of our literary imprint had actually known James Jones, the author of *From Here to Eternity*, a book I've read nine times. So I talked to her about Jones, and in the course of the conversation she mentioned that I was the only Vietnam veteran she had ever met.

My God that was stunning. This woman was in the upper reaches of New York society. Her husband tried cases before the Supreme Court. She'd had Caroline Kennedy Schlossberg and her husband to dinner the previous week. But she had never, either socially or professionally, knowingly met a Vietnam veteran.

But when our offices were moved in a corporate takeover, I stood in the halls and played Where-was-you-at? with the moving men. "Were you there for Tet?" "Were you in the Ia Drang?" Yes, they were.

About 10 years ago the armed services pruned all the Vietnam vets they could from their ranks. The Nammers had had that experience of being sold out by the people they risked their lives for, their lives expended needlessly by people who did not go and did not send their children. For the most part these men were still brave, still willing, if necessary, to die for freedom. But they were entirely too prone to ask the question, "Is this trip really necessary?"

It would probably be politically impossible to invade Iraq with an army of draftees. With the all-volunteer army we are spared those embarrassing questions about inequality of sacrifice.

I have heard and believe that during the entire course of the Vietnam War the son of only one congressman served. But those congressmen who did not send their sons and did not send the sons of their college-deferred big contributors voted with the Tonkin Gulf Resolution to send the sons of their less-affluent constituents. This is as grand a betrayal as I can imagine.

So we are now led by people who did not serve, and whose children do not serve. There is no Lieutenant Rumsfeld waiting for the new gas masks for his platoon. There is no navy pilot named Bush in this generation. Somebody's daughter will die, but it won't be Barb or Jenna. It's interesting to me that no Vietnam vet has achieved the office of president of the United States. Those who have climbed as high as the Senate have done so under special circumstances. One wonders if John McCain would have been elected if he'd merely been a fighter pilot and not a POW. One wonders if Bob Kerrey would have gone so far if he'd not lost a leg. But both of them know the full horror of war. I'd be far more comfortable if the decision to invade or not invade Iraq were being made by such a man. They don't see "collateral damage." They see dead babies.

Since Vietnam I don't think America trusts her military anymore. This is something of a mistake. There were next to no congressmen's sons in Vietnam, but every three or four weeks I'd pick up a *Stars and Stripes* and read where Lieutenant So-and-so, the son of General So-and-so, had been killed leading a Marine platoon. The military is probably the only segment of our society left that has that sense of noblesse oblige.

Saddam's military capabilities, compared to those of the United States, are almost laughable . . . unless we're right and he has poison gas and biological agents, and uses them. We'll still "win," but no one will be laughing because nothing will be funny.

The notion that we, the United States, can create "a stable democracy" in the Middle East strikes me as hubris of the highest order. But it's possible. We managed to create fairly stable, fairly democratic regimes in Japan and the Philippines after World War II, and they're still functioning more or less in that mode. So maybe this will work. But it's a very long shot. I'd just feel ever so much better if the people making the decisions carried the same risk as the people carrying them out. The only dogs they have in this fight are their money and their power. Bush won't personally know anyone who dies.

With the British upper classes the oldest son became lord of the manor, and the number-two son went to the army, and number three to the church. The British Empire lasted a long time. But I do not think America will long be top nation. The people will lose faith in a leadership that expends their sons and daughters like used Kleenex but sends its own to Harvard and Yale.

In Rome the Praetorians finally took to installing emperors from among their number. Then came the Visigoths.

BABY KILLERS

by Jim Morris

Jim Morris is author of the previous essay, "Chimps with Nukes." His biography is available under that title.

When I had a draft of "Chimps with Nukes" I e-mailed it to a bunch of old soldiers to see if anybody thought I had left anything important out. Only one person had a problem with the piece, and his problem was with my use of the term "dead babies."

The guy who objected to the term was Kenn Miller, author of my favorite Vietnam novel, *Tiger the Lurp Dog,* and also author of volume two of what is perhaps the most engrossing unit history ever written, *Six Silent Men,* the three-volume story of the 101st Airborne Long Range Patrol unit in Vietnam. All three authors of *Six Silent Men* were young NCOs, and the book covers the entire history of the unit from activation to deactivation. No self-serving general's memoir here, just the straight, painful, profane, fascinating truth.

I've also seen Miller's team picture from 1969. He was 19, and he looked older then than he does now, totally game-faced and grim as death.

When most guys came home from that conflict they caught a lot of flak. "Baby Killers" was a term that was bandied about a lot.

Probably the most hurt I ever was in my life was after the hardcover of my book *War Story* came out with a painting on the cover of a Special Forces guy holding a wounded child. Both my publisher and I had been in SF in Vietnam. (The book has been in continuous print since 1979 and has sold more than 200,000 copies, but at the time no conventional publisher would touch it.) He took the hardcover on a tour of paperback reprint houses in New York. The first editor he showed it to, a young woman, just took it for granted that the illustration suggested that we had killed that child deliberately, and that we were proud of it. When he told me that it was sort of like being chopped in the gut with an axe.

I missed most of that harassment by being wounded and coming home in hospital channels. I came home to Oklahoma, a conservative state where there was a lot of antiwar sentiment, but no anti-GI sentiment.

Miller went to the University of Michigan in Ann Arbor, one of the most virulently antiwar campuses in the country.

None of the GIs since Vietnam have been so vilified. For one thing, there has been no KGB disinformation campaign against American forces since then. And there has been no army of millions of draft dodgers projecting their collective guilt on those who served. I doubt that soldiers against Saddam will catch that kind of flak. But some will always believe that we do such things.

I have to assume that the people who have such grim imaginings have a vision of a bunch of power-mad thugs blasting everything in their path.

The truth is that when you go in on a combat operation you are scared to death. Nothing I've ever encountered in civilian life has scared me like that—not skydiving, car wrecks, cancer scares, or jealous husbands with guns.

Picture a company-sized (100 to 200 men) assault into a hot LZ. There's the *whop* of many helicopter rotors, choppers landing and disgorging men. There are gunships in orbit around all that, firing rockets into the bush. There are the explosions of rockets all around. There's automatic weapons fire coming from the jungle. In Iraq it would be from wadis and from behind dunes, or maybe from buildings, but you get the idea. And there's your trusty (I meant that satirically, but they're better now) M16, chattering its little song in your hands. Add to that the minor irritation of being sandblasted by dirt kicked up by the rotors. Under those circumstances fear becomes another thing, a live thing that takes your body for its own. The decision-making process so taken for granted in daily life is as forgotten as Ozymandias. An untrained man would simply cower and shit his pants, no matter how brave, because he wouldn't know what to do. A poorly trained man would—and many have—lie in the weeds and shoot wildly in the air. The well-trained man searches his sector for targets, takes up a good prone position, has a good sight picture and sight alignment, takes a breath, lets half of it out, and squeezes the trigger so slowly that when his weapon fires he's mildly surprised. Whoever he was shooting at then either dies or starts calling for a medic.

But the well-trained man is also on autopilot. If a psychiatrist, sitting calmly behind his expensive desk, could somehow examine an infantryman in the throes of combat, the only conclusion he could reach is that the man is clinically insane.

American troops are well trained. They're trained not to commit war crimes and seldom do.

In January of 1964 my commanding officer, Crews McCulloch, a brilliant slab of Missouri cotton farmer, was "advising" a company-sized patrol of Montagnards. He and his headquarters were behind the first platoon when firing broke out ahead. It was just a few rounds. He surged forward through the ranks and met the Montagnard company commander, Nay Re, coming back toward him. "We shoot two VC," Nay Re said, "One dead, one wound."

Crews continued forward to view the enemy casualties. The dead one was a 2-year-old baby boy; the wounded one was his mother. Crews has two daughters, one then a bit younger, one a bit older than the dead boy. He grasped Nay Re by the front of his shirt and jerked him a foot off the ground. "If any member of this strike force shoots another unarmed civilian I will kill him myself, on the spot. Do you understand?" Nay Re gulped and bobbed his head up and down. Then we broke a lot of rules to get a medevac chopper for the wounded mom.

But they view these things differently in Asia. Four months later Nay Re let a hard-core VC cadre we had captured escape. "Where is he?" Crews demanded.

"Oh, he run 'way."

"Why didn't you catch him?"

"He run very fast."

"Then why didn't you shoot him?"

Nay Re gave Crews a hurt look. "You say no shoot man he no have gun. This man no have gun. We take away."

The whole point of a rifle is that you can see what you're shooting at. There's no point in shooting unarmed people because they're not shooting at you. Most civilian casualties are caused by artillery and bombs, which are by definition area weapons, and indiscriminate. When they're used in conjunction with infantry attacks they're called "suppressive fires." Their function is to keep the enemy's head down so you can take his position without getting a lot of your own guys killed. When the enemy position is in an inhabited village, well . . .

The rules of engagement vary from war to war and battle to battle, but in Vietnam the rules were designed to minimize civilian casualties, very much at the expense of the GIs. When you don't use suppressive fires the enemy has a big advantage. There is nothing but what the GI has with him to keep the defenders from killing the attackers.

I was bemoaning the fact that our GIs were called Baby Killers when they lost so many trying to avoid civilian casualties to Mark Berent, a retired air force fighter jock and best-selling author (*Rolling Thunder, Steel Tiger*): "I'd say at least half the casualties on the Wall were a direct result of our efforts to avoid civilian casualties."

"I'd say all of 'em," Mark replied.

From an air force perspective we could have turned all of Vietnam into blasted earth and dead people and not lost a man.

If you knew all the relevant factors (which nobody ever does) beforehand you could just about work out the casualty figures on a calculator. So the question is, "How many GIs are you going to sacrifice to avoid how many dead babies?" Is it worth losing ten GIs to avoid one dead baby? Is one for one okay? One dead GI for a hundred dead babies?

If the combat actions since Vietnam are any indication, the determining factor is television. The American public will accept any number of dead babies if they're just numbers in a newspaper. But if they're a pattern of colored dots on a cathode ray tube, then we have to back off, a lot of GIs die, and we lose the war.

I was home on terminal leave when Lt. William Calley was being tried for the My Lai massacre. I was so outraged at what he had done, at the disgrace he had brought on the U.S. Army, that I actually thought about putting on my uniform and going to Ft. Benning to blow him away. I was being retired of wounds, but I still had my .45, and I shoot pretty well left-handed.

I cleaned the weapon and sat looking at it for about four hours. I didn't do it, of course. It would have just been more of the same. Now I'm glad I didn't. I'd rather be dead than have Lieutenant Calley's dreams.

Warriorhood
Reasons and Influences

Why do I do it? Because I have been blessed with being trained by the best to do what few have had the privilege of being allowed to do. I have been given much, and because of all the men who have influenced me over the years, I have been able to take the skills and talent granted me and stand in the breach, to place myself between my home and those who would do our families harm.

—Steel Parsons,
from "A Path that Began
with My Father and a Typhoon"

A PATH THAT BEGAN WITH MY FATHER AND A TYPHOON

by Steel Parsons

*Chief Warrant Officer (CW5) **Steel Parsons** is an active-duty army aviator with more than 6,200 hours of rotary wing flight time, more than 3,000 of them using night vision goggles (NVGs). He holds a commercial pilot (instrument) certification for rotorcraft and single-engine/multiengine fixed-wing aircraft. He is assigned to D Company, 1st Battalion, 160th Special Operations Aviation Regiment (Airborne). He has held various jobs ranging from assault pilot to flight lead to regiment standardization instructor pilot. He was named the Army Aviation Association of America Trainer of the Year in 1999.*

Mr. Parsons flew combat operations in the Persian Gulf area in 1987, 1988, and 1989 and participated in Operation Just Cause, Operation Desert Shield, Operation Desert Storm, Operation Uphold Democracy, Operation Enduring Freedom, and Operation Iraqi Freedom. He has 27 years of service.

Mr. Parsons is a pressure point control tactics (PPCT) staff instructor and has been working with PPCT since 1988. He has trained various law enforcement organizations in defensive tactics, including the Drug Enforcement Agency (DEA) agents who participated in Operation Snow Cap.

❖

I am the son of a soldier, and not just any soldier. My father joined the army in 1954 after graduating from high school. He led the life of a husband, father, soldier, and warrior, but most of all he led (and still leads) the life of a *man*. When he retired with 20 years of service at the rank of master sergeant (E-8), he had 627 static line parachute jumps, four tours of Vietnam, and had lived the early history of Special Forces. He was Special

Forces qualified in 1961, which was also the year of his first tour of Vietnam. His fourth tour there was in 1968. Who influenced me as a warrior? My father.

I attended first grade when my father was stationed on Okinawa; he would depart twice for Vietnam while we lived on that island. I learned to swim there, and one day in the middle of a typhoon, my father took me out into the storm, with me wearing a swimsuit, mask, and snorkel and attached to a tether line. We walked out into the howling wind and driving rain, and it was glorious. That may be why I enjoy flying and driving in bad weather. My father taught me that the weather (environment) was something you could deal with if you thought and planned for it.

My father's next duty station was Fort Bragg, North Carolina, and we lived in a little area named Kindlewood. All but one man in our neighborhood went to work wearing green fatigues, a green beret, and Special Forces patches on both shoulders. It would be many years before I learned the significance of the patch on the right shoulder. The one man who didn't go to work wearing a green beret was a North Carolina Highway Patrol officer. In 1969, after my father returned from his fourth and last tour of Vietnam, we would find out that the officer had been killed in the line of duty. It was after his death that a concept solidified in my mind. I realized the world was divided into two groups: us, and the others. Police fit into the "us" category. This man taught me that the police protect us at home like the soldier protects us overseas.

I was, and am, a prolific reader. I read *Starship Troopers*, written by Robert A. Heinlein, for the first time when I was 10 years old. Although it was beyond my age group, some things in it were understandable for a boy who had a father completing his third tour of Vietnam while war protesters were starting to make the news. As Lieutenant Colonel Grossman points out in his training, sheep don't like wolves, but they are also scared of the sheepdogs, at least until they need their protection and then only for as long as the danger is present. The point that Heinlein made in his book, one that I have always remembered, is that moral responsibility can only be demonstrated by action.

Being a warrior and willing to place your body between the horrors of war and your home demonstrates moral responsibility. It can't be forced on the unwilling, it can't be taught, and it can't be mandated into a program. In my opinion, those who are unwilling, who don't understand, and who don't wish to understand the concept of the warrior and moral responsibility are poorer in soul. On my most recent tour in Operation Iraqi Freedom, I saw a young Ranger reading *Starship Troopers*. I asked him about it, and he told me that his platoon sergeant had recommended it as a good book on leadership. (In my opinion, the movie did a great disservice to the book, and if you have only seen the movie, please, please read it.) Where did I learn about the concept of civic responsibility and being a warrior? My father, a North Carolina Highway Patrol Officer who died in the line of duty, and Robert A. Heinlein.

During my father's fourth tour of Vietnam, we moved to his hometown in Illinois. We settled in and he departed. It was the first time I had lived in a civilian community, and I didn't fit in. The children were not well behaved, they did not address adults with "sir" or "ma'am," and they were not disciplined regarding use of force (schoolyard fights). They also said a lot of bad things about soldiers. I resented that and came to realize that civilians were not in the "us" category and didn't know what they were talking about (ignorant, not stupid). That is where I learned that the warrior is not always appreciated and that it is the responsibility of our civilian leadership to use us wisely. I also discovered that I missed the military environment, people like me.

My father's last overseas assignment prior to his retirement was with the 8th Special Forces Group in Panama. During the three years and eight months that we lived there, from 7th through 10th grade, I would become an Eagle Scout, walk the Las Cruces Trail that the Spanish conquistadors used to transport their gold across the isthmus, climb a mountain that would let me see the Atlantic and Pacific oceans at the same time, and become SCUBA certified. I can think of no better place for a boy to start growing up.

Due to the nature of the assignment, the military supported the Boy Scouts for 50-mile hikes, canoe trips, and summer camp. Whenever we went camping, there were fathers with us who wore Green Berets at work and had a Special Forces patch on both shoulders. I knew these men were combat veterans who had done their duty in spite of bad leadership on both the civilian and military sides of our government. I realized that these men, camping with us, teaching us survival skills and how to "live with the environment," were also fathers, husbands, men dedicated to their families, and, most important of all, the warriors who kept the bad men away from us.

When my father retired and moved us to a rural farming community in Illinois, I spent three years realizing that I didn't know what I would do as an adult. The thought of working construction or a factory job depressed me, and I missed the military environment. I wanted to fly, but my grades weren't quite good enough for a scholarship, and my father made about $3 a year too much for grants (almost not a joke). One of his old Special Forces friends had left Special Forces and attended flight school as a warrant officer. After he explained how it worked, I went to an army recruiter in 1976 and asked him what I had to do to become a warrant officer helicopter pilot. I was starting on the road back to the environment I thought of as "home."

Basic training was conducted at Fort Jackson, South Carolina. Drill Sergeant Pankuk and Drill Sergeant Woodward made my life hell but introduced me to the concept of the professional and the amateur. On his worst day, a professional always performed to standard, but an amateur on his best day might meet the standard of the professional. During that time, I discovered what I was looking for: to serve and work in the company of professionals—soldiers/warriors. Who influenced me as a warrior? Standard army answer: my drill sergeants.

Initial entry into the warrant officer candidate flight school was a living hell for the first four months. Our class started with 33 candidates, but nine months later 16 graduated as warrant officer aviators. During that time, my flight instructors repeated over and over the importance of doing things right every time. Mistakes kill—not just you, but also your crew and, most importantly, the men who climb in the back of your aircraft putting their trust in your skill and judgment. My instrument instructor pilot (IP) was one of the first three helicopter pilots to fly a helicopter into the clouds intentionally to prove that the platform was stable enough for controlled flight in an instrument environment (no reference to the ground and all navigation using dead reckoning and radio navigation systems). Unintentional flight into the clouds is one of the greatest killers of military and civilian pilots (remember Kennedy?). That IP was a perfectionist. He would tell me over and over: "We do things one step at a time. We do each step perfectly, then we forget it and go to the next step." In April 2003, I would be using a special terrain-following radar system on my aircraft that would allow me to fly in the clouds at 300 feet above the ground with none of the standard instrument-flying air traffic controls and do it flawlessly. That flight would originate from our Forward Support Base (FSB) and terminate at a major Iraqi airfield where the shooting was still going on.

My instrument IP died more than 20 years ago in an accident. I know I was able to fly that mission because of the knowledge and skill he poured into me. One step at a time, each step perfectly executed, then forget it and go on to the next step. Executed in a professional, workmanlike manner.

When I graduated from flight school, I was 19 years old and held the rank of warrant officer one (WO1). I would be entrusted with a million-dollar helicopter but couldn't buy a beer in California. It was a sobering realization that I had legal authority over other men, but most importantly, I had responsibility riding heavily on my shoulders, since you don't get many mistakes with a helicopter.

My first assignment was in C Troop, 3rd Squadron, 4th Cavalry, Schofield Barracks, Hawaii. When I arrived, the youngest man in our platoon was 26, everyone was married (at least once), and everyone had at least one tour in Vietnam, with a minimum flight time of 1,900 hours. I was the first WO1 the unit had been assigned since their return from Vietnam. I was 19, single, and had 180 hours of flight time. Three pilots took me under their wings and pointed me in the direction I have been walking for 26 years of rated aviation service.

CW3 Rod Labrum was an old UH-1C/UH-1M gunship pilot who taught me how to finesse a UH-1H (Huey) helicopter into the air when it couldn't fly according to the performance charts. We would fly to the north shore of the island of Molokai, and he would teach me how to squeeze the maximum performance out of the aircraft for the minimal power applied by "gliding" on the thermals and vertical currents. I would learn by doing, making mistakes, and paying for my lessons in beer.

In 1989, during Operation Just Cause in the Republic of Panama, my crew pulled 28 Rangers out of a landing zone (LZ) using an MH-60A Blackhawk helicopter. They were literally stacked to the ceiling, and the aircraft was badly underpowered due to the temperature and the fuel load we carried. We performed the extraction of the Rangers after operating for 48 hours with less than 3 hours of sleep total. CW3 Dave Ambrose taught me about the importance of knowing the regulations and knowing when to apply them, as well as the importance of instrument flight proficiency. There have been many nights in my special operations aviation career when I was flying on top of the trees, working my way through low clouds with a formation behind me, trying to get our shooters into a target or get them out. Dave trained me to a standard where I had the proficiency and judgment for picking the time and place to "push the envelope." No one died when I was leading the flight.

CW4 Joe Taylor taught me how to be a maintenance officer and the importance of knowing the aircraft inside and out. The aircraft I flew had so many modifications made to them over time that it got to the point where they no longer resembled a UH-60, and a UH-60–qualified pilot couldn't even start the MH-60. It was at that point that I understood what Joe was trying to teach me: the importance of knowing "how does it know, and how does it do." This became critical to my ability to make the hard decisions on when I should fly that aircraft (it's broken, but is it *really* broken?) and when I shouldn't, allowing me to ensure that the missions succeeded. Most importantly, Joe taught me to be an officer, to be the can-do guy who motivates his troops to get the job done.

Two years later, I endured, and passed, a tough five-day assessment process to determine whether I was trainable for Task Force 160. There, everything I had learned about the warrior ethic, the soldier's creed, and flying would be pushed beyond the limits.

The same week I assessed for the unit, a Task Force CH-47 crashed off the coast of Virginia Beach, Virginia. The week I signed into the unit, another CH-47 crashed in the Great Lakes area. One month after I signed in, we had a UH-60A come apart in flight and kill the three men on board. Two of the three accidents could be summed up in one simple phrase: "failure to adhere to published procedures." During the month of October 1983, we would lose three more men in two crashes; only one was a combat fatality (Grenada). Our unit lost 18 men in 1983. We were pushing the edge of night vision goggle (NVG) technology. As in the law enforcement community, most of our tactics, techniques, and procedures (TTPs) are written in blood.

During Operation Just Cause, we had two combat casualties. The two pilots were rearming and refueling an attack helicopter at Ft. Sherman, Panama, when they got a call that the guys on the ground in Colón were in contact and needed close air support. They heard the call and went to help without their wingman, as he was refueling. They helped the ground guys but were shot down. They were heavy with ammo and fuel and tried to "stretch their glide." (Yes, a helicopter does glide, just not too well or too far.) Ten minutes later, I was looking down at a blackened, smoking helicopter and two dead aviators. Someone on the ground was in trouble, and these warriors didn't hesitate. They pushed it to the limit, saved the guys on the ground, and paid the ultimate price for their aggressiveness. To this day, I can only hope I would perform to the standard they did.

Most readers have probably seen the movie *Black Hawk Down*. I did not deploy for operation Gothic Serpent, but I knew all the men who died and the ones who made it back. CW4 (Ret.) Michael Durant did exactly as he had been trained to do. I learned another facet of being a warrior from him: *focus, and do what must be done to return with honor.*

During Desert Storm in 1991, or, as some are referring to it now, Gulf War 1, we conducted a medevac for one of the units we support. We lost an MH-60, four crewmen, two medics, and one of our shooters. The shooter was injured when he fell off a mountain. The weather was not what the forecasters had predicted. It was so bad the crew had to conduct a self-generated instrument approach on their return to the forward operating base. They were not successful, and the aircraft crashed, killing all seven men. I knew the technology existed that would allow us to fly that mission successfully, but we didn't have it.

In 1997, when our terrain-following radar system was certified, I was directed to develop a 17-day training program. During the qualification syllabus, the crews would not be available for support missions. The regiment commander asked me how he was supposed to justify so large a diversion of resources to the ground force commanders who would not have their standard number of airframes to support them for the next six months. I told him that all he had to do was tell them that if we'd had this system in 1991, those seven men would be alive today. He told me that he didn't think that was an accurate statement, and I told him that I did. My training syllabus was approved.

I can point to most of the technology and equipment improvements on our aircraft and give names of men who would be living today if we had only been able to give them then what we have now. That is another reason for my ruthlessness on training to standard. In the regular army, most aviation units have a lower accident rate than we do. However, when we go to combat, our accident rate stays the same, and the army accident rate goes up. We truly do *train as we fight*. There is a price to be paid, and it is always in blood. During his change of command, one of my commanders gave us a quote: "To those who are given much, much is expected." I believe that this is a very appropriate statement for all warriors. We have been given much, and after the events of September 11, 2001, most assuredly, much is expected of us.

I have been trained by the best, and I have worked with the best. During my aviation career I have gone from flying the UH-1H to flying the MH-60K. The MH-60K is a "glass cockpit" and has none of the traditional dials and gauges. Each pilot has two multi-function displays, and the aircraft is run by computer. It is capable of air refueling from an HC/MC-130 and can fly in the clouds as low as 100 feet above the ground.

I have stayed alive through more than 20 years in this unit because of the people I grew up with, who trained me and made me understand the importance and righteousness of the job I do. No other army, air force, navy, or Marine unit could do what we do. We're the best, and I have come up through the ranks to where I was the regiment standardization officer. I have seen two of my company commanders rise to the rank of major general and general. I have cried looking at the accident sites, feeling the pain of the families who will never see their husbands and fathers come home again. But I know that each death was not in vain. We train and push the limit because, well, as I was taught when I first got to the unit: *failure is not acceptable.* When you walk the edge long enough, sometimes you slip and fall. That slip might mean broken sheet metal, it might mean a totaled aircraft with injured crew, or it might mean a smoking hole in the ground. No, these warriors did not die in vain.

My unit has been in existence for 23 years, and we have lost, on average, more than two men a year to combat or accidents. From the time I assessed to the present, 51 men have died in training or combat in my unit. In aviation, you can die just as quickly in training as you can in combat.

Why do I do it? Because I have been blessed with being trained by the *best* to do what few have had the privilege of being allowed to do. I have been given much, and because of all the men who have influenced me over the years, I have been able to take the skills and talent granted me and stand in the breach, to place myself between my home and those who would do our families harm. Why do I do it? Because I can, and most can't. I am the son of a warrior who has showed me the path and, to this day, lives by the code of the warrior.

Since the day my father took me out into a typhoon, I too have been walking that path.

CHAPTER 12

Killing

"*When you bayonet someone, you pick a point on him, your hands slide up the stock and grip of your rifle, your feet skid. Training doesn't prepare you for that. The bolt pinches the web of your hand, cuts in, and barks your knuckle. . . . You feel the pop, it [the bayonet] slides in, the scrape of blade on rib, his movement, you feel it through the metal of your rifle, he goes down and you're spinning opposite him, rising as he goes down. You feel a heartbeat, his or yours. The last breath is hot and wet, it's blown out on you, you breathe it in. It's hard to pull the bayonet from a man's ribs with the stock slippery with blood and sweat.*"

—an old Marine,
talking with Tom Martin in
"What They Won't Tell Their Wives"

WARRIOR SENSE

by Sang H. Kim

Sang H. Kim, *born in Taegu, South Korea, served as a special agent in the South Korean Defense Security Command before coming to the United States in 1985. A lifelong martial artist, he has established himself as a leading figure in the martial arts world and traveled three continents extensively, giving seminars on tae kwon do and the combat art of junsado in Asia, Europe, and North America. Mr. Kim has written nine books on the subjects of martial arts and philosophy, including* Combat Strategy *and* The Art of Harmony, *published by Turtle Press (www.turtlepress.com).*

❖

Load . . . aim . . . fire! For eight weeks, my shooting instructor at Nonsan Military Training Center repeated this command, and for eight weeks I never hesitated to follow his orders. I enjoyed firearms training and prided myself on my abilities on the range. My training, I felt, was preparing me for what I would face in the DMZ as a member of the South Korean Defense Security Command, just as my years of martial arts training had prepared me for sparring matches, schoolyard fights, and combat survival training.

What I had not yet fully realized as a young soldier two years out of high school was how different training was from reality. Early one morning in the summer of 1981, I was assigned to patrol the South Korean side of the DMZ fence. While four other members of my team were having a cigarette break, I went into the woods to relieve myself. Suddenly I heard a movement behind a rock. I thought maybe it was a deer or rabbit, so I didn't pay much mind to it. The DMZ is home to everything from small animals to wild boar. When I heard it again, closer this time, I scanned the other side of the fence, M16 at the ready. On the other side, I was surprised to see a North Korean soldier aiming an

---

AK semiautomatic at me. He looked as young and as frightened as I was. We stood there aiming our guns at each other, neither of us moving.

In my head I could hear Sergeant Park shouting, *Load . . . aim . . . fire!* as if he were standing right behind me. *Fire! Fire, dammit!* I had my loaded weapon aimed at the enemy, but I could not bring myself to fire. I saw the tip of his gun shaking through the sight of my own shaking M16. I was ready to fire, I told myself, as I heard Sergeant Park screaming in my head. I considered calling my team members to alert them but realized that if I did, the North Korean would probably shoot me without hesitation. Once that happened, not only would one or both of us likely be dead, but all hell would break loose along what was already a volatile border.

We stood looking at each other for a long time. The truth is that when you look a man in the eyes, you can't shoot him without just cause. As members of opposing militaries, we were enemies sworn to shoot and kill each other on sight. For either one of us, it would have been an easy kill and a sure road to becoming a national hero.

It seemed that we stood there for a hundred years, until an unspoken agreement emerged. He moved a step back. At first I thought he was plotting something unexpected to distract me from shooting, but as he moved, he lowered his weapon just slightly. I took a step back and did the same. He moved again and I followed, step by step, until he felt safe enough to scurry off into the brush. When he finally disappeared from sight, I ran out of the woods like I was running for my life. When I reported the incident to my superior, he told me I was a coward for not shooting the enemy.

Maybe I was. I thought so, for a while. I'd had the opportunity to do what I had been trained to do, and I had not done it. It took many years for me to see the difference between acting out of cowardice and exercising my personal judgment. My superior officers trained me to have only one option—to shoot—and though I exercised that option on other occasions, this one particular time, I was given a second option. If I had reacted immediately out of duty or fear—both very real motivations for a young soldier—that second option, the option not to shoot, would not have been available to me.

The ironic thing is, my days of repetitive drilling on the range allowed me to load and aim my weapon, but not fire it. Drilling is like sight. When you look at a situation in combat, you take in the elements that appear before you. You might see what your enemy looks like, how close he is, what weapons he carries, how big or small he is, what expression he wears on his face, and the position of his body. If you're observant, you'll also see your surroundings—the surface of the ground, the location of doorways or walls, the presence of other people, the position of large and small objects. However, sight itself does not allow you to react to the situation. Through sight, you collect information that you will use to formulate a reaction, just as through drilling you assemble a collection of physical options. Each drill adds another piece to the puzzle of your combat arsenal, but in and of itself, drilling is useless without tasting reality. There were no North Korean soldiers standing at the other end of the firing range while my sergeant was barking out his commands. I shot faceless, soulless paper targets and thought I was prepared to shoot a living, breathing human. Drilling prepared me to execute the physical actions required to perform the task of shooting, but it did not prepare me to stare across the DMZ and decide the fate of another man.

To react to a situation, you need to do more than simply see what is in front of you. Based on what you see, you formulate a sense of the situation and make a series of conscious and unconscious decisions. Based on the North Korean's evident fear and uncertainty, I made a conscious choice not to be the aggressor and, perhaps sensing this, he felt he had the option to begin retreating first. What we each saw—an enemy soldier aiming an automatic weapon at us across a hostile border—said shoot, but our senses refuted that choice. I can't say what it was about the situation that made the other man choose to step back first. Maybe he was a rookie who was afraid of dying and decided to take his chances. Perhaps he thought about his wife or children at home. Maybe he was a highly trained warrior who sensed that this kill wasn't a necessary one. Or maybe the bottom line is that we were both selfish, fragile human beings who preferred our own lives to our mutual death. I clearly remember wanting to be done with the confrontation one way or the other, and surely he felt the same.

I think the ability to sense the nuance of a combat situation and to make sense of chaos is something that begins on the firing range or in basic training, but only confrontation with the enemy allows a warrior to fine-tune his senses and to create additional options. Not shooting, I believe, takes as much confidence in your training as shooting. Each has its place in the warrior's arsenal. The choice I made caused me to be labeled a coward at the time, but it gave me satisfaction in my soul. Although the North Korean soldier was my enemy by fate, I truly hope that he is now taking good care of his kids and wife across the border. There is a proverb that says the true master hits the enemy with the back of the sword rather than slicing with the blade. There is a time for using the blade and a time for keeping the sword sheathed as well.

Load . . . aim . . . fire! It's a definite process to eliminate an obstacle, but looking back at the changes over the past 22 years on the Korean Peninsula, it was not my best option at that time. Dialogue, humanism, and reasoning are more difficult but provide us with choices and, at times, solutions. In the end, I didn't mind being called a coward, but I resented those who called my enemy a coward. If he hadn't stepped back first, I might not be writing this. Though I was not ready to shoot, I was not ready to step back either. In some ways, I am ashamed that I did not have the courage to step back first and that I was so attached to my own political ideals and personal sense of duty to a cause that I barely understood. How can I not appreciate the courage it took to be the first to step back? In doing so, he saved two lives. Slicing the enemy is the most direct way to destroy the fear within and without. It is a response we can easily train for, learn, and apply without a great deal of thought. Turning the blade over and striking the enemy requires spiritual confidence, belief, guts, awe, and a willingness to put faith in your personal judgment.

Life, ultimately, is the goal of a warrior.

WHEN COPS KILL

by Loren W. Christensen

Loren W. Christensen's *biography can be found at the back of* *this book. This essay is based on* Deadly Force Encounters: What Cops Need to Mentally and Physically Prepare for and Survive a Gunfight *by Loren W. Christensen and Dr. Alexis Artwohl (Paladin Press, 1997).*

❖

"I went to work, I met a guy, we had a conversation, then I killed him."

That is how one officer summed up his shooting in a single sentence. It's simple, void of descriptive detail and emotion. Just the facts. Actually, the sentence describes most police shootings, except for those where the meeting is so fast and furious that there is no time for conversation. The irony is that the simplicity of the sentence belies the complexity of the event—especially the aftermath, which is often the deciding factor in whether an officer suffers from post-traumatic stress disorder (PTSD).

It was in the late 1980s when I first got the idea for writing a book about police officers who have killed in the line of duty. I had partnered with or worked around several who had been forced to defend themselves using deadly force, and each one had been changed by the experience, many profoundly so. Some sadly so. A few irreparably so, as many of the latter group sought solace in alcohol, several became problem employees, a few resigned early, and a couple ate their guns.

My plan was to create a book where officers would explain in their own words, without editorial interference, what had happened and how it affected them. I would write an introduction, and then each chapter would be a transcript of each officer's story as told to my tape recorder. To get a feel for the project, I approached an officer who'd had a recent shooting to see if he was willing to sit down and talk about his experience. It was actually his second fatal shooting, this one a teenage boy in a business district firing a rifle at anyone unfortunate enough to be in his view. The officer and his partner took cover and commanded the young shooter to drop the rifle, but they were ignored. There was no time to set up a perimeter or negotiate. The officers had no choice but to fire.

I told the officer of my book idea and asked if he would be interested in talking to me. He said that he probably would, but it was too soon for him, as he was still trying to work through what happened and come to terms with it. It had been only a few months since the encounter with the rifle-wielding boy, and two years since his first shooting. Maybe after a while, he said.

Later the officer went on a rampage, knocking over desks and threatening a lieutenant. He subsequently left the agency on a stress-related injury.

I put the project on hold for a couple of years while I worked on other writing projects, but then I started to get the itch again. One day I ran into my friend Deputy Chief Dave Butzer and told him about wanting to write a book on officers who have used deadly force. He said that his wife, Dr. Alexis Artwohl, who I knew to be a leading authority on the psychological implications of police officers using deadly force, had also been thinking about writing a book on the subject, and that I should give her a call. Although I had attended one of her presentations on officer-involved shootings, I had never met her. So making the call was a tad awkward. Until she answered the phone.

Dr. Artwohl has spent most of her adult life talking with combat soldiers and cops, and while her articulation clearly reflects her education, her use of cop slang and salty language reflects her years in the trenches. We clicked immediately and, after talking for only 15 minutes, agreed to merge our experiences and ideas on the subject to coauthor a book about how police officers can prepare for a deadly force encounter, survive it as it happens, and survive the often traumatic aftermath.

We began by interviewing officers who have killed. Dr. Artwohl contacted most of them, I assumed because she had seen them on a doctor/patient basis after their shootings, though I was to learn that she held the doctor/patient confidentiality next to her heart. Never once did she say whether an officer was currently, or had been, a patient. Sometimes an officer would say during an interview that he had seen her, but mostly I didn't know. Mostly it didn't matter.

We interviewed officers at her office, her home, my home, and their homes. Some sessions lasted two hours; most lasted longer. The first, which we did in Dr. Artwohl's office, lasted three hours, though it seemed like ten. It was grueling, heart-wrenching, and when it was over I was exhausted, drained, and unsure whether could do another interview.

"How can you do this day after day?" I asked her on the phone a couple of hours after I'd gotten home and had taken a nap. "I'm beat, emotionally drained. That interview depleted me. . . . I don't know if I can do this book."

The officer we had talked with had been one of three who had rushed into the bedroom of a 12-year-old taken hostage by a mentally deranged man after he had broken into the home, prowled about, and found the sleeping boy. Earlier, a number of officers had surrounded the place and tried to negotiate with him, but when he screamed that he had already cut the boy and was going to finish him off on the count of "one," and then began counting backwards from five, the three closest officers charged up the staircase to the boy's room. And burst through the bedroom door.

Into the horror.

The man sat on the edge of the bed, the terrified boy between his legs shielding the man's body, the knife at the side of the boy's throat. The man's maniacal voice continued the countdown: "Four, three, two . . ." He raised his arm to make the slice. The officers fired. A hail of bullets.

"I could see my rounds hit the man's chest," the officer told us, believing it.

The firing, the roar, stopped. A profound silence.

The man lay dead across the bed, his body riddled with holes. The boy, too, was slumped over, shot, close to death.

Despite desperate efforts by doctors, the boy died a few hours later.

"The officer was in so much pain," I said to Alexis on the phone. "He was crying. It was tearing him up. I just don't know if I . . ."

She talked to me for a long time about how indeed it was tough, but the book was important for officers and the public. I could do it, she said.

She was right: I kept writing and doing interviews with her, and they did get easier, but not by much.

The second officer, involved in the same shooting, had been involved in another four and half years earlier. In that one he had gone to back up an officer and ended up in a foot chase with a man high on methamphetamine. They fought, but the man was powerful and impervious to pain, even when struck by the officer's baton. A razor appeared in the man's hand, and he advanced on the officer, ignoring commands to freeze. When the man had advanced to within three feet, the officer fired, two in the head, two in the body.

The officer looked down at the body, at a trail of blood creeping toward a tattoo on the man's biceps, an image of two hands handcuffed together, the words underneath reading, "Mother tried." An image that burned into the officer's mind, forever.

At the detective's office, the officer was told that the hospital called to say the man was going to die, and that he should prepare himself for that. The officer went home and sat, smoked, contemplated—for three days. The shooting happened on a Monday. Friday the officer returned to work, hit the street, and went immediately to the hospital to check on the man. He had died, medical staff told him. Depressed, the officer returned to the precinct, only to be told by the desk officer that the hospital called and said they had made a mistake: the man was still alive but had slipped into a coma. They couldn't say when he would come out of it.

He would remain in the coma for four and a half years, and then die.

The day it happened the officer's supervisor called immediately and told him. "I didn't want to stay at home," the officer said. "I wanted to be at work with my pals."

He went to work that night, and a few hours into the shift, he would be standing with two other officers, firing bullets into a man holding a 12-year-old boy hostage. One of those bullets, from one of those officers, would kill the boy.

The officer sought out a psychologist after that shooting, but after a few weeks, he was dissatisfied with the man's help, or lack of it. He switched to Dr. Artwohl, and with her he began to come to terms with the two deadly force encounters. "I just felt I was surrounded in a cloud of death, and I kept asking what I had done to deserve this. In time I came to understand that I hadn't done anything, that these were just events that I happened to be part of. I began to realize that shit happens." One day, after seven months, he and the doctor decided he didn't have to come in to see her anymore.

That night he got into a third shooting.

All of the officers we interviewed had tragic tales to tell. There was the female LAPD officer with five years of street experience who moved to a relatively safer city and joined its smaller agency to escape the violence of the gang-infested streets of Los Angeles. Six months later, a 52-year-old woman ran toward her, pointing a gun, ignoring her commands to drop it. Three bullets brought the woman down.

There was the SWAT officer who had killed three people on three separate occasions. "There have been times," he said, "when I've wondered if for some reason it's my destiny to shoot people for the police department."

The first was a man who had just stabbed his second victim in 24 hours. The officer shot him just seconds before he would have been victim number three. A few months later his SWAT team confronted a bank robber holding a pregnant woman hostage, with one arm around her neck and a .357 pointed at her head. A flashbang tossed into the room startled him enough to make him stumble away from the woman, clearing a pathway so the officer and his partner could fire their MP5s into his face.

A few months later, the officer was back at work conducting a SWAT entry into a fortified drug house. Several things happened at once: one of the suspects came out on a back patio, saw the officers, shouted, "Police!" and then ran back inside; a SWAT officer on one side of the house confronted an attack dog and fired a burst into it; officers on another side smashed out the windows of a room where they knew weapons were stored so they could watch to see that no one got to them; and a SWAT armored car hooked up to the front door and ripped it from its hinges.

The officer who had already killed two people charged through the now open door with two other SWAT members. They advanced on a man and woman sitting on a couch and a lone man sitting in a chair next to them, watching the suspects over their MP5s and shouting for them to get on the floor. But in one swift motion, the lone man stood and thrust a derringer over the officer's MP5. All three officers fired, sending the stupid man to hell.

We talked to another officer who told us of how he and his partner had just cleared the precinct when a radio call sent them to a 7-11 convenience store on a fight between the clerk and a shoplifter. As they pulled into the store lot, they saw the clerk fighting at one corner and a small crowd at the other arguing with a very tall black man. Just as the officers stuffed the shoplifter into the back of their police car, the ruckus at the far corner became more boisterous. They looked over to see the black man hit another man in the chest. The police were to learn later that the black man, who stood six feet seven and weighed 275 pounds, had been preventing people from going to the clerk's aid.

The officer telling us the story said his partner approached the man from the front while he approached from behind. When the big man knocked his partner back, he grabbed the man and bent him backward, wrapped his arm around his neck, and applied a carotid artery sleeper hold. A moment later the big man lay unconscious at the officer's feet. But instead of sputtering awake a few seconds later as is the norm, the man remained motionless, and an awful rattling noise emitted from his throat. They asked dispatch for an ambulance but a third officer, who had just arrived, canceled it, thinking it had been ordered for the clerk, who was not hurt. The officers began CPR and continued it until another ambulance arrived. A short while later at the detectives' division, a call from the hospital informed them that the man had died.

We interviewed many officers over the months we worked on the book, most of whom had come to terms with what had happened, though some weren't quite there yet. The stories were all tragic, powerful, sometimes gut-wrenching. Some kept me awake at night; all instilled in me a heavy sense of responsibility to work with Dr. Artwohl to tell their stories true, to show what these warriors go through when forced to defend their lives or the lives of others.

Police officers solve problems and protect people. It's what they do. As a solver of problems, a protector of people, and a cop who loves his fellow officers, I often went to bed enraged that they had had these horrific experiences, had suffered afterwards—their families, too, and their friends. The suspects made the decision to fight, and the officers won. Seldom does the public say thank you; mostly they are ungrateful and couldn't care less. Then there are the squeaky wheels—citizens, politicians, and the media—who use the tragedy for their own agendas. Sometimes the lack of support comes from the officers' own agency, by upper echelon placating the media, the mayor, and the public, while walking on the officers in the process.

Warriors go toward the violence. Sometimes it lasts for a few minutes, though usually it explodes and ends in a few seconds. Its repercussions, though, can last for months, sometimes years. While there were some officers who had taken only a few days off after their deadly incident and said they had not had any lasting issues or repercussions, others we talked with had. Some had received months, even years, of therapy; one or two were still getting it years later.

But whether they had returned immediately to duty or had sought help for what they had gone through, all had grown from the experience. They had risen above the fray, the turmoil, and the politics that surround most police shootings and had arrived at a place where they were emotionally, spiritually, and intellectually stronger than before their deadly force encounters.

I have practiced the martial arts since 1965, rarely going more than a couple of days without training. I have always thought that my decades of study have developed an iron discipline, and my meditation and self-hypnosis have helped me become centered, calm, and introspective.

But I was humbled after working on *Deadly Force Encounters* with Dr. Artwohl, hearing these warriors talk about their experiences and the process they went through to survive the horrific aftermath and to grow in character and wisdom. The place I had risen to at that point, from my years of martial arts training and peripheral studies, paled in comparison to where these warriors had ascended to. Either through profound thinking, help from therapists, support and help from peers who have been in the same place, or a relationship with their God, these warriors had come to terms with what had happened and were ready to do it again should it be necessary. They had faced the dragon, dusted off the debris, and returned to the fight.

Why would they go back in?

It's what warriors do.

❖

Note: How well an officer recovers is determined by his physical and psychological makeup, the intricacies of the incident, and how he is treated in the days and weeks after the event by his superiors, investigators, media, community, friends, and family. Among those officers who develop PTSD, some experience problems immediately, whereas others won't experience them for months or even years. Many officers have problems afterward but won't recognize them as such, or will try to ignore or hide them. Some want help, but their agency won't offer it.

Dr. Alexis Artwohl says, "Assuming that officers are not treated inappropriately, most will recover from the psychological impact within about a month. However, a significant minority will go on to develop symptoms of post-traumatic stress disorder. It's essential that they have access to high-quality mental health care if that happens. Officers and agencies should seek licensed mental health providers who have expertise both with trauma and working with law enforcement personnel."

WHAT THEY WON'T TELL THEIR WIVES

by Tom Martin

Tom Martin, a former U.S. Marine; former combat arms officer, 10th Mountain Division; and current correctional professional, writes about survival and prison. A habitual and continual observer and recorder, he studies core motivations of people. In addition to teaching different agencies and groups about offender/criminal manipulation, Mr. Martin has also provided television, newspaper, and radio interviews on extreme survival situations. His book Behind Prison Walls: The Real World of Working in Today's Prisons *is available at www.paladin-press.com.*

❖

I waited until we were alone to allow for privacy and an anticipated reaction before I asked the question that should never be asked. The warm quiet of night in a correctional facility, with two veterans speaking, appeared as appropriate a place as any to have a conversation to cap my 20 years of studying an aspect of humanity.

"What is it like for a warrior to kill human beings?"

I would ask *the* question so that I might better understand one aspect of humanity, of being a warrior, and so that I might share the experience with others like me, who'd never taken a human life.

"I know I don't have a right to ask this, but have you killed people?" I'm not subtle, and I knew we'd come along enough in our discussions that William knew my intentions. I also knew what his answer was without its having been discussed before.

Perhaps this made my faux pas worse.

He looked down, quiet suddenly. Then his eyes flicked up; he frowned. William hadn't softened with age from being the early Vietnam War veteran and hero by definition of award. For a fraction of a second, I felt something I'd not admit was concern, but if he'd risen out of his chair I'd have been in trouble.

"You're damn right! You don't have a right to ask that question." He paused, settling a bit. "Fuck you," he added, but his tone was level, calm.

I gave William time.

I've done this before—studying, learning about different people, venturing into private thoughts and feelings where I didn't belong. In other cases, for other issues, the caution of interrogating criminals had directed the pace, or the sensitivities of questioning civilians had slowed my rate of discovery. This time my approach was tempered by my respect for a veteran, though I wanted and needed to know all he'd share.

His eyes stared past me into memories. He understood precisely where I came from, and he knew that by his answering the question, I'd be able to answer the questions in writing for others. Perhaps others who'd crossed the line, who'd killed, might not have to answer the question if it was in print. Perhaps men like him might be better understood. Perhaps he felt a need to discuss his thoughts and feelings.

He'd not taken opportunities to shift the conversation, and now he was ready to divulge.

"I've killed people."

He'd killed four people, to be more precise.

The man—still a skilled shooter, still working in a law enforcement role, although into his 60s, and also periodically moonlighting in armed security—had shot men in the past. He had a unique legacy.

He'd killed every man he'd shot.

"What did you feel?" I asked. *What did you, a warrior, feel when you did the killing and after you killed?* We were finally where I needed to be for my understanding.

"Anger and fear," he replied without hesitation. "Anger one time. Fear the other time. Afterwards, it was just something that happened."

"Why did you decide to kill?" I asked, knowing that William was a direct person; I didn't need a sophisticated question to convey that I wanted to know how he overcame any aversion to taking human lives.

I wanted the core.

"I didn't. I just did. If I didn't I'd have been killed." He almost laughed off the question as one with too evident an answer. He wasn't in a laughing mood.

"What was your motivation; what drove you?"

"Other guys relied on me. I didn't want to let anyone down." Then he told me about the incidents, providing details that are private and irrelevant to this piece, but he told me what I'd heard before.

He fought because of the men around him, not for the United States, or the abstract of bringing democracy to a foreign land, or to fight Communism.

"Any regrets?" I asked.

"No. No regrets," he stated casually, no hesitation.

"Thank you," I said quietly.

"You know, I've told you more than I've ever told my wife." He rose. "And unless you have any other deeply personal questions, I'm going out to have a smoke."

❖

Twenty years before I began that conversation with William, I'd become interested in the extremes of human experiences. I'd been introduced to a new reality during basic training at the Marine Corps recruit depot in San Diego. The Marine Corps loves its history, and they proudly share it with recruits whenever possible. I remember the drills bringing in an old vet who told us about his experiences in Khe Sanh, Vietnam.

What stunned me was the matter-of-fact means of describing combat—about being shot; of shooting back; of being wounded; of lying on the ground bleeding and cursing luck, the enemy, and the odd, idle thoughts that go through one's mind when someone bleeds until a loss of consciousness. I had no doubt combat veterans endured a rite of passage that changed them immeasurably, noticeably to those who knew them before they crossed a line, but it was the *ordinariness* with which they accepted what happened that fascinated me.

That began my study of the experience of being a warrior and of killing in war, and early exposure to the real individuals. The warriors, I learned over the years, were the ones who performed as required, perhaps beyond the call, but didn't have many regrets. I read the books as a preparation, and I began informally interviewing veterans, separating wheat from chaff.

I'd weeded through posers—those who claimed to be veterans and combat veterans but weren't. I spoke with the traumatized and found damn few true warriors who had actually fought there. One individual whom many considered to have gone through a personal hell in Vietnam turned out to have been a cook aboard a very large naval vessel off the coast of Vietnam. He wandered around in jungle fatigues he was never issued and complained of nightmares about Vietnam. I learned quickly that he didn't even see a shot fired except from the turret of his own ship.

I've spoken with those whose experiences, due to location and lack of enemy activity, didn't merit their being given the title of true warrior. The fighting they knew was always reported to them, heard in the distance, or beyond their immediate area. Many of them were glad not to have been through more.

I respect their service, in spite of their skewed portrayals of what it entailed, and they provided me more contrast when studying the *true* warriors.

I've talked to hundreds of veterans, but among the many I've spoken to, William and two others best illustrate the commonalities among warriors who have taken lives in that context.

They held few if any regrets; they didn't share their experiences with their wives; and they never spoke of patriotism, democracy, or heroism as motivators. They discussed killing directly. They mentioned the value of instinct, training, and reflex. One mortar man, I remember, specifically praised his weapon and the accuracy his crew attained in combat. He was pleased with the weapon, talked about fire missions, some within his actual sight. Unlike most veterans, he laughed and joked about the enemy but he grew less humorous when talking about when he conducted what was for him a rare battle damage assessment—actually walking amid those he'd helped eliminate. His awe with the power of explosions on human beings remained.

I spoke with many, many combat veterans.

Direct quotes are impossible, but I remember well what they shared.

Yet only some stick in solid detail.

A few years past basic training, an exposure to a warrior came unexpectedly and unsolicited.

While sitting in a Ford dealership in Tacoma, Washington, I impatiently waited for the upgrades and modifications to my new van. I was a young Marine back then with places to go, things to do. I sat on a couch, flipping pages of a magazine on the coffee table before me. I didn't pay too much attention to an older couple, no more than a quick glance and appraisal of the wife escorting her tall, silent husband to a chair with the care and patience that only love and acceptance of a condition can develop. He sat there rigidly.

I realized then he was "out of it," and I kept looking through the magazines.

"Tun Tavern." A man's voice broke, creaky and distant sounding.

I turned. The older man was focused on my Marine Corps ring. I realized it flashed each time I flipped a page.

He had good eyes to catch the image and logo on one side of the Jostens' silver.

"I served in the Marines," he stated proudly.

The woman, who'd been in line at the counter, turned and stared at him, her mouth half opened.

"Yes sir, *Semper Fi*," I responded, now more interested.

"I served in Guadalcanal."

Now he had my interest. I don't recall direct quotes, but I can remember pretty much what was said.

"When the Japs attacked, they came thick," he began. "We'd shoot and shoot and they'd be upon us, *among* us. When they came at you, they came hard. You could see in their eyes that most were ready to die. But some were ready to kill. We were like that, too. Some fellas just were right that day; others couldn't do anything. Different fellas, different times. Only a few on both sides were true killers, ready to scrap, determined at any time, so a few did most of the killing."

I had the images of wolves among the sheep, transforming to men, slaughtering each other in a jungle and tall grassy field.

"You didn't want to lock eyes with one of them so ready to kill; you wanted to kill the ones who were ready to die." He continued. The man didn't change his expression. He had passion in his tone, but his flat affect remained. I looked into his eyes. He wasn't alert; he was *focused,* but not on anything in the room.

"When you bayonet someone, you pick a point on him, your hands slide up the stock and grip of your rifle, your feet skid. Training doesn't prepare you for that. The bolt pinches the web of your hand, cuts in, and barks your knuckle." He touched his hand. "You feel the pop, it [the bayonet] slides in, the scrape of blade on rib, his movement, you feel it through the metal of your rifle, he goes down and you're spinning opposite him, rising as he goes down. You feel a heartbeat, his or yours. The last breath is hot and wet, it's blown out on you, you breathe it in. It's hard to pull the bayonet from a man's ribs with the stock slippery with blood and sweat.

"I found friends dead, heard others die. I wished I'd killed more Japs and saved my buddies. They were kids." He then became silent. I thanked him and rose, as the service manager had called my name a few minutes earlier. But I wanted to be polite and listen. I left him mouthing what I think might have been names, an indelible roster of slain and never forgotten friends.

More honestly, I couldn't tear myself away from the mental images he painted with shared memories and nightmares until he was done.

"He hasn't talked in years," the old woman said, grabbing my left arm tightly, examining me as if wondering what sparked the monologue from her husband. She was shaken. "And he's never told me things like *that.*"

"He zeroed in on my Marine ring," I said, holding it up, wondering how he got through whatever haze he was in to see the reddish flash of faceted glass.

She nodded numbly and let go of my arm. She sat on the couch by the old warrior, lovingly, and where she belonged, near him. But she stared at him a bit. She hadn't been as close to him as she thought she was.

I left.

Among the many, many veterans I informally and sometimes formally interviewed, I remember another from an incidental conversation. He was a contractor, checking on some of his employees' work. He looked about the house and saw evidence in the living room of my military service. He mentioned that he'd served.

My best opening is to ask what the man's MOS (military occupational specialty) was when he served. This eliminates an amazing number of posers, and it narrows the focus for questioning.

"Grunt," he said with some pride. "I carried an M60 in Vietnam."

He straightened up a bit.

Bingo! "Tough job, high casualties in Vietnam," I remarked, opening. Then I began the usual test questions concerning basic training and advanced individual training (AIT), and he was hitting on the mark. He grinned, knowing my casual questions were actually grilling to determine how much he really knew.

He wasn't a poser; he was sure of himself and apparently didn't mind talking about it. He patiently answered my test questions.

Then we shifted into combat and I flat out asked what it was like, as I'd not been there.

The shrug.

They often shrug. It's hard to describe certain things at first. We began a good conversation on the porch: the randomness of death, of mortars, of mines, but more importantly to him, of stupid vehicle accidents in the rear that still disturbed him.

The question—*why me?* or, more correctly, *why not me?*— came up now and then in such conversations.

On that day I was pushing on what still bothered him, as I wondered for myself what I should prepare and guard against, if it were possible. He paused, thought hard, not about the answer, but whether he'd share something that still gnawed at him.

"The LT puts the '60 where it needs to be, where it can do some good, and I assume I shot people. Shooting them saved GIs, and that's what mattered, and kept me going. But one still makes me wonder." He frowned. "We were walking across a field when I see a farmer suddenly reach down. I cut him down. The gun hit hard; the dinks are small. After I shot him, I wondered whether he was reaching down for a rake or a weapon. Either was possible there. I let them tell me to move on, and I didn't go over and look down, which I could have. It does bother me. Hell, I never even told my wife that. I don't know why I told you."

"Well maybe it's better that you're here telling me this story now," I responded, knowing exactly why he was telling me about the incident, "than Ho telling about how he shot an American machine gunner who hesitated."

Many of them say they don't give a crap what others thought, but many do.

He hoped I'd understand.

I think they hope we understand.

THE NATURE OF COMBAT

by Sgt. Rocky Warren

Rocky Warren is a U.S. Army veteran, former SWAT operator, and law enforcement veteran of more than 28 years, having worked as a military policeman, sheriff's deputy, detective, jail supervisor, and patrol sergeant. He has received two Bronze Medals of Valor.

Mr. Warren's complete biography is included with his essay "The Heroic Set of Shoulders" in Chapter 1.

❖

The vast majority of the movies you've seen about combat have prepared you for failure. If you look for the "glory" of battle and expect it, you're going to be disappointed. If you expect certain things based on the Hollywood version of fighting, the reality may well injure or kill you before you really have time to understand. Whether personal or collective, combat is not what you expect.

Combat is not pretty. It's not fun. It's seldom glorious. When you shoot someone at close range, or a partner gets shot next to you, you may get hit in the face, mouth, or eyes with blood or tissue. If that thought "grosses you out," how much worse is reality?

Combat is not sterile. It hurts and kills. It's loud and messy. You may find out that combat hurts—personally. With the current level of medical evacuation and medical technology today, should you get wounded and live long enough to know you're hit, you have a very good chance of survival. You'll find out that not every wound heals completely or by itself. Hospitals keep you a prisoner and hurt you to make you get better. Or, your squad mates or friends may well grieve as the zipper of a body bag hisses closed over your face. Almost unbearably, you may be the one left behind watching that zipper close over your best friend's face.

Then again, cancer, emphysema, accidents, and fire are often even uglier ways to die. Or you may die in bed of extreme old age.

What then, is the nature of combat? It is a lifetime of active training and running on "autopilot." You've trained long enough and shed blood in the hard work and sweat of the mind to prepare. You've lived, sometimes years or decades, with the expectation that combat will come. Sometimes it never does. Even then, by your service, willingness, and readiness, you've done your part. You weren't paid for what you did. You were paid for what you trained and might have to do. For what you stood ready to do.

For every warrior who hears a bullet crack overhead or sees the shine of a naked blade bared in anger, there are thousands who never do. However, should you and your friends get within range of hostilities, you now have the first problem of the encounter: the realization that someone actually dislikes you enough to want to do you harm! If you survive that first two-tenths of a second, you've come face-to-face with the second problem of the encounter—namely, "I'd better do something really harsh and final to this person before he does it unto me or mine!"

In a warrior society, whether soldier, sailor, airman, Marine, police officer, fireman, EMT, nurse, doctor, or good citizen, the warrior takes up the burden and carries it. Cops, soldiers, Marines, and others carry arms so the rest of society doesn't have to. Most people wouldn't know how to bear arms, so it's a good thing, and a service, that there are those who can and do. Ponder that thought a while the next time you go to bed in your sleepy house.

If not for those armed people on watch day and night, year after year, our civilization would not be. It would be overrun with criminals, and the strong would constantly prey on the weak just because they could.

Doctors, EMTs, and nurses defend against the ills of society and the inhumanity of mankind to itself. Firefighters, pilots, and sailors are just plain crazy. They fight the natural elements that uncaringly and unconsciously kill without a trace of remorse or moment of warning. The sea, air, fire, flood, mudslide, and so on are their primary opponents. Firefighters conquer the element they battle and partly clean up the mess to restore some sense of normalcy. Sailors and pilots, on the other hand, go on after conquering the air, gravity, and ocean and go into armed conflict, where they're expected to fight and bring force to bear on land and shore. These folks are a trace different, and thank God for them.

And that's another thing. This recycled material from a bull that says, "Don't shoot someone in the back," or "Don't hit from behind" is rubbish. Say you are a sniper with a high-power rifle in the edge of a wood line, and you see an enemy soldier walking toward the opposite side of the clearing. He has a rifle, plenty of ammunition, and grenades. He's 100 yards away and you almost can't miss. Your orders are that you have a free-fire zone, meaning you can kill him where he stands. All you see is his back . . .

Are you going to fire?

If you said no, let's suppose that tomorrow, back in your cozy camp, you wake up to loud noises in your bivouac area. You rouse out of your slumber to see the same enemy soldier having a high old time. He and his friends are cavorting through your encampment throwing grenades and firing off their rifles, killing many of your squad mates. Might you bear some responsibility for the deaths of your friends?

Let's put you back in that clearing. Again you see the enemy walking away. Only this time you know that a squad of your comrades-at-arms is resting and taking a break in the far tree line. You know the squad is getting some shut-eye, and there's no chance they can wake up and fight before some of them are gravely injured or killed. If you don't shoot the enemy soldier, your squad will get attacked. Will you fire now?

Let's put you back into that clearing for one final time. You see the enemy walking toward the wood line, but now you know that your family is over there, unarmed and defenseless. Will you fire now? If you never fired before, ask yourself some hard questions: Do the soldiers in your squad deserve less than your family? Are their lives worth less? Do they feel that way about you, too? If they do, how much have your chances of survival dropped within the course of this conversation?

Let's use a final scenario and bring it home. To your home. You're going to bed one night and hear glass break downstairs. You don't own a gun because you just know you couldn't possibly shoot anyone. You haven't had the foresight to pick up one of your son's baseball bats because if you can't punch nice, clean holes in someone who's trying to break in, the thought of scattering someone's brains over the carpet makes you nauseous. Since you're in your jammies in the master bedroom, you don't have a knife from the kitchen. You try to dial 911. The line has been cut. You reach for your cell phone and breathlessly try to tell the operator there's someone breaking in. The call goes to the highway patrol, who don't know much about home-invasion robberies or hostage situations, and they cannot do a fast cell phone trace for location. You drop the phone as two armed, masked criminals burst into the room. They put a knife to your throat and tie you up. You may well spend the next few minutes listening to the gruesome noises, or even being forced to watch, as the crooks beat, rape, abuse, torture, or kill your family.

You may spend many hours listening to those same repetitive noises before they decide whether to kill your family or let you all live with the nightmares and horrid memories. But the choice will be up to the criminals. Not you. A situation that could have been well met and ended with two loud noises from you was allowed to occur because *you* decided to hold the suicidal beliefs of a totally nonviolent victim.

Your family will also have to live with the nightmares, scars, and consequences of your decision. As Winston Churchill said, and you just found out, "There are worse things than combat . . . and all of them come with defeat."

If someone shoots at you, what are you going to do about it? There are places in the world where a child 12 years old or younger is a full-fledged fighting member of a gang of "technicals" or other armed force. Let's suppose that child charges at you with an AK-47, a weapon he's held in his hands almost since infancy and decidedly knows how to use. Are you going to hesitate to shoot? If you don't and the child kills your comrade-at-arms, does that make you morally superior . . . or morally culpable? If you hesitate and the child kills you, will there be less grief on your family's part because you hesitated to kill a child? Or would they prefer that their warrior not hesitate and come home alive?

Let's make the assailant a pretty young woman. She sees you in the street, puts down her bowl of food, and reaches for the rifle propped against the wall near her. You point a rifle at her and warn her in your quavering voice. The warning has no effect. She picks up the rifle and begins to swing it into line with your pretty, unscarred skin. You're six inches and a finger twitch away from death. Are you going to fire?

After you wound or kill her, are you going to drop your weapon and react in horror and disgust? If she's trying to kill you, other unfriendlies in the area are probably somewhat disposed to take an active dislike to you. You might want to keep your eyes open and your rifle near, and have friends there who think like you do. Lots of them.

When a person is armed and can kill with a twitch of a finger, you need to make as many of your decisions ahead of time as you can. You draw these decisions from your active training and your own ethical and moral decision-making.

As a warrior, you need to answer these questions, and the best time to do it is right now, while your rump is planted in a chair and you're not full of adrenaline. If you can't come to the conclusion that lets you survive in combat, there's absolutely nothing wrong with your becoming a medic. If you don't have the stomach for that, you might want to remain in insurance or used-car sales. You surely don't need to be a warrior.

We in the United States are fortunate. Our warriors believe in the ascendancy of law and service. We believe in our Constitution and Bill of Rights, and we'll go into a foxhole or anywhere in the world with anyone who defends them with us. Warriors in the United States are different from fighters in third-world countries. The technicals of Mogadishu, Somalia, are out in the streets for themselves and their warlord. The Hezbollah and Islamic Jihad are serving themselves in the afterlife and out to please their imam "teacher" and religion. However, you hear "duty, honor, and country" from Americans and true warriors everywhere. The common theme of the warrior in the United States is service to others.

You cannot give an illegal order to a "moral warrior" and force him to obey it.

In the recent Iraqi conflict, there were many pictures sent back that depicted American soldiers and Marines holding and comforting babies and young children. There were pictures of women and children walking along on patrol through Baghdad streets, taking protection from our military presence. The look on those young soldiers' faces says it all: "I am willing to risk my safety and even die to protect you. To free you. To help make sure you stay safe, and the children continue to grow up young and strong."

So, why would you willingly go into combat? If you know what you will die for, you also know what you will live for. When values have been thought out ahead of time, it is a source of comfort to a warrior and a valuable commodity in today's world.

When you have a squad around you, a squad that you've shared blood with, you can rest easy. You know you're among the closest brothers and sisters you can have. When your captain walks past and loudly proclaims in front of your friends, "Hell of a job you did there," your chest swells with pride. When you say, "Hey! Remember when . . ." everyone does remember, and it's a shared bond between you. When you've saved a life, you'll get "the feeling." You will come to understand that you've shaped and forged yourself into a tool. How good a tool is limited only by the amount of action, pain, and training you are willing to undergo. You finally come to know that when other people lose their nerve, you are just getting into familiar territory. You have useful skills and abilities that others do not. Skills and abilities that work in a crisis and bring order out of chaos. As a warrior, you are the only one who can bring control out of havoc and civilization out of anarchy. Negotiation never works unless there is force to back it up.

Some may call you crazy for what you do, this thing about being a warrior and going into struggles, fights, and combat. I've long contended that it's not whether you're crazy that counts, but whether you're *usefully* crazy. Strive to be usefully crazy in the most uncontrolled and trying environment in the world: combat.

That, dear friend, is the nature of combat. It is enduring the seemingly unendurable for the sake and safety of those who cannot endure or who have not the strength to struggle. For those who survive combat, life is more treasured, drink more pungent, bed softer, and love more sweet. When you've known just how hard combat can be, almost nothing in your life will ever test you more.

You are successful when you've lived to pass on the lessons to the next generation. More and more as we come into the modern age of combat and increase our knowledge of warrior science, we realize that when we reach the slipper and rocking chair stage, it's our duty to tell the tale. Time to pay it forward. You will have earned that right.

AFTER THE KILLING

by Dave Barrows

Dave Barrows retired in June 2003 from the Kane County (Illinois) Sheriff's Office with the rank of commander, the highest nonpolitical rank in the agency. In the course of his 29-year career, he worked in all divisions but served primarily in patrol and administration. Mr. Barrows was awarded every medal authorized by the agency, including the two highest, a Medal of Honor and a Medal of Courage, and he was named the agency's Officer of the Year in 1985. The Kane County Chiefs of Police Association named him Countywide Officer of the Year in 1982. A founding member of the SWAT team, Mr. Barrows later became its commander, serving a total of 18 years with the team. He was also a charter member of the Illinois Tactical Officers Association and served on its executive board. Prior to retiring, Mr. Barrows served for two years as vice president of the Northern Illinois Critical Incident Stress Management Team. He is currently employed as a consultant and writes in his spare time.

❖

THEN

The nights are the hardest.

When the lights go out and the sounds stop.

And that night comes flooding back in vibrant Dolby stereo and vivid Technicolor freeze-frame memories . . .

It is 5:30 on the evening of November 26, 1981; it is Thanksgiving, and people all over the country are enjoying the holiday. And I am standing over the body of the man I've just shot.

The neighborhood is silent, but from somewhere within me there's a shrill voice screaming that there has been some kind of mistake. This feels nothing at all like what I had imagined during those long midnight-shift hours of fantasy gunplay and heroic arrests of armed felons.

I am on my way home for Thanksgiving dinner with my family. As a supervisor I have no area assignment; I am free to roam wherever the mood strikes me.

At 4:52 P.M., communications dispatches two units to an unincorporated residential area five minutes north of me on "shots fired." No big deal; we often have this type of call in our two-thirds rural county jurisdiction, and the area of the call is notorious for its drunken celebrants' loud activities with firearms and fireworks on weekends and over the holidays.

Indeed, this is apparently the case, since the first unit finds nothing after a search of the neighborhood and advises the other unit to disregard the call. I have also responded and am still close by when there is a repeat of the same complaint 20 minutes later.

As I arrive, I have a chance meeting with one of the other squads and flag him down without using the radio. I don't want to transmit because if the offenders have a scanner they will know when we are coming and hide the fireworks. I will simply, silently be another pair of eyes and ears.

We decide that Jim, the other officer, will search the area first, conspicuously using his spotlight up and down all the streets. He will then clear the call on the radio. I will do my search covertly, and we will both remain in the area, exercising radio silence for as long as it takes to flush out the bad guys.

Jim precedes me by a couple of blocks. I roll down all the windows and decrease the volume on the police radio.

Bang!

The sound is from somewhere behind me, and not far away. I pull off to the side of the street in the darkest area I can find, using my emergency brake so the brake lights don't reveal my position. I turn off the ignition and exit the squad and stand there in a silence that is broken only by the soft whisper of clicks and creaks from the cooling car. I am a statue, listening, waiting.

Jim announces on the radio that he will check out several subjects in a vehicle around the next corner from where I am. I am about to leave and back him up when I hear another booming, whip-crack sound to the south. It is very close to my location. Now I'm getting mad. They are taunting us; they obviously know that we are in the area by now, and they are continuing their activities regardless.

Well, this time I am going to catch them.

I work my way down the block using trees and darkness for concealment. When I am halfway to the next intersection, the front door of the house directly across the street from me opens, spilling a broad wash of light across the yard. I duck behind a tree, peering around it at the porch, which is now illuminated by the light from the open door. I am excited. Without knowing exactly why, I am firmly convinced that I have located the source of the fireworks. The thrill of victory races through my veins.

Then the hair prickles along the back of my neck as I see a human shape step out onto the porch, a shape that is clearly holding a long-barreled revolver.

Not fireworks. A gun. A big gun.

As the figure moves out onto the porch, I can see that it is a shirtless male. It's not all that much above freezing. Isn't he cold? He points the gun into the air and thumbs back the hammer.

I don't actually see the billowing smoke or blinding muzzle-flash, as I have my face buried into the tree bark.

Bang! Bang!

Okay. It's time to do some crime fighting.

"Police! Drop the gun!" I bellow like they do on TV, then peek around the tree.

Unlike on TV, however, the suspect does not obey; in fact, he turns slowly to go back inside the house, undoubtedly to hide the gun and feign innocence when we come a-knocking on his door. No cooperation with the script from this guy. Why am I suddenly so scared?

"County, from K-Seventy-two," radios Jim. "These are the wrong subjects. Assignment completed, nothing found."

Huh?

My somewhat distracted mind is slow to comprehend that Jim is using the ploy to catch the offenders that we had discussed earlier. Didn't he hear those last shots? How could he not hear them? They were so loud and so close! Or is he going around the block to sneak up on them from behind? Where is he going now? What is he doing? Is he . . .

It doesn't matter. Stop thinking about him. Get your head back to the problem at hand. Don't let your mind wander. Keep it simple, stupid. Do your job.

"Negative! Negative!" I say into my portable radio. "I have the offender spotted! K-Seventy-two, go back to the corner, block the intersection. . . . K-Thirty-two," I radio to the third car that is just now coming into the area, "take the south end and stop traffic."

Following the tactically sound doctrine of varying my location from where I had challenged the suspect previously, I sprint across the street to a utility pole near his residence. The area around the base of the pole is shrouded from the view of anyone in the house by some large bushes, and from this position I begin planning how to confront and arrest the offender for reckless conduct, and probably for not having a valid firearms owner's ID card.

I observe that directly in front of the suspect's house there is an area for perpendicular parking with room for about six cars. There are two vehicles there, parked nose-in. There is no actual driveway. The front yard is about four feet above street level with a stone wall forming a terrace at the border of the parking area. A series of steps is cut into the middle of the wall, providing access to the sidewalk leading up to the door. The cement porch with wrought iron railings is also about four feet high. The front door is centrally located on the street side of the house with windows on either side. The left one appears to be a picture window.

The door slowly opens. My heart jackhammers out of my chest as the suspect steps out onto the porch only fifty feet away and eight feet higher than me. He is still holding the revolver.

I stand immobile, pressing against the rough wood of the utility pole, reaching down to turn off my portable radio so routine transmissions do not reveal my position.

Bang! Bang! Bang!

I cringe into my jacket, flinching as each echoing blast erupts, wondering what the hell is wrong with this guy. He is supposed to have already hidden the gun and be preparing his alibi.

Bang! Bang! Bang! Click.

Click? Oh, yeah. Right. He has fired all six shots.

I peek cautiously around the pole and see him standing there with the gun pointed into the air, again thumbing back the hammer and clicking the trigger of the obviously empty revolver.

"Police officer! Drop the gun!" He hesitates. Apparently he hears me. I exult. Now we are getting somewhere. "Drop the gun. *Put it down, now!*" I hope my voice doesn't crack.

He pivots and begins to open the door. He is getting away.

I do not consciously make a decision (in fact, I don't remember how I reach the front yard, whether I crawled clumsily over the stone wall or hurdled it in a single bound), but I suddenly find myself running to the porch in an attempt to catch him before he gets inside.

Too late. The door closes behind him. I don't know how many offenders or weapons may be inside and wisely decide not to follow him. Through a partially curtained window, I see his head and shoulders move into a room to the right of the porch. He hunches over, and it takes little imagination to project either another gun or more ammo for the cannon he already has.

I am suddenly acutely aware that I am standing in the middle of the yard with no cover. I turn to run back to the utility pole, but it seems a mile away. I can see him moving across the window in the direction of the door. I am running out of time, so I dart around the corner of the house and flatten myself against the wall.

I hear the aluminum storm door open and close.

He now stands on the porch 15 feet away. I feel hollow, brittle. I can't catch my breath.

"Hey, you out there!" he yells. "I want to hear your voice again. Come on, talk to me."

He wants me to reveal my position. My hands are shaking. So are my knees. I need to know where he's at, but I am too afraid of exposing myself to peek around the corner. I try to judge his location from the sound of his voice. I don't remember unholstering it, but I become aware that I am gripping my gun with both hands.

"Hey, you! What have you got in your hand?"

Time stops. I am frozen solid. Unable to move. Unwilling to move.

If I don't react, maybe he won't shoot me. How could he have seen me?

It dawns on me that this is a different voice, coming from the direction of the street. I stare into the darkness, just barely able to make out the image of some idiot neighbor standing in the middle of the road shouting at the suspect, asking him questions.

I feel an incredible rush of hatred toward this fool. He's going to get me killed.

Now I have no choice but to peek around the corner. If the suspect points his gun at the street, I'm going to have to challenge him. He will ignore me, so I'll be forced to shoot at him, undoubtedly miss, and he will come down here and kill me. I resignedly peer around the corner.

The pedestrian stands in the street, hands on hips, impatiently awaiting a reply.

The suspect boldly waves his gun in the air. "I have this, and I want to be left alone," he answers.

The neighbor, now aware he has blundered into something he wants no part of, sprints off into the darkness. I start breathing again, peeking one-half of one eye around the corner of the house.

Bang! Bang! The suspect fires two shots into the air. Pauses. *Bang!* One into the ground.

He swivels his head. I detect the motion and pull back, staring at the base of the steps. I won't let him sneak up on me. I hear the door open, close. A quick peek confirms he's inside.

I run up the street past the empty lot adjoining the suspect's residence, find a large tree next to the driveway of a house two doors down, and cower behind it, catching my breath. It's easily 60 yards away from the porch where the suspect is apparently determined to take on the world, but I am able to observe his house. I will watch from here.

Okay. Relax. Calm down. You're safe now.

I slide my portable radio from its holster and call in. I advise Communications that we have a drugged, drunk, or crazy man with a gun holed up in a house, and I want the sheriff notified, the SWAT team, the negotiators, and some more patrol units . . . I run out of breath.

They acknowledge.

Maybe we can talk him out, maybe he will pass out, maybe the SWAT team can go in and get him, but I'm not going near that house again until everyone gets here.

Jim sprints over to me and we confer briefly. I will take over stopping traffic from the north and watch the area directly in front of the suspect's house. Jim leaves to circle the block to find a location from which to observe the rear of the house. Joe, the third officer, still has the south intersection blocked. Until we get more assistance, this is the best we can do.

I am considering a dash to my squad to get my shotgun when there is a piercing cry from up the street. The door to the suspect's residence has slammed open and a female bolts out, screaming for help. She crosses the yard, launches herself off the wall, and flees down the block away from me. Mere steps behind, the suspect pursues her, gun in hand. He stumbles down the steps onto his knees, then lurches to his feet and continues to chase the shrieking woman.

I find myself running after them, with no awareness of having left the safety of the trees—in fact, with no thought of safety, period. I am completely exposed. I begin searching for cover. Okay, over there is a parked car; get behind it and challenge him from there.

He stops, raises the gun with one hand, and points it at the rapidly escaping female.

"Freeze! Drop the gun!" I yell as I skid to a stop about 60 feet from him, with nothing but air between us. How did I get this close when he had such a big head start?

He turns, with his arm still extended, pointing the gun at me.

Without conscious decision, without hesitation, in mortal fear for my life, *I am going to stop him from hurting me.* I raise my gun in a standard two-hand grip and squeeze the trigger and keep squeezing until he falls down.

He curls into the fetal position and lies there, unmoving.

I approach him warily, see the gun lying on the pavement, and step up, intending to kick it away. I pause. The action seems unnecessary, even drastic, since he hasn't moved since going down. I settle for reaching down carefully to pick it up without taking my eyes off him. I try to tuck it in my waistband, but it is too big to handle until I holster my own gun and use both hands to slide it between my pants belt and utility belt. It is a Ruger Super Blackhawk .44 Magnum revolver with a barrel that is 10 1/2 inches long. The barrel is still hot.

I hear voices. My radio is on. Joe is reporting a series of gunshots and a woman fleeing past him. Jim is calling for my status, and I realize no one else knows what has happened.

"County, get an ambulance up here. Joe, get up here . . . Jim, get up here." I can't remember their car numbers.

Later, listening to the radio tape, I realize my voice was breathless and strained, as if I had been injured. I should have announced that the offender was down and I was okay, but I did not want to admit to the world at large that I had shot someone. I'm not sure I was admitting it to myself.

The offender is motionless, but breathing. When Jim pulls up next to me we open his first aid kit; place a dressing over the oozing, bloody hole at the edge of the suspect's rib cage; and cover him with a blanket.

Joe begins to search for the screaming woman, who is now long gone.

After an interminable wait, common in county area but even longer tonight, the ambulance arrives. Jim holds up a plastic IV bag as the paramedics start an intravenous line, place electrodes on the suspect's chest for the cardiac monitor, and then begin to apply special trousers with inflatable air bladders that reduce the effects of shock due to blood loss, which has been significant.

The guy stops breathing; one paramedic checks the cardiac monitor and reports that his heart has also stopped beating. They frantically begin various critical medical procedures. Jim's hands are still full, and I am the only one left. Habit and prior training take over. I kneel and begin basic CPR, pumping his chest rhythmically, mindlessly. After several minutes the man's respiration and heartbeat resume. The paramedics stabilize him and depart for the hospital.

My pants feel damp. I see a wet, purplish stain soaking the material of my uniform pants from my knee to the top of my boot. I have been kneeling in a large pool of blood. His blood.

Assistance begins arriving; I have disrupted a dozen Thanksgiving dinners.

My good friend Ramsey, a detective, demands my gun as evidence and for ballistics tests. A panic-stricken refusal is on the tip of my tongue. I am not going to walk around here defenseless, and I have done nothing wrong. Standard procedure, he explains. How can there be a standard procedure? No one on this department has ever done this before. Suddenly sensitive to my dilemma, he extends his own gun as a replacement. Rationality returns, and I am able to turn my weapon over to him, refusing his offer. Once I'm able to give up mine, I have no need for his.

I reenact the scene again and again for the sheriff and the detectives and the evidence technicians, until I am released and ordered back to the office to complete my reports.

Once I'm there, everyone, official and unofficial, wants to know what happened. The story is repeated over and over, including once for the record on the investigator's cassette tape. The ending never changes; I still shoot the guy.

Just after midnight I prepare to leave for home, but the midnight shift sergeant, who has been arranging for personnel to guard the prisoner at the hospital, walks in and congratulates me.

"Well, Barrows, you did a better job than we thought. That guy just died."

A numbing shiver travels along my spine, across my shoulders, up my neck. I feel hollow, like a strong wind could send me skittering down the street like an autumn leaf.

Died. Oh God, he died. Sudden wash of relief.

At least I won't have to keep looking over my shoulder for the guy to exact his revenge.

I go home, tell the story once again to my wife, and go to bed. I cry myself to sleep.

The next few days are a blurred kaleidoscope of ragged stimulation. Everything is more vivid: colors are brighter, sounds louder, the very surface of my skin more sensitive, tingling. I'm told later this is a typical post-combat reaction; apparently, the tidal wave of adrenaline flooding the system enrages all the neurons to a fever pitch.

I go back to work the very next night, hear a call of a prowler, maybe armed, and I can't remember what roads to take to get there. I grew up here, learned to drive on these roads, went parking with girlfriends on them—and for several moments can't remember what streets intersect. It doesn't matter because the call ends peacefully. It was just the homeowner's son.

On Saturday I am at a camping gear show when several kids bump into me while dodging for cover, screaming imaginary gunshots. I cringe and feel the world closing in; I have to leave.

I cry myself to sleep again.

But I'm okay. I'm dealing with this okay. I am.

Except for the first night, when everything was clear and focused, I find myself having trouble writing reports. I begin, but soon discover I am staring at the second line and 20 minutes have gone by: my watch hands have moved but my conscious thoughts are static. It takes forever to complete reports covering even the most mundane police activity.

It is the same with newspaper articles and television shows: halfway through I find that I do not remember the topic or the plot.

I am often updated on the shooting investigation. We discover that the guy had previous arrests for burglary, aggravated assault with a firearm, and aggravated incest. He is divorced, and his family lives out of state. His body is to be shipped for burial. If this were not the case, I would go to the cemetery to try to explain to his son and three daughters why I killed their father.

I feel I should explain it to his girlfriend. When she was eventually located that night she told the detectives that he had invited her over for dinner and to watch football. During the late afternoon he began drinking whiskey and playing with the gun. About two hours before the neighbor called us, he began firing into the walls and then intermittently stepped outside to fire shots into the air. When she asked why he was doing this, he wouldn't explain. She told him that she was frightened and wanted to leave, but he threatened her and told her to stay because he needed her. Fearful, she remained. Later, hearing me outside, she waited for the first good opportunity to escape. When he became distracted loading his gun, she made her break for freedom. But all in all, she said, he wasn't a bad guy, and she had no clear idea why any of this happened. Neither did we.

A week later I am watching TV, a cop show in which a divorced cop tells his son how much he loves him and doesn't want to be apart, though sometimes he must. I begin crying uncontrollably, weeping for one son who will never again hear words like that from his father.

Regardless of his background, he was somebody's father, brother, son. Somewhere they were still grieving for him.

Or maybe I am weeping over the loss of my innocence.

I am no longer immortal. I have felt the breath of my own imminent death on my cheek.

Over the years I have seen others die, some violently and unexpectedly, and I have experienced the deaths of family members and close friends. But this was different. It was me who was going to die, and at the time I felt totally powerless to prevent it. On that miserable street, for no good reason, I was going to die.

Instead, I am alive. Someone else has died. Died at my hand.

Not a day goes by without that particular tape being played in my mind.

As I walk in public I sometimes wonder what the people around me, complete strangers, would think if they knew that I had slain another human being. Would they recoil in horror as if I were unclean, something from the primordial jungle not fit to interact with civilized people?

But I only did what I had to do. He left me with no other option. It was him or me, and I was only protecting myself.

As the years pass the recollections will dim. Time will coat the events of that night with layer upon layer of new events and occurrences. I know this. This part has happened before.

Until then, there will be the nights.

When the lights go out and the sounds stop and sleep is far, far away.

And the memories come.

NOW

The previous words were written over two decades ago in the weeks immediately following the event. The writing is essentially unchanged; it is an accurate representation of what was in my head and heart at the time.

After it occurred, I thought about the event several times every day, intrusively so.

I was disappointed in myself. I had been so afraid that at one point I had run away from the threat. It didn't matter in my belief system that I had ultimately done the right thing. I should have done better.

I grew up a somewhat ragged Christian but knew that the Sixth Commandment, as written in the King James version of the Holy Bible, the Bible of my youth, orders not to kill. But I had.

Late in that first year, a vague recollection from a college lecture seeped into my consciousness. I remembered suddenly and very clearly that I had been told by a knowledgeable professor, an ordained minister, that in the original language of the Bible, Aramaic, the commandment was to not *murder*, rather than to not *kill*. I found several other biblical translations that included the earlier and more accurate language. This moral sanction of the act, when judged in context, made a huge difference in my healing process.

Lt. Col. Dave Grossman covers this issue more completely, as well as the overall human reluctance to kill one another, in his fine presentations. But again, this came to me much later.

Eventually, enough calendar pages turned, and I began to think about the event only every other day, then once a week, once a month. Life went on.

I have since completed a 29-year career and have retired from active service, a graybeard with numerous knowledge-bumps and scars, a perspective matured by blood, sweat, and fears. I have experienced and learned many things that might have changed my reactions had I been exposed to them before or immediately after the event.

But this is now and that was then.

The contributors to this book might be described as warrior scholars and warrior trainers, to use the terminology of Lieutenant Colonel Grossman. They are experienced, knowledgeable participants and instructors in the art of war, combat of all types—the best in their respective fields.

While not in that class, I, for example, instructed in firearms, tactics, officer survival, and use-of-force issues for many years. I led and ordered others into harm's way. I was a SWAT team member or commander for 18 years. Over the course of my career, I was awarded every medal my police agency had available, including a Medal of Valor for driving a squad car into the field of fire of a subject armed with an H&K MP5 to rescue two officers pinned down by gunfire. The outstanding service award for our agency's SWAT team was named after me when I retired, which may be the greatest honor of all.

Certainly, I could pontificate on the value of tactics and training.

Yet I feel the most important contribution I can make is the power of this statement: each of us was a human being before becoming a cop, a soldier, a warrior—and (however reluctantly) remains one now. Armored with Kevlar and professional demeanor, it may not often appear that way, but there it is.

True warriors live by a code, mostly unspoken. They choose to run toward the sound of gunfire rather than away. They swear oaths and live by them. They stand their ground, morally, physically, and ethically, to protect each other and those who are unable or unwilling to protect themselves.

There is a strong bonding between warriors—we few, we brave, we band of brothers—that infuses all we do even when we are alone. We subjugate self for the good of the team.

True warriors have a sense of duty that works something like this: A warrior driving alone in a car down a narrow, twisting mountain road comes around a bend and there, in the middle of the road, is a young child. Safe evasive action is not possible, so the warrior swings the steering wheel to avoid the child, even if the action includes the potential to drop off the edge of the cliff. However, if driving a school bus filled with children, the warrior may steer directly toward the child in the roadway instead, hoping to make that end as quick as possible—because the greater duty is to the many children on the bus who have been entrusted to the warrior's care. Everyone may tell the warrior it was the only thing to do—and the warrior may believe this to the core of his or her being.

Yet the warrior may then go home and be confused by the overwhelming desire to cry.

The warrior/survival culture does not foster the expression of emotions—it is often confused with weakness, especially among young or newer members. There is so much competition, so much desire to be considered "one of the team," and such a high demand to prove themselves (both from within and from without) that the exclusion of emotional vulnerability is almost a requirement.

And most warriors actually in the field *are* young (as I was) when first tested in mortal combat. Many do not have "old warrior" experience, and the destruction of their illusion of immortality and self-worth belief systems comes as a shock. A statement uttered frequently after the event is some variation of "I couldn't believe it was really happening to me . . ." Even if they have done their expected duty and acted with great honor, their emotional and cognitive reactions are often not what they expect.

The huge dump of adrenaline into the body common to these events serves to heighten all the physical senses and memories to a very intense level. A sudden stark realization that one is truly mortal, that fear can be overwhelming, that behavior might be less courageous than expected, that moral or ethical ambiguity may set in despite the most crystalline clarity of intent, can all be surprising next-day visitors.

Certainly, some will read this and say, "Huh?" They survived a close encounter of the violent kind and did not have any of these reactions. So it goes. Each of us comes from a different background and brings unique past experiences and beliefs to the table. But many *will* have some or all of the reactions I've described.

Progressive training programs include warnings and methods to deal with these reactions, yet most young warriors stubbornly expect they will react only in a preconceived image of professional aplomb and studied indifference. I certainly believed that.

Beyond the culture, there is the training.

The rigors of physical fitness, regular practice with weapons and techniques of unarmed combat, the study and rehearsal of tactics—these types of training, by their nature, tend to minimize emotional responses.

This is as it should be.

The primary function of the warrior is to contain or eliminate the threat of the enemy and complete the mission, whether that is protecting the innocent, enforcing the law, or defending the country and the Constitution from all enemies foreign and domestic. Allowing emotions to interfere or impede or impair the survival response is a bad thing.

But afterward, when time and circumstances permit, a healthy warrior should deal with the emotional responses inherent in each of us, just as he or she cleans a weapon, critiques tactics, and prepares for the next mission.

Over the last several years, much has been written about critical-incident stress and post-traumatic stress disorders. There are highly effective techniques that can be used to combat these issues, both before and after the event. For example, teams made up of mental health professionals and (more importantly) experienced peers exist in many areas to respond and provide critical-incident stress debriefings for police officers following traumatic events. These teams also provide preincident training.

There are studies, both statistical and anecdotal, that show the techniques work. The aftermath of my event might have gone more easily had something been in place years ago.

So, as I said earlier, warriors are people, too.

Special people who, when walking down a jungle path with ordinary people and attacked by a tiger, stand their ground—in fact, place themselves between the tiger and its intended victims. Without regard for the beauty of nature and secondary recognition of the big cat's need to eat to survive, without regard for his or her own shaking knees and draining bowels and bladder, armed with only a sense of duty that does not allow flight as an option, the warrior stands his or her ground to protect those less able to protect themselves.

Special people that I have been honored merely to serve beside.

But people nonetheless—burdened with hopes and fears and a strict sense of self that often considers the admitting of fear a weakness—who, in the aftermath of an event in which they acted honorably, may still feel they have not cleared the bar because they experienced more intense emotions than they ever anticipated or were prepared for.

Yet that makes them special as well.

To all warriors, I humbly offer three essential rules: prepare for every encounter as if it will be a fight to the death; do everything necessary to survive and accomplish your mission; and when the threat is contained or eliminated and the mission is completed, allow yourself to experience it emotionally and honestly, and share those reactions with your comrades.

Take care of yourself as you take care of others. Your emotions make you strong, not weak. Anger and fear, often two sides of the same coin, are among the most powerful motivators for survival. Do not deny them; just don't let them control you. Expect to have emotional reactions; it is only human. But remember: to expect them is to accept them, and that is a valued goal.

So go in peace, my friends, while being fully prepared for war.

And what comes after.

THE COST OF IT
MEMORIES FROM VIETNAM TO PANAMA TO DESERT STORM

by John R. Finch

Lt. Col. John R. Finch (U.S. Army, Ret.) served 22 years as an intelligence officer, participating in the Easter Offensive in the Vietnam War, Operation Just Cause in Panama, and the latter stages of Operation Desert Storm in the Persian Gulf. He was awarded the Silver Star for gallantry in action at Kontum, South Vietnam, in May 1972.

Mr. Finch served as a reserve police officer in Kansas and was an instructor and author at the U.S. Army Command and General Staff College, Leavenworth, Kansas. He is a graduate of Massad Ayoob's Lethal Force Institute training system, including his instructor classes. Mr. Finch holds an MA in history from the University of Kansas.

❖

The title of this essay was inspired by the famed World War II artist Tom Lea's painting from the invasion of Peleliu titled *The Price*, which graphically depicts a terribly wounded U.S. combatant still moving forward.

Many of us view the loss of life or limb as the primary risk involved when humans engage in deadly conflict, and there is logic in this perspective. However, there are other costs, especially psychological ones, associated with such conflict, and my purpose here is to describe some of these from engagements I participated in during a 22-year U.S. Army career.

KONTUM

In 1971, after a tour in Germany as a tank platoon leader, I arrived in the Central Highlands of Vietnam as a captain and a G-3 air advisor with the 23rd ARVN Division. The goal then was captured in this ditty: "I went to war at 24 and came home alive at 25," since the year-long combat tour was still the requirement.

From April through June of 1972, the 23rd ARVN Division was heavily involved in the defense of Kontum during the North Vietnamese Army's (NVA's) Eastertide Offensive. There were U.S. advisors with the division headquarters (HQ) and also at regimental level. Additional U.S. military members were involved with ARVN Rangers, Airborne, and Regional/Popular Forces (RF/PF).

Shock and Awe

Remember the bombing attacks against the Tora Bora Mountains during our recent campaign in Afghanistan? Remember the huge multiple explosions from the B-52s that we could view from the safety of our TV screens? Well, I remember . . .

- The sometimes-hourly B-52 Arc Light strikes in support of the Kontum defenses (as many as 20 sorties a day, or 300 B-52 sorties during a three-week period) and the resulting "shock and awe" then when we declared tactical emergencies (Tac-Es) and ended up violating the safety margins. The regimental folks felt it worse, but we felt it too: the concussion, shock waves, and noise.
- The resulting smoke and dust, followed by the bomb damage assessment (BDA), when you would find everything from unidentified body parts to weapons parts scattered over ground that resembled moon craters.
- Blood pouring from noses and ears—the usual result when

a Tac-E bomb line got within 300 meters (rather than the 1,000 meters for troop safety specified by the secret document on Arc Lights that I carried in my pocket). You learned not to "love the smell of napalm in the morning," or any other time. But at least you were alive, although you might never be the same emotionally.

Seeing and smelling roadkill today can still bring unpleasant reminders of past combat. There was no live coverage in 1972, but the "replays" are available in the minds of those who witnessed, smelled, and felt the impacts.

Timing
For some vets, the collective experiences of combat engendered a lifelong commitment to *being on time*, and thus, years later, being late can trigger an angry outburst that is difficult to explain to your spouse or others. I recall . . .

- The time my friend Capt. "Pat W." was airlifted out after his "combat skyspot" (normally four fighter-bombers dropping on the command of an accompanying control aircraft for greater effectiveness) bombing mission hit an ARVN patrol that had fibbed on its real location. Although Pat had done nothing wrong, ARVN blamed him for the resulting serious casualties and threatened deadly reprisal against him. Our counterparts also made it clear that if the remaining advisors tried to leave by helicopter, ARVN soldiers would stop us by force.
- Times like May 14, 1972, when the NVA began its attack on Kontum, and our stomachs twisted into knots as we tried to "in-flight divert" an Arc Light and other air strikes because two regiments were in trouble. And I said a silent prayer—*Oh God, please don't let me fuck up*—that the coordinates encrypted off the 1:50,000-scale map using cardboard cutouts from C ration box tops for templates were

accurate enough for eight-digit, 3 x 3 kilometer target boxes. *Will the bombs hit in time? On target? Not too close? And then I thought, screw the secret regulations, because it's a Tac-E, and the calls on the radio are desperate!* A so-called "big belly" B-52D could drop 84 500-pound bombs internally and another 24 750-pound bombs from the wings. And each B-52 strike cell normally consisted of three planes dropping upwards of 30 tons of bombs each. A mistake anywhere in the sequence of individual actions and decisions that got the planes over target could have horrific consequences. Couple that with an intelligence report that says the NVA have a $2,000 price on your head (dead) because you're the Arc Light guy.

- The "make the pickup point or be left behind syndrome"—know where you are at all times, just in case you need fire support, medevac, or shift from a known point. Each U.S. advisor was instructed during the battle for Kontum to select an emergency pickup point using the face of the clock so we wouldn't all go in one direction. If we were overrun, each of us was to evade and escape to the position we selected. A helicopter would then make one pass over that spot to see if we were there. If we made it to our personally selected pickup point, then there was a good chance we would be evacuated. If we didn't make it on time for that one pass, we would likely be listed as missing in action.

- That time a frag grenade came through a window when I was eating in Ban Me Thout. The media described it as enemy terrorism. But I later learned it was a disgruntled ARVN soldier, angry at his girlfriend for talking to co vans (American advisors). All these years later, I still do not like to be seated in a public place with my back to a door or a window. My spouse has adapted and now naturally selects a seating position with my needs in mind.

Eventually, there is an awareness that the odd quirks you may have developed, like the insistence, even now, on being "on time," are an outgrowth of the incident where help was late and people died or a unit failed in its mission.

Triggers
For some vets, there are triggers that serve to reawaken long-forgotten memories of past events. I think of . . .

- Hearing the Vietnamese language spoken now, decades later, in the United States, and how it causes "combat words"—a combination of Vietnamese, French, and English—to tumble back into my mind.
- Seeing a certain face in a crowd and thinking, "He looks like . . ." only to realize "he" has been dead or missing since *that day.*
- Seeing a recent news report of a U.S. Navy combatant conducting the first port call to Vietnam since 1975 and realizing why I feel a twinge of betrayal still—and perhaps gaining an understanding of why some of the U.S. Pacific theater vets still cannot reconcile with our now allies in Japan and their aging World War II veterans.

Pain and memories can run deep for some, perhaps too deep to ever be reconciled. They are part of *the cost of it.*

Truth and Lies
Vietnam veterans tend to stress the importance of ensuring that events are recalled and recounted accurately, that imposters be exposed, and that those who wear medals they did not earn be held accountable. I think of the cost, even years later, of . . .

- That photograph in *The New York Times* by Matt F. that

depicted me with a helmet on a rifle while hiding in a ditch with a grenade in my left hand. One media caption later read, "U.S. advisor waves his helmet to advancing South Vietnamese troops in Kontum." That was a nice editorial spin at the time, but also false. In reality, sappers from D-10 (an enemy sapper battalion that was used to make holes in our defenses so that infantry and tank units could more easily attack and exploit) were trying to kill me and the AP photographer as they infiltrated to blow holes in our wire defenses. I "John Wayned" the helmet in order to find the guy who was heaving stick grenades in our direction and "send him a baseball grenade back." Problem was, I saw him with a Chicom stick grenade almost primed. So I pitched the helmet off the barrel and shot him, one time, in the head. That single M16A1 5.56mm bullet made for a Kennedy assassination-type moment that I have yet to dispel from my memory. No AP photo of that, except in my mind.

Sometimes I catch myself seeing that face and wondering, *Who was he? What might he have become and done? What did his family think when he didn't return? Did he have a wife and kids?*
You usually don't see up close the ones you kill with bombs and artillery; they are just blurs in the distance tossed like rag dolls by the force of the explosions. But this incident was, and has remained, different for me: not just a dead body, but one *I* killed, just me. And circumstances didn't permit examination of the body. No chance to see if he had any papers. Just an unknown teenaged face that remains clearly etched in my mind these many decades later. But, as a friend recently reminded me, "That 'kid' was about to make you very dead or terminally fucked-up. That was clearly a 'him or you' event. You were better, or faster, or luckier. So that's it.

That was just part of your war; it was the end of his war. It is over, Jack. Just be glad that the kid is not today a 50-year-old NVA veteran sitting in a teahouse in Ho Chi Minh City telling his buddies how he whacked this tall American with a Chicom grenade during the siege of Kontum."

"Souvenirs"

And still, there are the sights, sounds, smells, and other reminders of the victims (on all sides), such as . . .

- The souvenirs kept either on private display or packed away in "storage." It all comes rushing back when looking at or touching a faded photograph, patch, letter, or diary entry, or when hearing music from that time.
- The experience of going to see the acclaimed and award-winning movie *Platoon* in 1986 and then realizing that the clever director and technical advisor had provided numerous subliminals to enhance the viewing impact on certain audience members. For example, there was the sequence with the gekko lizard, known as the "fuck you" lizard because of its call, during the night ambush scene. Hearing that sound during that scene triggered a Condition Orange (heightened awareness) response in a number of vets I spoke with. Capt. Dale Dye (USMC Ret.) of Warriors, Inc., was the technical advisor for *Platoon,* and we spoke by phone about the potential costs for Vietnam vets in the movie audiences. He acknowledged there were a couple of dozen such subliminal moments in the film and said that director Oliver Stone had insisted upon their use. These triggers were so effective that some Vietnam vets were unable to sit through the film because of the memories rekindled by the realism portrayed.
- The mental image of the French female correspondent who hitched a helicopter ride into Kontum (probably as a

result of sexual favors) and soon ended up dead. I never learned her name; never saw what became of her body. At the time we suspected she was killed by ARVN because of the possibility she was a spy and could leave with useful targeting information on a later helicopter flight. There were apparently many bitter memories of the first Indochina War that may have played a part in her death 20 years later. The thinking at the time was that if Kontum fell, Pleiku was next, and then the country would be split in half. You wonder at *the cost of* perhaps making the decision to murder her rather than accept the risk. But in such a chaotic situation, with known spies within the perimeter helping target command posts for very accurate NVA M46 130mm artillery fire, what would you have done? It is war on the lowest common denominator and no unnecessary chances taken when the fate of a country is at stake. An example, perhaps, of, "Ya pays your money and ya takes your chance." She lost.

- The concrete and steel water towers, common where I live, that sometimes bring back memories of our fight for the Kontum water tower. I think of the seven ARVN soldiers who followed me and died or were wounded attempting to eliminate an enemy heavy machine gun emplaced there that had downed a Vietnamese Air Force (VNAF) A-1E Skyraider and damaged an F-4 Phantom. And that day when we eventually employed the then-revolutionary TOW antitank missile fired from a UH-1B Huey gunship in its first combat use. Records indicate 73 hits for 89 missiles fired during the siege, with 26 T-54 Chicom Type 59 or PT-76 tanks destroyed. The TOWs were a key and timely response to the NVA's initial use of Sagger antitank missiles when the B-3 front units had earlier destroyed the 22nd ARVN Division at Tan Canh north of Kontum in April.
- The sight of an AC-130 gunship today, which brings back

memories of the "fabulous four-engined fighter" AC-130 Spectre E and H models and how they also contributed vital support in Vietnam, from laser designating for F4s to providing pinpoint fire support against troops or tanks at night. The NVA tried to counter the Spectres with Soviet SA-7 Strellas but failed because the AC-130s just flew higher.

Part of *the cost of it* is the realization that sometimes mere flesh, blood, and will are not enough to do the job. The engagements against those 40 NVA tanks in the Kontum battle and the water tower fight were costly lessons in that reality. Such recollections are just some of the emotional or psychological costs of remembering past combat.

Rages and Nightmares

At times the current speeches and "spinning" by various factions can bring about a visceral response as you recall the results of earlier campaigns against enemies now deemed friends. At the forefront of my mind are . . .

- The rage that can surface when elected leaders vote for military action that they themselves or their families have never risked.
- The memory of having killed and then suffered the "mark of Cain" effect in dealings with those civilized citizens you live with who know what you have done (maybe not the "baby-killer" comments, but the looks and glances can cut just as deep, as can viewing the old videos and seeing the war protests against what you participated in and did).
- The nightmares that you can't or don't explain to your spouse.
- The potential for angry outbursts over something that seems trivial to others but for you clearly triggers a remem-

brance of *that moment* when your life changed forever.

- The recollections of the dead, like the legendary John Paul Vann, who saved my life and the lives of many others before he and his passengers died in the crash of his OH-58 on June 9, 1972, while flying to Kontum at night. It took me a long time to finally read Neil Sheehan's *A Bright Shining Lie: John Paul Vann and America in Vietnam.* The resultant recalled memories came at an emotional cost, but one that I and others paid willingly in order to learn more about this flawed but dynamic "civilian warrior" who led from the front like the two-star general he was the equivalent of in his civil position at the time.

- The haunting images of the horrible wounds suffered by close comrades whom you were to never see again. *Did they die of their wounds? If not, then aren't their names on The Wall? Where are Col. R., Bill B., Col. Ba, Rich G., "Bear" B., Wade L., Ray H., and the others? What happened to the slick pilot named Lobo with the Maltese cross on the nose of his Huey?* (Sounds like a line out of the movie *Rambo,* but perhaps it is echoed in real life more than you might think.)

From the dark spaces of the rage, the nightmares, the recollections, and the haunting images, the question emerges: *where are they?* They are in the memories of those who survived, and those memories are a key component of *the cost of it.*

Luck

In considering *the cost of it,* there is always a sense of irony, or luck, or whatever word or phrase you use for "there but for the grace of God go I." Combat is rife with inexplicable twists of fate:

- While I was flying with Lobo checking for NVA tanks from their 203rd Regiment, a radio call came from Vann (call sign: Rogue's Gallery) on the "guard" frequency telling us we were flying into a B-52 in-flight divert box and to "turn now!" Question was, *which way?* Lobo turned left, and we were able to watch the "eggs in the air" as they fell and detonated to our right—right where we would have been. Despite the best efforts, training, and awareness, the phrase "shit happens" is a keen philosophical insight that warriors ignore at their peril.

- One day my friend Capt. Ray H. showed me a piece of shell fragment that hit his chest but was stopped by his M69 flak jacket. I remember him saying, "Well, Jack, they've had their chance. I'm gonna make it." Sadly, a short time later he was badly burned when the Huey he was in crashed and we couldn't get him free from the fire in time. Gathering his belongings and writing the letter to his wife were part of *the cost of it.*

- Then there was the unfortunate Special Forces soldier who triggered a friendly "toe-popper" antipersonnel mine, and the resulting mangled foot. So suddenly was one of our most highly trained warriors removed from combat because of an unfortunate step on one of our own defensive weapons.

- And there was the ARVN soldier equipped with an M-72 light antitank weapon (LAW), who by accident destroyed the first NVA tank with that LAW. We had many problems with the LAW warheads fragmenting rather than penetrating when they struck a target, possibly from improper storage. In this encounter, the ARVN soldier aimed correctly but when he fired, his aim shifted and the rocket hit the tank's track, but the defective warhead still succeeded in breaking it. With the NVA driver chained to his seat, the tank could only pivot helplessly while other ARVN soldiers then peppered it with enough additional LAWs to destroy it. I've always wondered what would have happened if the LAW had been fired correctly and the warhead had shattered on the tank's turret ring. Probably we would have been overrun in that sector on May 14. The phrase "For want of a nail . . ." comes to mind when I recall that incident.

- And there was our good luck that the NVA never elected to shoot a barrage of their 122mm rockets at the huge troposcatter communications screens at Pleiku, where our requests for tactical air and Arc Lights were routed. I was later told that if those screens had been destroyed it might have crippled our air support because of increased response times and limited ability to do three-hour lead time in-flight diverts by the Pleiku G-3 air folks like Capt. Chris S. Part of *the cost of it* is that all sides make mistakes that get people converted from living to dead; this case being perhaps roughly parallel to the Japanese failure in not destroying the Pearl Harbor fuel depots when they could have easily done so on December 7, 1941.

Finally, I go back to the death of John Paul Vann. Is the old saying, "Guts will get you just so far and then they'll get you killed . . . luck runs out," true in his case? He was the soul of the Kontum defenses, along with ARVN commander Colonel Ba. His death on June 9, probably caused by pilot vertigo in sudden night IFR conditions (instrument flight regulations, where the visible horizon is lost and the pilot must rely on instruments to fly), was a severe blow to our morale and a chill reminder of how vulnerable can be the warrior's moment to the vagaries of weather.

PANAMA

In the United States' efforts to remove Manuel Noriega from power during "Operation Just Cause" in December 1989, some of the old *cost-of-it* memories resurfaced. Take, for instance, the effort to secure Noriega's personal safe and remove it from his headquarters in the Commandancia. After much effort by various intelligence specialists, the safe was removed to a secure location where, under the gaze of CIA and military representatives, it was opened via "brute force and ignorance" techniques, since the required "technical expert" was still stranded at Pope Air Force Base due to the infamous foul weather at that staging point. As the safe door was finally opened, we were crestfallen to find not the key documents we had expected but just a bag of anticorrosion powder! All that effort, including the sacrifice of warriors wounded during the Commandancia fight, and the ultimate prize was desiccant powder. Such is the irony at times for those in fluid combat situations.

Later, we had to identify the remains of wanted Panamanian military members. Even in December, the heat in Panama quickly turns enemy dead into an unpleasant "forensic situation." The images, smells, and tactile sensations that go along with unzipping body bags and grimly, but not always quickly, confirming that, "Yeah, this is one of the guys we're looking for," tend to stay with you. As I look at an old Panama Defense Force (PDF) ID card from that period as I type this, it comes back to me like only yesterday.

OPERATION DESERT STORM

During Operation Desert Storm, while we were in the vicinity of the so-called "Highway of Death" near Al-Jarah, Kuwait, the *cost-of-it* memories resurfaced again in an odd and—I think—unnecessary way. Our British allies were initially loath to bury the seemingly countless dead in the area because of religious differences between the Shia and Sunni Muslims with regard to burial. Consequently, the scent of human roadkill would waft in your face from time to time, depending on the direction of the wind. A smear of vapor rub compound under my nostrils helped, but the legions of flies descending on the remains was a grim reminder of what can happen to the dead.

But the cost of our U.S. units sending unbloodied troops in to view firsthand the handiwork of U.S. technology was one I think we are paying interest on in homes and VA centers to this day. Our troops were sent wandering through this carnal house of burned vehicles and bodies so they could get a "feel for what U.S. high-tech weapons combat results looked like." Imagine the impact of this experience on the human psyche. No amount of spray-painting "U.S. is # 1" on the burned-out hulks could overcome the subconscious horrors that were possibly planted in the minds of many. And for what real warrior gain? Did the exposure make some of them better warriors? Did they extract better payback in Somalia, Afghanistan, or Iraq in later years? Or do they pay the price today in some other form? Ask the VA for statistics, or ask some of the suffering spouses.

MEMORIES FOREVER

In a few short pages I have tried to provide a glimpse of some aspects of *the cost of* being engaged in lethal combat from Vietnam to Desert Storm. Other participants, especially those on the opposing side, will have additional or possibly even conflicting viewpoints. But what I've written here is enough if you take away from it the realization that warriors who risk their lives pay a price that in many cases, in some form, is for life.

I have come to realize that when you take a human life as a warrior combatant, be it from afar with an air strike that you direct or up close and personal, you carry those moments with you. They may become hazy or even suppressed in your mind, yet seem to resurface or become uncomfortably clear during unsuspected or unguarded moments conjured up by some psychological trigger: a scene on TV, a movie sequence in a darkened theater, the sound of an approaching storm, or even the distinctive *whup whup* sound of the blade of a passing UH-1-type helicopter.

Where I live now, there are C-130s passing by most days because of a nearby training base. I hear the sound and always look up and usually smile as I remember the brave crews of the Spectre gunships and the transports that did the airdrops. And then my mind sometimes lingers on the image of the one that burned at Kontum's airstrip.

There is an old commercial jingle that went, "Is it real, or is it Memorex?" For combat warriors, it is real, and the tape of *the cost of it* can be replayed without warning, possibly for life.

May most of any such memories for you be welcomed and good.

CHAPTER

Family

Every single one of them told me that the images they saw when they looked at their imminent demise were the faces of their mothers and their fathers and their lovers and their sons and their daughters.

And the lesson from all those flashing lives is this: the people we love are our raisons d'être. Our reasons for being. The ones for whom we fight.

—Massad Ayoob,
from "Why We Fight"

WHY WE FIGHT

by Massad Ayoob

*In his 30th year as a sworn police officer, currently serving at the rank of captain with a municipal police department in northern New England, **Massad Ayoob** has been a firearms and use-of-force instructor since the early 1970s. He has chaired the firearms committee of the American Society for Law Enforcement Training (ASLET) since its inception in 1987. Mr. Ayoob also serves on the board of the International Association of Law Enforcement Trainers (ILEETA) and has lectured for the International Association of Law Enforcement Firearms Instructors (IALEFI) at regional, national, and international seminars. He has lectured for the International Homicide Investigators' Seminar, the National Association of Criminal Defense Attorneys, and the DEA Academy at Quantico, Virginia, on investigation of officer-involved shootings and management of trial defense in justifiable homicide cases.*

Cross-trained as instructor and trainer of instructors in firearms, straight baton and PR-24, kubotan, advanced Taser, and unarmed defensive tactics, Mr. Ayoob founded the Lethal Force Institute in 1981 and has served as its director for 22 years. He has held several state, regional, and national titles in combat handgun competition and was voted the Outstanding American Handgunner of the Year by his peers in 1998. He is the author of numerous books and thousands of published articles on weapons, law enforcement, survival tactics, and appropriate use of force. Mr. Ayoob's book In the Gravest Extreme *is generally recognized as the authoritative text on judicious use of lethal force in self-defense.*

Information on Lethal Force Institute training and on Mr. Ayoob's many books and training tapes produced for Police Bookshelf is available online at www.ayoob.com.

❖

It is not enough to teach a practitioner *how* to fight. It is essential to teach him *why*. History is replete with ragtag patriots who kicked out of their homelands hardcore professional soldiers who had invaded them, a history we Americans celebrate every Fourth of July. Skill and knowledge aren't enough. There's that thing called motivation.

The warrior skills, truth to tell, are so involved that they can become their own raison d'être. Why else would martial arts be a sport that creates a lifestyle, and why else would combat shooting be something practitioners do in a competition arena for their primary avocation? Let's admit the dirty secret: learning to fight, with or without a weapon in hand, can be *fun,* and sometimes the fun and the self-esteem of achieving a certain skill level can become the tail that wags the dog. When that happens, the result can be a national champion *karateka* or pistol competitor . . . but not necessarily the best-prepared warrior.

If you have been in this business long enough, you have come across the person who looks you in the eye and says, "I'd rather die than kill my attacker." If you get that from a cop or soldier, your duty is to remove him from The Job, because he's obviously not ready to perform it. When you hear it from an ordinary citizen, you have a little more room. My answer has always been, "That's OK, because it's your life . . . isn't it?"

They morally answer, "Yes." Fine so far. Then I ask them the litmus test question.

"Tell me something. If that same guy you'd rather die than kill was standing over your baby's cradle holding a knife, ready to sacrifice your child to Satan, what would you do then?"

When you ask that question, the answer comes boiling up out of them in pure reflex, before they can think about it, more than nine times out of ten: "I'd kill him!"

Then I pause for a moment, to let them reflect on what they've said, and ask them the final self-probing test question: "*What's the difference?*"

All who are writing for this book, and a great many reading it, know the answer to that question. We know it because we have stood at the precipice of Death and looked down into the abyss, and it is a knowledge we have an ethical obligation to impart to those we teach.

The answer is, there is no real difference at all. Death is The Great Separator. Whether it is the parent who dies, or the child, either way each is lost to the other forevermore, at least upon this earth.

You reading this, you who have been there at the edge of the Darkness and looking into the Void . . . remember. Did it not happen—at that moment, or very shortly thereafter—that you thought of your loved ones? How long did it take for the realization to hit you that you almost didn't see your children grow up, almost lost your last chance to say good-bye to your parents?

This tells us something, something we need to share with those we teach in the art and science of survival of violence. Hold that thought, and let's look to some analogous concepts to see how they fit in.

The survival disciplines are multidimensional, and each interrelated discipline can be a lifelong study in and of itself.

A conflict involving lethal force is, by definition, a near-death experience for the survivor. We can learn a great deal about how to face imminent death by studying not just combat survivors but all survivors of near-death events.

Virtually all of us contributing to this effort are familiar with the splendid work done by Dr. Alexis Artwohl when she was police psychologist for the Portland Police Bureau, as published by her and her colleague Loren Christensen in *Deadly Force Encounters*. Few are aware of a corollary study done about a decade ago by Dr. John Woo, chief of psychiatry at the University of California, Irvine.

While the Artwohl study focused entirely on officer-involved shootings, the Woo study was geared to the perceptual phenomena of near-death survivors at the time of their incidents and covered a broader spectrum. I came into it when Dr. Woo approached me to arrange interviews with Lethal Force Institute graduates who had survived gunfights. They would join a much greater body of research participants who had survived falls from high places, automobile collisions, train wrecks, plane crashes, near-drownings, sudden and cataclysmic medical emergencies, and other immediately life-threatening situations.

The same phenomena I had been studying, writing, and teaching about since the 1970s were all there when I read the results of the Woo research: tachypsychia, the sense of everything going into slow motion; tunnel vision; auditory exclusion, or "tunnel hearing"; and more. But Woo's study asked one question that I had never thought to ask the gunfight survivors I interviewed. I wanted to kick myself when I realized the oversight.

The question was, "Did you experience a sensation of 'your life flashing before your eyes' at the moment you looked Death in the face?"

A significant number of the participants in the Woo study had experienced exactly that. It's something we've all read or heard about. "My life flashed before my eyes." It's a perception so common that almost everyone who has experienced it uses virtually those exact same words to describe it.

Since learning that, I've made a point of polling my own students when we talk about the altered perceptual phenomena that occur in violent encounters. I ask how many have heard of "the life flashing before the eyes"; virtually all have. Then I ask how many have experienced it themselves, and in a class of any size there are usually at least a couple.

And then I ask one more question, a question so obvious I've never heard anyone ask it in these discussions: *What were the images?* You were 20, 30, whatever years old; there wasn't time for all of it. When you thought you were about to immediately leave this world, what were the images that computer between your ears thought were so important they had to be reviewed one last time?"

The answers have been strikingly uniform. I'm still waiting for one of them to tell me, "I flashed back to the cutest gal I ever picked up in a singles bar," or "I saw myself back at the podium receiving my life achievement award."

No, every single one of them told me that the images they saw when they approached their imminent demise were the faces of their mothers and their fathers and their lovers and their sons and their daughters.

And the lesson from all those flashing lives is this: The people we love are our raisons d'être. Our reasons for being. The ones for whom we fight.

Medical literature is replete with examples of "surrender death," patients who shouldn't have died from what ailed them but did, because they simply "gave up." And any experienced trauma doc, ER nurse, or paramedic can describe cases of the opposite: the patient who was torn apart by outside trauma or rotted away by disease from inside who managed to stay alive long enough to accomplish something important.

We've all heard the stories of the little granny who manages to lift up the car that is crushing her grandchild. No one ever mentions that she tore loose every muscle in her back and suffered two or three compression fractures of the spine. It suffices to know that superhuman physical ability is there on tap, triggered by supernormal need to act.

I tell my students of two police officers in Ohio. Terry, a county deputy, remembers being down on his back, being stomped into the parking lot of a roadhouse by a veritable giant. Kicked in the groin, battered about the head, and almost fading out of consciousness, unable to breathe because his ribs were broken, he was ready to let go. "It wasn't just the pain," he told me much later. "It wasn't even the humiliation of being beaten. A big part of it was despair, looking at the faces of the people I was dying to protect. They had their faces to the window, watching me get kicked to death, and not a God-damned one of them was willing to come out and help me."

Terry paused and added almost in a whisper, "And then I saw in my mind's eye, as if I was there, my two sons standing at my grave."

The witnesses inside the roadhouse saw something close to a miracle then. One of them told an investigator later, "The deputy climbed the big guy's body."

They saw a hand rise up and grab the big man's jeans, and another reach up and clutch his belt. One of the sheep inside had at least called 911, and when the responding deputies arrived, Terry was on top. The big man's eyes had rolled back in his head, and Terry was somewhere else behind a face covered with blood and grime, and it took three of them to peel Terry's hands from his antagonist's throat and pull him off . . .

Jimmy was a big-city cop in the same state. Armed only with a little five-shot Smith & Wesson .38, he responded from off-duty status to join the manhunt for a suspect who had shot and wounded two cops. Jimmy was searching an apartment when he jerked open a closet door, and—*bang!*

The suspect had been waiting inside. At a range measurable in inches, he shot Jimmy in the face with a .357 Magnum. The bullet entered just to the side of his nose, shattering the maxillofacial structure; traveled under the brain; and exited just to the side of his spine and under the base of the skull. At the hammerblow of the impact, the young officer toppled onto his back.

He told me a long time afterward, "Mas, you cannot *imagine* the pain. Picture a great big railroad spike. Heat it white hot. Now suppose someone hammers it through the front of your face and out the base of your skull and nails you to the floor with it.

"I wanted to die just so the pain would stop.

"And then I saw my daughters being told that I was dead."

It was as if something from outside his body had entered and reanimated him. Something unseen lifted him up off the floor. He reached down and picked up his fallen revolver and went after the man who shot him. Jimmy emptied his revolver into that man, hit him four times out of five, and killed him where he stood. By now, the other cops who had heard the shots were there.

It was clear that Jimmy had sustained a perforating, large-caliber, close-range gunshot wound to the head. They knew he could not possibly live, but they had to do everything they could. Rather than wait for an ambulance, they put him into a squad car and raced to the hospital.

Jimmy was calling for his daughters. A good supervisor knows his personnel and their families, and Jimmy had a good sergeant. It was day shift, and the sergeant rushed one patrol car to the high school and another to the middle school to pick up each of the girls.

By the time the kids reached the hospital, Jimmy was on a

gurney outside the OR, about to undergo emergency surgery. In each of his bloodstained hands, he took one of theirs. The inside of his shattered head was so full of blood he sounded like a man talking underwater when he told his two daughters, "I'm gonna live! I'm gonna live for *you!*"

And he did.

It's as if inside each one of us there is a reserve battery for desperate moments, a last-ditch source of superhuman energy that is tapped only in the gravest extreme of crisis. And I have often wondered how many people couldn't use it because by the time that hidden battery kicked in, their body was already too broken to take advantage of it.

Remember the mother who has been conditioned by her society to die rather than protect herself but is triggered to homicidal response by the mother wolf instinct when someone attacks her cub. Most humans will fight harder to protect someone who depends upon them than they will to protect themselves.

Those of us responsible not only for training but for motivating individuals to fight for their lives cannot lose sight of this. The next time you train your warriors, remind them what they're going to be fighting for.

Not for the next drink at the bar. Not for the next plaque on the wall.

Remind them that they're fighting to spare their parents the unnatural grief of burying a child. Fighting to return to the person they swore a covenant to live out their life with. Fighting to come back to every child they have brought into this unforgiving place, to be there for as long as they can be, to shepherd them through it. Because if they allow themselves to be killed, they will be separated from those loved ones as surely as if the loved ones had been murdered instead.

If they know from the beginning of the conflict that this is what they're fighting for, they'll be stronger, more determined, more likely to prevail. Let that reserve battery be triggered at the beginning of the fight, so they can fight from the beginning at maximum strength, and they will be more likely in the end to emerge from that fight unscathed.

WARRIORS AT HOME

by Daniel L. Christensen

Daniel L. Christensen has been surrounded by warriors his entire life. Son of Loren W. Christensen, he grew up hearing long discussions by martial artists, police officers, and soldiers. As a boy he worried about his father, who worked some of Portland, Oregon's most dangerous streets as a patrol officer, mingled with brutal white supremacists as a gang specialist, and bodyguarded a host of high-profile personalities. Mr. Christensen watched his father and many of his police cases on the 5 o'clock news, and he read about them in the newspaper.

For the past several years Mr. Christensen has been entrenched in academia. Having earned a bachelor's degree in biblical studies and a master's degree in exegetical theology, he is now a doctoral candidate in theology.

Mr. Christensen's work in sharing his faith has taken him into the streets of Portland, South Central Los Angeles, San Francisco, Las Vegas, Baltimore, Washington DC, and Juarez, Mexico. He has worked diligently with the homeless and the mentally ill.

As a writer, Dan is a regular contributor to Christian News Northwest.

❖❖❖

She is the little girl who cries as her head rests on the shoulder of a man who has knelt down to her on the tarmac. She has on her pink Sunday dress; he has on standard-issue military fatigues. Telling her he will be back in a year does not comfort her, because he is either with her or he is not. Cries of "daddy!" will now go unanswered, for her stronghold is leaving. She used to be concerned about getting ice cream after dinner, or whether the kitty would let her pet him. Now she prays nightly, "Please God, don't let the bad guys kill my daddy."

He is the boy who shakes his dad's hand though he desperately desires a hug. His face reddens and his lip quivers as he holds back tears. He is worried but tries not to show it. He does not talk because he is unsure of how to express what he is feeling and because he does not want his mom to worry. Before he learns algebra, he will learn the difference between chemical and biological weapons. Small countries with names that are hard to pronounce become part of his everyday language. He will not have a good night's sleep until his father returns home.

She is the woman who sees her elderly father fight silent, invisible battles from a war that history books say ended many years ago. She knows he fights to sleep at night, losing the struggle to the dreadful images of suffering and death. She believes he is incomplete, having had part of himself stolen in a hostile, foreign land. She cannot talk to him about his struggles because he will not expose her to such demons.

He is the young man who brags to friends that his father is an important man who dons a uniform and badge. Yet when his father is at work, every siren the boy hears in the distance causes his heart to flutter and his palms to sweat. He turns on the television to escape the anxiety, but in too many shows and movies, as sure as the credits will roll at the end, police officers are injured and killed.

Together, they are the children of warriors. They count among them the sons and daughters of military personnel, police officers, and everyone who runs to the dangerous ground that all others are fleeing. As this malicious ground turns red with stolen life, children are left wanting, ignorant of the bigger picture by which the battle is justified, awaiting the return of those they need most.

Unlike traditional warriors, these children fight a battle without artillery and intelligence, receive no training or instruction, and have no choice. Fear, pride, worry, and excitement, all tread upon the same soul without concern for its innocence or vulnerability. These children have a warrior in their family and have, therefore, been drafted into a complex labyrinth of emotions. The children's battle is to live with this confusing and paradoxical reality. Their war is to know the warrior whom they love.

Children of warriors often line the parade route of patriotism and champion national attributes such as freedom and bravery. They are often those waving flags and leading the cheers. Particularly for boys, there is an excitement about the life of a warrior: fighting bad guys, rescuing people, carrying a gun. To them, their warrior is like the hero on a television show. He fights raccoon-masked robbers who are as physically weak as they are dumb, and he drives cars at high speeds and rides horses at full gallop. At the end of the hour, the bad guys are caught and no one is hurt; that is, unless the bad guys are knocked out cold by a telegraphed, from-the-next-town-over roundhouse punch.

For most of these children there is a pride within. That a member of the family is partially responsible for capturing a dangerous criminal or halting the progression of a hostile regime makes children hold their heads high and puff out their chests. As the child grows older, these positive emotions are aligned inevitably with new ones that understand better the reality of danger and violence to which their warrior is subjected. Then, inside, there are no more fireworks or victory parades.

When their warrior's environment is truly understood, childhood becomes one long gasp for breath. It is not uncommon for them to struggle through school, church, extracurricular activities, and at home. In their sleepless, infinite midnight, their attempt to think good thoughts fails as their minds wander into that dungeon of fear where childhood naiveté and innocence are attacked mercilessly.

For as much good as the warrior does—that is, the causes for which he fights and the positive changes that he makes—it is inevitable that warriorhood changes him. The transformation from animalistic predator on the battlefield to gentle teddy bear at home is difficult. What does that mean for the children? At times, they see only a stranger. They know something has changed. Their warrior may get angry frequently, spend more time alone, or not get along as well as he did with other members of the family. Warriorhood to these children is a tiptoeing, approach-by-night life-stealer, robbing them of a part of their warrior, a part that is rightfully theirs.

Those whose parents are warriors have had constructed around them a shield, the intention of which is to keep the danger and violence of the world far from them physically and mentally. However, the shield is porous and flimsy. It is almost impossible for the warrior to speak to his spouse or his children and not mention work, exposing what childhood psyches are not ready to experience. In the warrior's defense, because warriorhood is often stressful, it is important to be able to talk to get release from pressure and frustration.

Children may sincerely enjoy an interesting or humorous story about military or police life, but the next time the warrior is working, the story takes on a different meaning in their mind's eye. This time it's replayed with a bad ending. Ultimately, any story provides the compartments by which children organize their fears.

Children of warriors often understand the world better than other children. They know in part because they want to know their warrior, but this truth has negative aspects as well. When they keep up with current events in their community, country, and the world, they become experts at self-absorption. They think that whatever conflict is happening is related to their warrior. From wars to gunshots to car accidents, all dangerous occurrences are potential environments for their warrior, but on a collective level, which means to the children it never feels like *it's my warrior against one bad guy*. It feels like *it's my warrior against the world*.

Children of warriors have also exposed a grave weakness in the information age. The Internet, cable and satellite television, news radio, and numerous literary publications make available the smallest details of military conflict. The current era is one where 24-hour media outlets are plentiful and news organizations fight over violent wartime images like vultures over a game carcass. Though too much information can be bad for children, and they may not want to see the images or read the articles, they do because there exists in them a curiosity concerning the environment and welfare of their loved one. Today, the children of military personnel can watch a war on television while news anchors give the play-by-play as if it were a football game. Cringing at every bomb that is dropped and every gun that is fired, children can have their emotional turmoil turn into panic attacks or some other physical instability.

Entering adulthood, children get more clarity on why their warrior does what he is called to do. This is not to say that they are comfortable with the activity, but that they understand the actions taken. Many reason that there are people somewhere with names they have never heard and faces they have never seen whose lives are better in some way because of their warrior.

Being the grown child of a warrior does not bring as many answers, but it does provide a greater depth to the questions. More often than not, the children are caught in an endless cycle of answer-seeking. They search desperately for the man behind the curtain, only to discover he is not there. But instead of walking away in an act of desperation to escape their paranoia, they shut the curtain and quickly open it again with the hope that this time someone might be there.

The children of warriors live with two realities. The first is one of patriotism, pride, and excitement. The other is one of fear, anxiety, and worry. Neither is to be ignored or exalted. The realities are seemingly opposite, yet not contradictory.

Instead of trying to control the children's emotions and feelings, people would do well to let them simply feel and experience this paradoxical reality. They do not need a this-is-the-right-way-to-feel-and-think life preserver from an adult. Rather, they need to ride the current in whatever direction it may take them. To experience these two realities is to hold them in tension. To hold them in tension is to acknowledge them as they take turns manifesting throughout childhood. They are not to be fought; rather they are to be invited to run their course. For the child, to acknowledge them is to communicate their existence in order to distribute the burden to those who have offered to share the load.

In light of their struggles, there are two common paths that the children of warriors travel. Variations are plentiful, and a child may wander down each at different times in life. Although some people have taken the first path and some the second, no two people can walk the same path in the same way. Each traveler brings his own uniqueness and specific intricacies to the journey.

The theme of the first path incorporates resentment, anger, and loneliness. On this path, gaps in the parent-child relationship are not uncommon, for when that negatively influenced part of a warrior surfaces, many children, no matter their age, instinctively withdraw to protect themselves emotionally and, for some, physically.

Travelers on this path would benefit from finding that place within their relationship where the negatively affected part of the warrior does not manifest. That place is not a physical location, but an emotional environment where the child, young or old, feels nurtured and loved. Perhaps sharing the mutual enjoyment of a recreational activity, such as a hobby, sport, literary or movie genre, or restaurant can act as a foundation of interacting in a relationship that will open the door to further depth throughout life. Without such a place in such a relationship, the lack of emotional intimacy will be reduced to an occasional meeting of two physical beings, their souls having been divorced from one another, and their bond severed by a gloating enemy.

The theme of the second path is trust. It is natural for the parent to be desirous that his child would trust his decisions in all circumstances, and natural for a child to want to trust his parent. However, this is not to advocate trust in the parent's decision to enter warriorhood, since he was probably young when he entered it. In many cases, the decision may not have been his, such as during the years of the draft. In others, it may have been the result of young, idealistic 18-year-old ambition. Only the parent knows how he perceived warriorhood before he entered it versus how he perceives it after making a career or a life out of it.

What "trust" suggests in this context is a belief in something higher. Coupled with this suggestion is a sense of purpose. Sons and daughters traveling on the second path have, as an aspect of their worldview, a belief in a reality that is not seen. They believe there is a greater and higher cause to which their finite understanding may not be privy. They observe that their warriors have special abilities in relation to the responsibilities they have been asked to carry out and tasks they are to complete—attributes most people do not possess.

The questions, Why is the world such a dangerous place? and Why did my warrior get called to this particular role in it? will, in most cases, go unanswered. Yet, what is transparent is that the way of the world and the way of the warrior fit together like two pieces of a jigsaw puzzle.

The children's consciences, like the rhythmic beat of a war drum, continuously whisper to them, "The world is not supposed to be this way." The world is full of violence, death, malice, suffering, and pain. In this world, the warriors are called to confront the physical manifestations of such evil. Their children are called to withstand the consequences of these battles.

If warriors were to look behind them as they run toward the hostile ground from which everyone else flees, they would see their children running after them. For it is better to be in danger and *with* daddy, than to be safe *without* him. The children run, driven by love and strengthened by courage. The bravery and ambition of the parent and child in this picture would leave an outside observer to remark, "They are both warriors."

And when the guns are silent and the family is safe and together, only then can it be said, "We were victorious."

TRIBULATIONS OF A WARRIOR'S FAMILY

by Dave Rose

Dave Rose retired from the Placer County (California) Sheriff's Department after 25 years of service, with 28 years total law enforcement experience. He is a certified instructor in defensive tactics, impact weapons, firearms, survival shooting, less-lethal munitions, submachine guns, distraction devices, Tasers, incident command, and WMDs. Mr. Rose has 23 years of SWAT experience, including entry team, entry team leader, assistant team leader, team leader, and team commander.

Mr. Rose's complete biography is included with his essay "You Scare Me" in Chapter 1.

❖

"Just shoot him! Don't talk to him, shoot him!" Responding to these statements in the darkened theater was my bride's sharp elbow into my rib cage. I had once again embarrassed her immensely by reacting to the screen hero's actions as a warrior, forgetting that the movie was designed for entertainment, not reality.

A warrior's family and friends have to endure many hardships, embarrassments, rude or inane questions, and lonely times. It is the resiliency of the warrior family that enables the warrior to focus on the responsibility of his chosen profession. It takes a great deal of give and take among members of the family to weather the various stresses the warrior path places upon all of them. It is no surprise that many warriors' personal relationships suffer if they are not able to adjust their professional lives to their personal and social lives. It is unfortunate that many warriors of my generation have had to learn this the hard way, after experiencing a divorce or two.

One of the larger stressors on a warrior family is the work schedule or assignment. Shift work, undercover assignments, surveillances, heavy caseloads, or long-term deployments can have a deleterious effect on a family. A spouse is forced to perform in both the father and mother roles while the warrior is engaged in his professional role. Any family emergencies that occur are oftentimes handled without direct input or support from the warrior. An excellent example can be found in the daily news coverage of our military forces—regular, reserve, and National Guard—that are deployed all over the world fighting the War on Terror. These warriors and their families experience tremendous financial and emotional hardships as a result of their professional responsibilities. Combine that with missed holidays and family gatherings due to professional obligations, and the stress builds.

The holidays are an especially important time of year for most Americans. Family gatherings can be of tremendous significance to a stable family life. Missing too many of these valuable social events can have a harmful effect on family life. There have been many holiday family dinners where I have fallen asleep on the living room floor and family members had to step over and around until it was time to awaken me for dinner. I was present in body but not in conscious thought. Other times the only way to attend a family gathering or seasonal dinner was to drop in while on duty, even as the family attended without me.

Perhaps the most bizarre examples of times my family had to adjust to my warrior schedule were two Memorial Day holidays in a row. The entire family gathered to celebrate three family birthdays that all fell on that weekend, one of which was mine. Both years my SWAT unit was activated for emergency callouts, and both times I anticipated returning within several hours to enjoy the family festivities. But each year I missed the family gatherings, much to my late father's dismay. My wife pulled them off magnificently without me.

These trials of working hours, training, or assignments can also have detrimental effects on the children, particularly if they are involved in extracurricular activities. How many back-to-school nights; recitals; football, basketball, or baseball games; wrestling matches; track meets; or plays has a family had to participate in without the physical presence of their warrior? It can be especially difficult for younger children or teenage children when all of their peers' fathers or mothers are present but you are not. The stress of missing these growing experiences of one's children can cause even the toughest warrior to suffer emotional pain.

Friends and acquaintances often inadvertently add to the stress placed upon the family. Sometimes they are just curious, and other times they just don't realize what they are doing. For example, when the warrior is involved in some notable incident, usually one involving high-risk issues or use of high-level force, word gets around through media or gossip. Curious friends or neighbors ask family members what it is like being related to the warrior, or they simply state, "Boy, I bet he is a hard-ass, isn't he?" Occasionally, someone asks questions such as, "What's it like being married to such a potentially violent man?" Or the children are queried, "Did your dad/mom really shoot that guy?" I lost track of how many of my sons' friends would admit, after having been around the family for some time, that they were afraid of me at first. Even some of their girlfriends would tell my sons how intimidated they were when I was around or when they had first met me. This obviously had some effect on my sons' and wife's social interactions.

Warriors and weapons go hand in hand, and having weapons in a residence is routine. Firearms, particularly in gun-restrictive states like California, are subject to voluminous regulations. Children and firearms are always of concern. Controlling unauthorized access to weapons in a warrior household places additional pressure on the family unit. Rules are necessary, as is the strict adherence to them. There can be no room for bending of the family unit's rules on weapons access. Education of all family members in proper weapons handling and use is imperative. My four sons were subjected to several trips to the firing range, and after many rounds fired downrange and many plastic bottles destroyed, the mysteriousness of firearms was gone, replaced with a proper respect for the tool. In my entire 28-year law enforcement career, the family never committed a weapons rule violation.

Intensity is my wife's favorite noun to describe my personality, and it has been a source of particular stress on our married life. The inherent intensity required in training, job performance, and daily preparation can bring about unintended strain on the family unit. This is particularly true if other family members are involved in activities at the opposite spectrum of the warrior way. Transferring the intensity required to perform as a protector to everyday events can be overwhelming to family members, not to mention the general public. Just reverting to command voice can chill many family discussions or get-togethers. Not consciously realizing that the tone of your voice just clicked into intense mode can inject unintended friction into an otherwise normal conversation. You must maintain a constant check on the intensity expressed both in voice and body language when you are not in an action mode. However, the family needs to be trained to respond without hesitation as directed in times of crisis or danger. This apparent dichotomy causes anguish within the family unit unless the family understands the importance of the need to respond correctly when dangerous situations are confronted.

A gathering of family or friends in public can result in another type of difficulty. A family member or friend can inadvertently put the warrior and his family in danger, or at least discomfort, by identifying him. Most often the family member or friend doesn't realize that distinguishing him as a member of the warrior class might force him to take an action that otherwise might not be suitable in the circumstance. These incidents only serve to put the peace officer or military member on the spot when, say, antiwarrior types who feel secure within the social environment berate or challenge the warrior.

A more problematic situation occurs when some family member or friend becomes involved in a verbal or physical confrontation and identifies the warrior as someone in authority. Now he has to put on his professional face and interdict. Invariably, some will decide that whatever action, or nonaction, was taken did not meet their expectations. The immediate family members find themselves being interrogated by other family members or friends about why the warrior did or did not do something.

How does a family overcome these many trials and tribulations? I have found that truly expressing your love and feelings for them, as often as possible, is a great antidote. Not being afraid to show emotion for and to your family, either in public or private, demonstrates to them that you have a soft side as well as a hard side. For my family and me, having a solid grounding in our Catholic faith is a tremendous asset. Practicing that faith as a family whenever possible is the cement that holds the unit together.

Having integrity within the familial relationships, as well as the professional ones, exhibits your true strength as a warrior, one whose family will withstand all trials put to it.

THE WARRIOR PARENT

by Sonayia Shepherd

Sonayia (Sony) Shepherd *currently serves as the bioterrorism exercise coordinator for a state public health agency. She previously served as a school safety coordinator and as the state antiterrorism planner for the Georgia Emergency Management Agency–Office of the Governor.*

Ms. Shepherd is also one of the nation's top experts in the field of school safety and childcare facility safety. She has coauthored 14 books on school safety issues and authored numerous articles, and her monthly column Sony Says *can be found in* Campus Safety Journal. *Ms. Shepherd is currently writing a book on childcare facility safety. In addition, she is the lead author of the book* Jane's Citizen Safety Guide *by Jane's Information Group Publications.*

Ms. Shepherd is a nationally recognized presenter who has provided training for national organizations including the Boys and Girls Clubs of America, The National Association for School Security and Law Enforcement Officers (NASSLEO), the Israel Police, and many others. She is certified in grant writing, adventure therapy, play therapy, juvenile and adult case management, managing aggressive behaviors, crisis intervention, and crisis counseling. Ms. Shepherd is a regular presenter at state, national, and international professional conferences. She holds an MS in child and adolescent psychology from Cameron University in Oklahoma. Ms. Shepherd also serves as chief operating officer of Safe Havens International, Inc., a nonprofit safety center (www.safehavensinterntional.org).

❖

Many children innately possess a warrior mentality during their youth, but some event squelches their ability to hold onto their inner warrior. Sometimes this event is internal, such as a decline in self-esteem, or the event may be external, such as a bullying incident that had a lasting effect. In any case, the war riorlike mentality must be fostered in children, and a balance of discipline and love must occur for children to prosper. This balance is an important aspect of warriorhood. If children are not instilled with both unconditional love and a disciplined mind, then a potential *warrior* will grow up to become a painstakingly annoying *worrier*, and a great opportunity to effect a positive change in a child will be missed. As research demonstrates, if a child can identify and connect with just one adult, he or she is less likely to engage in risky behavior. Everyone reading this statistic should become overjoyed at the fact that *you* can be that one adult or parent who can raise a warrior!

Parents must first notice that their child is a warrior and build upon that notion.

Look for a natural talent in your child.

Most men and women who have achieved success will relay childhood experiences that led to their current position. For example, many great athletes had a natural talent in their youth. Someone saw this talent and fostered it by enabling the child to get proper coaching and opportunities to hone his or her skills. Likewise, the most powerful speakers typically have always had something to say, even as children (this has happened in shy children also). However, with the help of others, they realized that their message must be packaged and presented in the best possible way, and thus a great orator emerged. Whatever the talents of the child, if proper guidance is not provided, the talent will become a simple dream that will never be achieved.

Helping children find their purpose by teaching them to assess *who* they are instead of *what* they want to be is a great step in warriorhood. In other words, parents must discard the proverbial question, "What do you want to be when you grow up?" and ask them, "What type of person do you want to be?" Instead of getting the typical answer of firefighter, police officer, doctor, or lawyer, you can expect answers like "a caring person," "someone who helps people," "a strong person," and so on. Helping children find out who they are will help them avoid building their life around the goals and expectations of society. This is an important point because if they build their lives around things that they can see, the impact can be devastating because the meaning of their lives will shift as society changes. And instead of becoming strong-anchored warriors, they will eventually be in need of an anchor themselves and latch onto things beneath them. Building a high-minded mentality in children is crucial because as adults they must understand that just as a compass has two ends, they need to know their current position in order to know where they are going. In order for a child to figure out what he will be, he must first understand who he is and, by continually assessing his purpose, he will inevitably lead himself to the path of warriorhood.

Develop a regular weekly routine for doing something special with your child.

Not only will this help keep open the lines of communication with your child, but this can also help you discover exactly what types of activities your child is interested in, which will in turn give you insight into your child's natural talents. Expose your child to a variety of activities—don't limit her mind. Eat together often. Meals are great for bonding. It is a fact that parents who spend quality time with their children will reap the benefits of an open relationship. Meals are a perfect avenue for sharing. Showing your willingness to listen will make your child feel more comfortable about opening up to you. So talk to your child. Seek input from her about family decisions. Sometimes, you will be shocked by what your children will tell you, but don't react in a way that will cut off further discussion. If your child says things that challenge or shock you, turn them into a calm discussion and look for a lesson in every situation. There are other activities that you and your child can partake in besides meals. Reading, walking, playing, and cleaning house are also great ways for spending time together and bonding.

Create an environment that exemplifies a warrior mentality.

Warriors will beget warriors, right? Not necessarily. There are some warriors who happen to be parents. But will this mean that they will parent like warriors? Obviously, you don't have to be a warrior to have children with a warrior mentality, but parents or guardians who already possess this mentality will have a distinct edge in raising children to become warriors.

An environment that expects excellence is key. Your expectations must be clearly expressed to your children, and you must not yield to less-than-desirable results. Now it must also be noted that when a child makes a mistake it's your job to unveil a lesson in that mistake. Remember, affection and respect will reinforce good (and change bad) behavior. Embarrassment or uneasiness won't. This is important because most warriors have an uncanny sense of understanding about how to turn life's lessons into positive energy. They know the world well and do not succumb to naiveté.

Tell your children they are what you want them to be. I remember my mother telling me when I was young that I was smart and beautiful. I grew up believing both, and I have lived my life as if they were true. I never saw the connection until I studied child and adolescent psychology and learned that children believe what they are told about themselves. Telling a child, "You are a bad kid!" may cause him to grow up believing it and allow him to feel comfortable doing the things a bad person would do. The extreme case of this was a mother who repeatedly told her son, "You are just like your father, you are all bad." The father was in prison for murder. As a man, that former little boy is proud to be a killer. He is now on death row for multiple murders. One woman told her four-year-old to "be a good boy" every day when she dropped him off at preschool. He is 15 now, and she wishes she had done the same with her older son, who is now on probation. Each parent must decide which positive things to say to his or her children. Remember that parents who say negative things eventually pay for it later. But parents who are continuously feeding their children an emotional diet of positive energy will reap the benefits of becoming proud parents. Remember to constantly show your love. Every day, tell your children: "I love you. You're special to me." Give lots of hugs and kisses and children learn to love every day.

Lead by example.

Show the compassion, honesty, generosity, and openness you want your child to have. Remember that the warrior adult will often possess these attributes, so they must be fostered in children. The best way to instill these warriorlike qualities in children is to show them by modeling this behavior. Each day is an opportunity for you to provide your children with examples of all of the qualities you want them to have. Always praise your children. When they learn something new or behave well, tell them you're proud of them. Reward good behavior consistently and immediately. Expressions of love, appreciation, and thanks go a long way—even for kids who think themselves too old for hugs. Accentuate the positive. Emphasize what your kid does right. Restrain the urge to be critical. Create rules and enforce them fairly. Discuss in advance the consequences of breaking them. Don't make empty threats or let the rule-breaker off easy. Don't impose harsh or unexpected new punishments. For older children, set a curfew. Enforce it strictly, but be ready to negotiate on special occasions. By providing this type of structure and discipline, you will teach your warrior child how to be gentle yet firm. She will understand the difference between assertiveness and aggressiveness. She will grow up to be an honest adult and a positive person.

Be a guide for your children.

Offer to help with homework, in social situations, and with concerns about the future. Be there to help them direct and redirect their energy and to understand and express their feelings. Provide an environment for your children with a foundation of mutual appreciation, support, and respect as the basis of your relationship into their adult years. Correct your child's behavior when necessary. Remember to criticize the behavior, not the child. When your child makes a mistake, don't say, "You were bad." Instead, explain what the child did wrong. For example, say, "Running into the street without looking isn't safe." Then tell the child what to do instead: "First, look both ways for cars." Teach your child that you love him even when his behavior is untoward. Doing this teaches the most important quality of a warrior—unconditional love.

Once the child has discovered his purpose and understands what it takes to succeed, he will in turn exude warriorhood. Children are by far the best-known warriors. Their resilience and innocence should be noticed by all adults as basic characteristics of warriorhood.

WARRIORS' KIDS

by Loren W. Christensen

Loren W. Christensen's biography can be found at the back of this book.

❖

Once on the job I found a dead baby in a dresser drawer. She was a couple months old, cute, and blue. The parents were huddled together on the front steps of their dilapidated apartment, holding each other and weeping. They couldn't afford a crib, or much else for that matter. So the baby slept in the drawer. The last I heard was that the medical examiner was going to declare it SIDS, sudden infant death syndrome.

That night I hugged my kids extra hard; my boy wasn't much older than that baby.

For two years I investigated child abuse cases. One case involved a father who beat his eight-year-old boy bloody with a belt each day, hung him on a closet hook each night, and occasionally stuffed feces in his mouth. The father was apprehended before he killed the boy, but still the child stopped speaking and growing for a couple of years.

I hugged my kids extra hard after that was over.

We have all heard the expression "man's inhumanity to man." There were many times on the job when I thought it should be "man's inhumanity to children." It's abominable what adults do to their kids and to kids who aren't theirs. Molest, rape, kick, punch, burn, and drive mad. One guy dangled his six-year-old boy by his ankles over the edge of a parking structure across the street from my precinct, just to "tease him." The father lost his grip and the boy fell three stories. When the officers got there, the father was telling his still-conscious son, who at the very least had a broken back, not to tell the cops anything.

Children, their purity and innocence, suggest hope that maybe everything will be okay, like the way a beautiful sunset suggests that tomorrow will be a new, better day. Often, I found it a confusion of emotions to first handle a call involving crude, despicable, and stupid people who were ruining their lives, or already had, and then drive around the corner to see kids squealing with delight as they chased one another in a school-yard. It would sadden me to think they shared space in this world with those wretches I had just left. But then I would feel better thinking that just maybe these kids would grow up to make a better world.

Like most parents, warriors love their kids. But unlike most parents, warriors experience that love along with the ugliness and violence of their duty. The contrast can be disconcerting and profound. Many times I wondered, after lodging some salivating beast of a human being into jail, how could the same God who made my beautiful children have made *that*?

One time I had to work when my eight-year-old son had a soccer game. I couldn't get time off, so I went and watched from inside my police car. It was a miserable day, cold, gray, and windy, but the little dudes ignored it and played hard anyway. As I watched, I thought back to when my little buddies and I were that age—full of life, energy, and innocence, not knowing that in 10 years a miserable hell in Vietnam would devour us and change us forever. I prayed that they would never have to experience such horror. I wonder now as I type this if any of my son's soccer pals are in Iraq.

As a military policeman in Vietnam, I patrolled the streets and back alleys of Saigon, where thousands of little children played, begged for food alongside their mothers, or hustled soldiers to follow them to meet their sisters. "She virgin girl. Number one." Sometimes the hustler was no more than six years old. Cherub-looking pimps.

Countless times I saw half-naked kids playing alongside a dirt road as a convoy of dark green military trucks lumbered by, filling the air with thick dust and black exhaust that settled on the laughing children. Sometimes their laughter was nearly drowned out by the ever-present thumping of heavy artillery in the distance. I often played with them, hoping desperately that they would survive their present world to make a better future one.

Sometimes after a long day of patrolling the extraordinarily violent streets of war-torn Saigon, I'd see an exhausted off-duty MP retrieve a crumpled photo from his wallet and smile wistfully at an image of a toddler. "It's all for you, punkin. See you soon." Many a footlocker, barracks post, jeep dash, chopper ceiling, PBR boat, and jet cockpit was covered with photos of babies and toddlers. Most of the troops were too young to have older kids.

Most warrior parents show two faces—one at home and one at work. Sometimes they overlap. Once as I walked through the report-writing area of a police precinct, I heard this in baby talk: "Hi Tiffany. This is daddy. *Daddy.* No, no, don't hang up. What's wrong? Fifi ate your cupcake? Did you put it in the dog dish again? No wait, I don't want to scold the dog . . . hello Fifi. Don't eat Tiffany's cupcake. Tiffany? Tiffany? Listen, sweetie. I have to work late again. But I will come into your room when I get home and kiss you. But I won't wake you. Okay? Love you a whole bunch." The speaker was a 240-pound, beef-fed SWAT man with a buzz cut, 19-inch biceps, and veins that snaked across his forehead. A couple of the guys teased him after he hung up, but he just smiled, picked up his MP5, and left.

I worked the gang unit for four years during the late '80s and early '90s when street gangs were at their worst. Part of our job was to patrol gangbangers' funerals to prevent the opposing gang from doing a drive-by on the mourners, which we had to do nearly every week. We also executed lots of forced-entry warrants, performed saturation patrols in areas where we knew there was to be a drive-by, and rolled up on clusters of gangbangers to disperse them before things got hot. Before each mission and after we had donned our bulletproof vests, strapped on primary and secondary guns, and checked out a shotgun, we called home. If it was in the afternoon, we got to speak to our kids. *"Just wanted to tell you that I love you."* If it was late, we spoke to spouses, telling them they were loved and to give the kids a goodnight kiss for us.

Most warriors hide the horror of what they do from their children in an effort to keep the evil outside the doors and maintain the peace and sanctity of the home. They also do it to preserve, for as long as possible, that sweet innocence that radiates from an often jelly-covered smile.

I once asked a partner, after we had arrested a particularly grotesque manifestation of evil, which is real: the brutal world of the mean streets or the beauty of my kids in the relative quiet of my home. "They are both reality," my partner said simplistically, as if it were a stupid question. He was right, of course, though it's hard to fathom that the merciless asphalt of violent urban America and the dusty, mean streets of volatile Baghdad exist on the same plane as a young daughter's pretend tea party and a red-, chubby-cheeked boy's soccer game. But they do. And it's a difficult task to function well in the two worlds; indeed, it's a warrior's task.

The young kids don't know of this dichotomy. To them, the warrior parent is a hero, a vanquisher of "bad guys," just like the bad guys on television. But when the kids get older and evolve into the dreaded teenagers, the warrior sometimes wonders how he is perceived. Do they know what I do? Do they understand? Do they care?

Perhaps more than we know.

Jessica Blankenbecler, 14, e-mailed this final letter to her father, Command Sgt. Maj. James Blankenbecler, at 1:29 A.M. on Friday, October 3, 2003, two days after he was killed in a convoy in Samara, Iraq:

> Hi Daddy,
>
> Sorry I haven't written to you in a while. A lot of things have been going on. I miss you so much. How have you been? Is heaven everything it says it is? I know it's probably that and more. I can't wait 'till I can come join you again.
>
> I miss you so much—just being here for me to hold your hand and you calling me "princess." But one day we can do this again.

But it will be even better because Jesus will be with us.

I keep going in your office to see all your things and your awards that you have gotten over the years. You accomplished so much. I am proud you were my daddy; I would not have chosen anyone else. I like to go into your closet, too, and just touch and smell all your clothes. . . it gives me so many memories that I miss so much.

Sitting at this table I see your writing on a little piece of paper telling me and mom what e-mail and address in Iraq to write to you . . . CSM JAMES D. BLANKENBECLER, 1-44 ADA. I love to just look at your handwriting so much.

I have your military ring on right now. It's kind of big for my little finger, but it makes me feel you're holding my hand when I have it on . . . It's been on since we found out the news. I have your driver's license with me, too, so I can just look at you whenever I want. You have a little smile this time. When we went to get them done in El Paso I asked you to just smile this time . . . and you did it just for me. I also was looking at your car keys and that little brown leather pouch you always had on your key chain. It made me cry a lot when I picked it up.

Everything reminds me of you so much. When we pass by Chili's I remember you sitting across from me eating your favorite salad. You always told the waiter to take off the little white crunchy things . . . because you hated them. And when we drive by billboards that say "An Army of One," it makes me remember you in your military uniform. How you always made a crunching sound when you walked, and how you shined your big boots every night before you went to bed. I miss seeing that all the time. Little things that I took for granted when you were here seem priceless now.

One thing that I regret is when you wanted to open my car door for me, but I always got it myself. I wish I would have let you do it. And when you wanted to hold my hand, I sometimes would pull away because I didn't want people to see me holding my daddy's hand . . . I feel so ashamed that I cared what people thought of me walking down the parking lot holding your hand. But now I would give anything just to feel the warmth of your hand holding mine.

I can't believe this has happened to my daddy . . . the best daddy in the whole world. It feels so unreal, like you're still in Iraq. You were only there for 17 days. Why did they have to kill you? Why couldn't they know how loved you are here? Why couldn't they know? You have so many friends that love you with all their hearts and you affected each and every person you have met in your lifetime. Why couldn't they know? When I get shots at the hospital I won't have my daddy's thumb to hold tight. Why couldn't they know I loved for you to call me "princess?" Why couldn't they know if they killed you I would not have a daddy to walk me down the aisle when I get married? Why couldn't they know all this? Why?

I know that you are gone now, but it only means that I have another angel watching over me for the rest of my life. That's the only way I can think of this being good. There is no other way I can think of it.

All the kids at my school know about your death. They even had a moment of silence for you at our football game. A lot of my teachers came over to try to comfort me and mom. They all ask if they can get us anything, but the only thing anyone can do is give me my daddy back . . . and I don't think anyone can do that.

You always told me and mom you never wanted to die in a stupid way like a car accident or something like that. And you really didn't die in a stupid way . . . you died in the most honorable way a man like you could—protecting me, mom, Joseph, Amanda, and the rest of the United States.

In the Bible it says everyone is put on this earth for a purpose, and once they accomplished this you can return to Jesus. I did not know at first what you did so soon to come home to God. But I thought about it—you have done everything. You have been the best husband, father, son, and soldier in the world. And everyone knows this.

One of my teachers called me from El Paso and told me that when her dad died he always told her, "When you walk outside the first star you see is me." She told me that it is the same for me and you. I needed to talk to you last night, and I walked outside and looked up . . . and I saw the brightest star in the sky. I knew that was you right away, because you are now the brightest star in heaven.

I love you so much, daddy. Only you and I know this. Words can't even begin to show how much. But I tried to tell you in this letter, just a portion of my love for you. I will miss you, daddy, with all of my heart. I will always be your little girl and I will never forget that . . .

I love you daddy, I will miss you!!

Jessica

P.S. I have never been so proud of my last name.

Sunrise – June 27, 1963
Sunset – October 1, 2003

Jessica's letter appeared originally in a Killeen Daily Herald *(Killeen, Texas) article titled* "Hood soldier's family thankful for community support and help," *written by Debbie Stevenson for the* Herald. *It was reprinted here with permission from the Blankenbecler family.*

CHAPTER 14

An Oath to Justice

Earn it. Be worthy. Don't waste it. Two centuries of warriors look up from their graves in this dark hour, they look up from the rubble of the World Trade Center, and their message is, "Earn it." We can never truly earn what has been purchased at the ultimate price, but we can do our best.

—Lt. Col. Dave Grossman
and Loren W. Christensen,
from "Survivor Guilt:
Life, Not Death; Justice, Not Vengeance"

THE WARRIOR ETHIC IN LAW ENFORCEMENT
COURAGE OF THE THIRD KIND

by Philip J. Messina

Phil Messina, president of Modern Warrior Defensive Tactics Institute in Lindenhurst, New York, is a highly decorated New York Police Department (NYPD) officer, both plainclothes and uniformed assignments. He finished his distinguished (active) law enforcement career as a trainer and supervisor in the research and development section of NYPD's police commissioner's office before retiring in 1987. Since then, Mr. Messina has conducted training seminars for police trainers and officers from across the United States and abroad. He currently serves on the advisory board of ILEETA.

Mr. Messina has taught defensive tactics for more than 20 years, drawing from his unique street experience as an active police officer, his martial arts background of more than 40 years, and extensive research. His unique research and methodology have led to the development of key concepts now being used in defensive tactics training including goal-oriented training, time framing, combat stress conditioning, and physiokinetics.

The National Institute of Ethics honored Mr. Messina with its award for Moral Courage in May 2000. You can learn more about Mr. Messina and Modern Warrior by visiting www.ModernWarrior.com or e-mailing info@ModernWarrior.com.

❖

A dozen years ago, it wasn't PC to refer to our law enforcement officers as "warriors." The public, and politicians in particular, preferred to think of their police as simply "public servants." Thankfully, however, today it appears that things are changing as the general public learns to accept the broad, holis-

---

tic definition of warrior, as opposed to the narrow and shallow Hollywood definition, which simply identifies the warrior with violence, cold-heartedness, brutality, and revenge. True warriors in law enforcement view themselves as protectors of those they serve and of society in general. They have a powerful belief system and a willingness to sacrifice for those weaker than themselves, even if that sacrifice includes their own lives. Each warrior may have a slightly different view of good and evil or legal and illegal, depending on environment, education, and upbringing, but all true warriors believe in the basic concepts of right and wrong, fair and unfair, and loyalty and honor. It's the latter two that often create the true warrior's greatest turmoil.

Although true warriors must have the courage to perform their duties as law enforcement officers, many do not understand the full meaning of courage, even when they display it every day. Courage is shown in various ways, although when all is said and done, there are three basic kinds.

The most commonly recognized form is physical courage, the kind a warrior displays when he enters into a physical battle with life and limb on the line. We often honor those acts of physical courage, especially when the warrior knows the odds are against him, yet he enters the battle anyway. The true warrior understands that physical courage is not the absence of fear, but merely the belief that certain things are worth more than anything one might fear.

As most normal human beings fear injury and death, so does the warrior. The difference is that none of this supersedes a warrior's fear of losing a worthy battle, except, of course, the fear of not being worthy enough to enter into it. In other words, the true warrior's worthiest opponent is the very fear that may cause him to turn his back on his perceived duty as a warrior. This kind of courage is often referred to as bravery, and when others note it they usually reward it with some type of public or private acknowledgment. So although true warriors don't perform brave acts just to receive such admiration, they do know that the reward is often there, especially if their act succeeds.

The second kind of courage is emotional courage, which is often displayed when one is terminally ill, handicapped, or close to someone who is either. Recognition for this type of courage is not so easily come by and sometimes never truly given. It requires a kind of strength that goes far deeper than the strength often required for physical courage, because there is almost always a feeling of hopelessness, and the enemy is one that cannot be harmed or sometimes even seen.

To continue to focus on your duty after giving aid to an abused child, losing a partner, or taking the life of a violent assailant in front of his family, knowing you will change their lives forever, are some other examples of emotional courage. The true test of this type of courage is fighting the fight you cannot win. Although the reward is rarely public recognition, there is often a private recognition of those who display this type of courage—and sometimes even a kind of immortality for those who face it or even those they face it for. Those who display emotional courage tend to be those who care more about the feelings of others than they do about their own. They know that their duty is more important than how they "feel" or how people close to the battle might feel about them, and they recognize that in the long term, the greater good must always take precedence over future battles they may have with their irrational emotions. This kind of courage is often referred to as dignity.

The third kind is moral courage; in many ways this is the truest form. Moral courage is almost always tested during ethical battles rather than physical or emotional ones. Sometimes just the act of entering an ethical battle takes a great deal of moral courage. Unlike other battles, ethical ones are fought alone by the time they are completed, and it's the warrior's willingness to fight such a battle alone that truly tests his moral courage. Unfortunately, most ethical battles are lost by those who initiate them. This is usually because unethical conduct often has the loyal support of those who have gained from it. Ethical conduct rarely has such support because there is no tangible benefit for those who would support it, and most people feel that without a promised reward, the inconvenience and ridicule often heaped upon those who identify unethical conduct just isn't worth the effort. In other words, for every reason there is to "do the right thing," there are usually a hundred reasons not to.

Then there are those who, although ethical by nature, still allow themselves to profit from the unethical conduct of others. Some even put up token resistance against such conduct initially but, in the end, fall back on the old "well, I tried to change it" excuse and continue to reap benefits from the very acts they once fought against. Unfortunately, there is no rule as to how long one must continue to fight unethical conduct while still allowing oneself to benefit from it. It is a decision each person must eventually make. Unfortunately, there are too many otherwise ethical people who call themselves warriors who will never make this decision and, in failing to do so, will in fact be endorsing the very conduct they are trying to condemn. It is these internal conflicts, plus the fact that even in victory moral courage is rarely recognized either publicly or privately, that make it so difficult for even the most heroic warriors. Warriors aren't born, and they aren't made. Rather, they create themselves through trial and error and by their ability to conquer their own frailties and faults.

Unfortunately, because law enforcement personnel are held to such a high standard, the public evaluates us more by our standards of moral courage than by our standards of physical or emotional courage. Many honest and decent citizens feel that while we are quick to condemn the wrongdoing of others, we are very slow, and even reluctant, to identify the wrongdoing of our own. Unfortunately, many of our law enforcement leaders and representatives act in a manner that verifies this perception.

One way to address this is to simply argue that those who criticize us also ignore or simply give lip service to unethical conduct within their own professions. The problem is that they are not the ones who want to be thought of as warriors. We are. The other way we can address this issue is to simply refuse to tolerate unethical or immoral conduct by our leaders, our representatives, or our peers. We can acknowledge that this lack of credibility with many honest citizens may be at least partially justified, that with a lack of credibility there is a corresponding lack of support, and that because of this lack of support more officers than necessary may die in the long term. We may in fact have to concede that, as true warriors, we are bound by a duty within ourselves to display all three kinds of courage and that in doing so we will regain the respect and support of all those honest and decent citizens who do not give us that support now.

Law enforcement officers are not superior to those they protect, but they are quite special. They are special because they do things that others are unwilling or incapable of doing. They are special because they are among a few who are willing to risk their lives for a total stranger. And they are special because they see themselves as warriors in a world where warriors are often resented and ridiculed by those who need them.

However, being a warrior means more than just saving lives. It even means more than dying with honor. It means living with honor as well.

Loyalty and Honor

The true warrior knows the meaning of loyalty.
The true warrior knows the meaning of honor.
And the true warrior knows where loyalty ends and honor begins.

SURVIVOR GUILT
LIFE, NOT DEATH;
JUSTICE, NOT VENGEANCE

by Lt. Col. Dave Grossman and Loren W. Christensen

Lt. Col. Dave Grossman *is a West Point psychology professor, a professor of military science, an Army Ranger, and author of* On Killing: The Psychological Cost of Learning to Kill in War and Society; Stop Teaching Our Kids to Kill: A Call to Action Against TV, Movie, and Video Game Violence, *coauthored with Gloria DeGaetano; and* On Combat: The Psychology and Physiology of Deadly Conflict in War and in Peace, *with Loren W. Christensen. In the wake of the 9-11 terrorist attacks, he is on the road nearly 300 days a year, training elite military and law enforcement organizations worldwide about the reality of combat. His complete biography is included with his essay "On Sheep, Wolves, and Sheepdogs" in Chapter 1.*

Loren W. Christensen's *biography can be found at the back of this book.*

"Survivor Guilt: Life, Not Death; Justice, Not Vengeance" was taken from the book On Combat *and has been edited slightly for this book.*

❖

Much has been written about survivor guilt among Holocaust survivors, war veterans, police officers, and even relatives spared from an illness that has struck down other family members. It is not unusual for the survivor to think that he was spared at the expense of another and feel a heavy sense of debt to the one who is gone. Some survivors make every effort to stay in the shadows to avoid drawing attention to the fact that they survived. Some may suffer from a distorted sense of self-worth and feel that their daily concerns are of little matter; they may even feel guilty for having needs at all. Survivor guilt can be extraordinarily toxic.

There is a bond of love among the men and women who put their lives on the line that the average person cannot comprehend. Shakespeare wrote:

> We few, we happy few, we band of brothers;
> For he to-day that sheds his blood with me
> Shall be my brother; be he ne'er so vile,
> This day shall gentle his condition:
> And gentlemen in England now a-bed
> Shall think themselves accursed they were not here,
> And hold their manhoods cheap whiles any speaks
> That fought with us upon Saint Crispin's day.
> —*King Henry V*

That is the bond of the men and women who put their lives on the line every day. Lose one and it is the same as losing a spouse or a brother, and when it is a human who causes the loss of a fellow warrior's life, it becomes personal. If you are a survivor and you do not proceed carefully, there are two ways you can spin out of control: through inappropriate aggression toward others and through inappropriate aggression toward yourself. Warriors must guard against both. The last two pieces of what Lieutenant Colonel Grossman calls the "bulletproof mind" are "justice, not vengeance" and "life, not death."

JUSTICE, NOT VENGEANCE

Don't dehumanize those who disagree with us, or even hate us. Filling ourselves with hate is neither necessary to combat those who hate us, nor productive. The professional soldier is one who is cold, dispassionate, and regretful in his duty when forced to kill.

For our purposes, "justice, not vengeance" simply means that the soldier and police officer swear a solemn oath to justice. Should they violate that oath and seek vengeance, it will destroy them. Know that the surest way to a dose of post-traumatic stress disorder is to commit an atrocity or a criminal act that violates your code of ethics.

Let us look at the factors that can contribute to stress disorders so that we can place the impact of atrocities into the equation.

First, remember that unmanaged stress is a major destroyer and disabler of warriors.

The way to be psychologically predisposed to becoming a stress casualty is to be a sheep: live in denial, fail to stay on the warrior's path, avoid training, don't prepare, and don't equip yourself for that moment when the wolf comes.

The way to physically predispose yourself to becoming a stress casualty is to allow your body to be stressed already when the traumatic moment arrives. This includes poor nutrition, dehydration, and, most importantly, sleep deprivation.

The key to avoiding stress casualties at the moment of truth is to not enter Condition Black, a catastrophic condition where your adrenaline boils and fear causes your heart rate to rocket to more than 175 beats per minute. This is avoided ahead of time through stress inoculation—learning to apply tactical breathing and undertaking training that develops an autopilot response to ensure that even under high stress you do the right thing.

Ahead of time, the warrior must confront that dirty four-letter word "kill" and the responsibility to use deadly force when the situation requires it. This ensures that at the moment of truth you will not panic, you will be more likely to deter your opponent, and you will be better able to live with your actions afterward.

Thus the warrior's mind and body must be ready, but there is one other component that must be covered: the spirit. The warrior must address the spiritual or religious aspects of killing.

Afterward, the key to preventing a stress disorder is to conduct debriefings so the participants can delink the memories from emotions, multiply the joy of the success, and divide the pain of errors and losses.

There is one last ingredient in the equation, and that is to understand that of all the actions you could take in combat, the one most likely to destroy you is to commit an atrocity or a criminal act. In their article, "Post-Traumatic Stress Disorder in the Police Officer: Paradigm of Occupational Stress" (*Southern Medical Journal*, May 1990), Francis L. McCafferty, et al., wrote:

> The officer can eliminate or reduce much of the stress related to police work with foreknowledge and understanding of the job. The police officer must lessen stress by avoiding: excessive alcohol consumption, drug use, gambling, poor nutrition, lack of exercise, working too many hours, taking the job home, or performing illegal acts.

This concept was communicated most eloquently by a warrior leader on the eve of invading Iraq in 2003:

> It is a big step to take another human life. It is not to be done lightly. I know of men who have taken life needlessly in other conflicts, and I can assure you they live with the mark of Cain upon them. If someone surrenders to you then remember they have that right in international law and ensure that one day they go home to their family.
>
> The ones who wish to fight, well, we aim to please. . . .
>
> If you harm the regiment or its history by overenthusiasm in killing or in cowardice, know it is your family who will suffer. You will be shunned unless your conduct is of the highest, for your deeds will follow you down through history. We will bring shame on neither our uniform nor our nation.
>
> —Lt. Col. Tim Collins,
> 1st Battalion of the Royal Irish
> March 22, 2003

Two centuries earlier, Longfellow wrote:

> Every guilty deed
> Holds in itself the seed
> Of retribution and undying pain.

You can almost think of "justice, not vengeance" as what the Bible calls the "Breastplate of Righteousness." As long as you are doing the right thing, as long as you are following the rules and doing what your duty calls you to do, then there is true legal and mental protection in that. Again Shakespeare said it best, calling this "a peace above all earthly dignities, a still and quiet conscience." For those seeking more information on this topic I strongly recommend Jonathan Shay's excellent book *Achilles in Vietnam,* which is a superb analysis of the tragic price that warriors pay for committing atrocities, engaging in berserker behavior, and violating the ancient code of the honorable warrior.

When a warrior tells of his righteous acts with his peers, he is sharing his pain, and pain shared is pain divided, a powerful psychological tool. But when a warrior commits a criminal act, he cannot share that pain. You are only as sick as your secrets. If as a warrior you commit a crime or an act of vengeance, you cannot share that secret with anyone, and it will only eat away at you.

When we are young and hard, we think we can get away with anything. A World War II veteran once sat across from Lieutenant Colonel Grossman, wracked with sobs. He was a magnificent, noble American, but he had made one tragic, horrific mistake in his life, and it was eating him alive. He looked at Lieutenant Colonel Grossman, tears streaming down his cheeks, and said, "Colonel, I'm an old man now, and I'm going to have to answer to my maker soon. I'm going to have to answer for that day it was inconvenient to take those German soldiers back. The day we shot them while they were 'trying to escape.' I murdered those men that day; we murdered them. We didn't have to kill them. We murdered them, and soon I will have to answer to my maker for what I did."

What do you tell a man like that? No one is beyond redemption, but I know what that old soldier would advise us: "Don't do it."

Now, many will say, "Colonel, you're crazy. I'm not going to commit some criminal act." Good, but the reality is you do not know what you are going to do when your world comes unglued unless you prepare your mind, soul, and spirit ahead of time. Unless you have rehearsed it, you do not know for sure that you can dial 911 when your world comes unglued and your adrenaline and heart rate scream into the red zone, nor do you know for sure that you can make a magazine change in your weapon under these conditions unless you have rehearsed it ahead of time. Likewise, when you have rehearsed and prepared to always do the right thing at the moment of truth, you are more apt to deal appropriately with whatever comes your way.

The key is to work this matter out ahead of time because at the moment of truth, making the right decision might be difficult.

Justice, not vengeance. You have sworn a solemn oath to justice. Some swore it as a peace officer, but all Americans swore it from their youngest days. It went like this: "I pledge allegiance to the flag of the United States of America, and to the republic for which it stands, one nation under God, indivisible, with liberty and justice for all."

Vengeance will destroy you. Know that post-traumatic stress syndrome is the gift that keeps on giving. It impacts not only you in the years to come but also your spouse and your kids. So now, ahead of time, while you are calm and rational, think it through: whomever you think you are avenging does not want you to pay the price of your life and your loved ones' lives in the years to come.

Consider this incident that happened to a young Marine captain in Beirut in the spring of 1982. The Israeli army was advancing into Lebanon with tanks in the lead when word came down to a small band of Marines to stop them. An entire army, one of the most competent in the world, was rumbling up the road, and the U.S. Marines were waiting for them, armed with nothing bigger than M16 rifles. But orders are orders, and

Marines are Marines, so a young captain, holding an M1911 .45 automatic pistol in his hand, walked out into the middle of the road before the advancing army. He stopped the lead Israeli tank, turned it around, and sent them all back.

Did that pistol in his hand deter and frighten the entire Israeli army? No. But that pistol represented the might, the majesty, and the authority of the United States of America in the hands of a very brave man who was doing what his nation wanted him to do. Those Israelis knew that if they continued forward they would have to kill that young Marine and, along with him, all his friends—a whole nation of friends bringing a whole world of hurt, a price that was too high for the Israelis to pay.

As a warrior, understand that when you awaken every morning, strap on your weapon, and take it into combat, it represents the might, the majesty, and the authority of your city, your county, your state, and your nation, but only as long as you do what your nation wants you to do. Step out from under the umbrella of your authority and you become just another criminal.

Not too many years ago a police officer used to be given a lot of leeway. Perhaps there was a day when, if a man was asking for an ass-whooping, it was an officer's job to give it to him. Well, that day is gone. If it ever existed, it is gone today.

The Nazis and the Imperial Japanese in World War II committed many horrendous, brutal, and large-scale atrocities. Unfortunately, the Allied side also committed some. Many prisoners were "shot trying to escape" when it was inconvenient to take them back, an atrocity that was often winked at. That day, too, is gone. Like the police officer, the modern soldier is likely to have his every act videotaped and reported on national TV, and there is no tolerance for any deviation from the rules of war. Today our soldiers are held to the highest standards, and that is a good thing.

It is as if we had been playing football but now it is basketball season, and some fool is out there trying to tackle people on the basketball court. Tackling people on the basketball court!

What's going to happen? He is going to foul himself out of this game. And if he is not careful, he is going to lose this game.

Whether you are a soldier or Marine in close combat, a peacekeeper in a distant land, or a police officer working in the mean streets of America, you are held to a far higher standard than that of the average person. As such, you must dedicate yourself now, ahead of time, to the concept of justice, not vengeance. As individuals and as a society, we must walk the path of justice, not vengeance.

LIFE, NOT DEATH: "EARN IT"

When someone gives his life to save your life, you must not waste it. Repeat: if someone buys your life at the price of his life, you do not dare waste it. Your moral, sacred responsibility is to lead the fullest, richest, best life you can. We cannot fill his shoes, nor can we replace him, but we can do the things that he did. We can remember and honor him by being good officers, good husbands and fathers, and good friends. We can take seriously our life's work and be faithful servants.

Think about this right now, ahead of time, while you are calm and rational. If you were the one to die and your partner lived, you would want him to have the best life possible. You died to give him that.

Now, should your partner or your buddy die in combat, leaving you to drive on, what would he want for you? The same thing. He would want the fullest, richest life you can have. That is what he died to give you, and that is your moral, sacred responsibility. Your mission.

That means that right now you need to make a conscious effort to set aside all self-destructive thoughts and dedicate yourself to leading that full life. Now, you might say, "Colonel you're crazy, I'm never going to eat my gun." Good. But according to the National Police Suicide Foundation, the number of suicides among police officers is two to three times greater than line-of-duty deaths. And many other warriors in their hour of despair have done the wrong thing, seeking a permanent solution to a temporary problem. They too would have sworn that they would never consider suicide. At the moment of truth, however, they did the wrong thing because they had not, with all their heart and soul, worked through it ahead of time.

Steven Spielberg's motion picture *Saving Private Ryan* not only gives us an incredibly realistic depiction of the violence and horror of combat, but it also provides us with a wonderful model for behavior when we talk about choosing life, not death. Here is how Lieutenant Colonel Grossman interprets *Saving Private Ryan*:

> A band of U.S. Army Rangers goes behind enemy lines where each man, one by one, dies to save one young paratrooper: Private Ryan. That band of Rangers represents every American warrior who ever willingly gave his life to give us the freedom, lives, and liberty we have today. Those Rangers are the boys who fell at Lexington and Concord, and they are bloody windrows of bodies at Shiloh and Gettysburg. They are trenches full of blood in the Ardennes forest, and they are a bloody tide of bodies at Normandy and Iwo Jima. They are more than 300 police officers and firefighters rushing up the steps of the World Trade Center, and they represent the officer who died yesterday, alone and afraid on a dirty street somewhere in America.
>
> Private Ryan is us. He is every citizen who is alive and free today because two centuries of warriors have gone before us and purchased at the ultimate price what we have today.
>
> Do you remember the end of the movie, when the last Ranger, Captain Miller, lay dying on the bridge? He looked up at Ryan, he looked up at us, and what were his dying words? "Earn this . . . earn it."

Earn it. Be worthy. Don't waste it. Two centuries of warriors look up from their graves in this dark hour, they look up from the rubble of the World Trade Center, and their message is, "Earn it." We can never truly earn what has been purchased at the ultimate price, but we can do our best. Our model is Private Ryan.

Do you remember the old man at the very end of the movie standing over the grave of his comrades with his grandbabies and his great-grandbabies bouncing all around him? He looks over at his wife, and says, "Tell me I've led a good life. Tell me I've been a good man."

As a warrior, your mission is to man the ramparts of our civilization honorably and well in this dark hour; to retire honorably and well; to raise your grandbabies and your great-grandbabies straight, tall, and true; to raise the next generation straight and tall and true; to crack the bones and suck the marrow from every single day you have been blessed with; and at the end of your days, to look into the eyes of your loved ones and say, "Tell me I've led a good life. Tell me I've been a good person."

As warriors, we dedicate ourselves to a lifetime of service to our civilization. We make the choice, the conscious decision to take the path of justice, not vengeance and life, not death. Almost 2,500 years ago, the Greek poet and philosopher Heraclitus talked about making this choice:

> The soul is dyed the color of its thoughts. . . .
> The content of your character is your choice. Day by day, what you choose, what you think, and what you do is who you become. Your integrity is your destiny . . . it is the light that guides your way.

In Lieutenant Colonel Grossman's presentations he shows a photograph of a young firefighter wearing his heavy protective equipment and helmet. You can see vasoconstriction causing white areas around his eyes, nose, and mouth—clearly the face of a frightened young man. The photo also shows several other people in the background, their backs to the camera as they scramble *down* a stairwell. What makes this firefighter—this young warrior—different from everyone else in the photograph is that he is going *up* the stairs.

The photo was taken in a stairwell in one of the Twin Towers on September 11, 2001, where in one horrific morning 3,000 Americans died. Most of them did not have a choice that day, but there was a group of warriors—police officers and firefighters—who did. They were willing to go up the stairs because that was their job and there might have been a chance to save a life. They went up, but most of them did not come back down. Many lives were taken on that tragic morning, but some were given freely.

How can we equip ourselves, train ourselves, and prepare ourselves so that we will not be found wanting at our moment of truth? How can we "earn" this? As warriors, we can learn, strive, and prepare ourselves, but in the end we can never truly earn it. None of us can ever be worthy of what two centuries of men like the frightened, courageous young firefighter in that photo have done for us. We can, however, strive to do our best, like Private Ryan, and dedicate ourselves ahead of time to master survivor guilt and lead the full, rich, and productive life that has been purchased for us at such a dear cost.

About
Loren W. Christensen

*In 500 BC, Heraclitus . . . wrote to his comman-
der, "Of every 100 men, 10 should not even be here,
80 are nothing more than targets. Nine of them are
the real fighters. We are lucky to have them, they the
battle make. Ah but the one. One of them is a warrior
and he will bring the others back."*

—Brian Willis,
from "The Warrior Pyramid"

❖

Loren W. Christensen began his law enforcement career in 1967 as a military policeman in
the army and then joined the Portland (Oregon)
Police Bureau (PPB) in 1972, retiring in 1997.
During his years on PPB, he worked street patrol,
child abuse, dignitary protection, intelligence,
street gangs, and in the training unit.

Mr. Christensen began training in the
martial arts in 1965 and continues to this day.
Over the years he has earned a total of ten

black belts—seven in karate, two in jujitsu, and one in arnis. As a result of his tour in Vietnam and nearly three decades in law enforcement, Mr. Christensen's focus in the martial arts—in his writing, teaching, and training—has always been on street survival, not competition. He has starred in five martial arts training videos.

A professional writer since 1978, Mr. Christensen has penned 27 published books and dozens of magazine articles and edited a police newspaper for nearly eight years. He has written on the martial arts, missing children, street gangs, police-involved shootings, nutrition, exercise, prostitution, and various street subcultures.

Mr. Christensen can be contacted through his LWC Books Web site at www.lwcbooks.com.